FLOYD CLYMER'S MOTORCYCLIST'S LIBRARY

THE BOOK OF THE MATCHLESS

Fully illustrated and containing much valuable data concerning the construction, intelligent handling, maintenance, and overhaul of Matchless machines, with general advice also on engine tuning, lubrication, trouble diagnosis, touring, and legal matters.

BY

W. C. HAYCRAFT
1931
With 1933 & 1936 Supplements

There is no edition number stated on this 1931 publication.
However, it precedes the 1950 1st edition of the
'New Book of the Matchless'
which was the subsequent publication in this series.

ANNOUNCEMENT

By special arrangement with the original publishers of this book, Sir Isaac Pitman & Son, Ltd., of London, England, we have secured the exclusive publishing rights for this book, as well as all others in THE MOTORCYCLIST'S LIBRARY.

Included in THE MOTORCYCLIST'S LIBRARY are complete instruction manuals covering the care and operation of respective motorcycles and engines; valuable data on speed tuning, and thrilling accounts of motorcycle race events. See listing of available titles elsewhere in this edition.

We consider it a privilege to be able to offer so many fine titles to our customers.

FLOYD CLYMER
Publisher of Books Pertaining to Automobiles and Motorcycles

2125 W. PICO ST. LOS ANGELES 6, CALIF.

INTRODUCTION

Welcome to the world of digital publishing ~ the book you now hold in your hand, while unchanged from the original edition, was printed using the latest state of the art digital technology. The advent of print-on-demand has forever changed the publishing process, never has information been so accessible and it is our hope that this book serves your informational needs for years to come. If this is your first exposure to digital publishing, we hope that you are pleased with the results. Many more titles of interest to the classic automobile and motorcycle enthusiast, collector and restorer are available via our website at www.VelocePress.com. We hope that you find this title as interesting as we do.

NOTE FROM THE PUBLISHER

The information presented is true and complete to the best of our knowledge. All recommendations are made without any guarantees on the part of the author or the publisher, who also disclaim all liability incurred with the use of this information.

TRADEMARKS

We recognize that some words, model names and designations, for example, mentioned herein are the property of the trademark holder. We use them for identification purposes only. This is not an official publication.

INFORMATION ON THE USE OF THIS PUBLICATION

This manual is an invaluable resource for the classic motorcycle enthusiast and a "must have" for owners interested in performing their own maintenance. However, in today's information age we are constantly subject to changes in common practice, new technology, availability of improved materials and increased awareness of chemical toxicity. As such, it is advised that the user consult with an experienced professional prior to undertaking any procedure described herein. While every care has been taken to ensure correctness of information, it is obviously not possible to guarantee complete freedom from errors or omissions or to accept liability arising from such errors or omissions. Therefore, any individual that uses the information contained within, or elects to perform or participate in do-it-yourself repairs or modifications acknowledges that there is a risk factor involved and that the publisher or its associates cannot be held responsible for personal injury or property damage resulting from the use of the information or the outcome of such procedures.

WARNING!

One final word of advice, this publication is intended to be used as a reference guide, and when in doubt the reader should consult with a qualified technician.

PREFACE

THE author has, over a period of many years, ridden numerous types of motor-cycles (including one of 1912 vintage!), and he finds that such accumulated experience enables one quickly to become familiar with and competent to handle new mounts, especially if one has a good "mechanical sense." He realizes, however, that to-day there are hundreds of young men taking over modern machines with no previous practical experience—in other words, absolute novices. It is this and the fact that the author has lately been lucky enough to take over a "Silver Arrow" Matchless (a machine, by the way, which is a revelation to the confirmed "hot-stuff" single-cylinder, O.H.V. exponent) that has induced him to write this practical handbook for the benefit of Matchless owners and prospective owners, inexperienced and otherwise.

In this handbook the reader should find all he requires to enable him to keep his mount in perfect condition, and it is also hoped that he will derive considerable pleasure and interest from its perusal, for some of the recent Matchless models are obviously very clever engineering jobs, and a study of their design and construction is recommended to all interested in motor-cycling developments as well as prospective buyers.

Special attention is directed to that remarkable car-type design, the "Silver Arrow," which is substantially the same as when first introduced amid enthusiasm at the 1929 Olympia Show, and some particulars are given of the new "Silver Hawk," a remarkable four-cylinder development of the "Arrow," having an exceptional turn of speed and general performance.

For the benefit of the absolute novice for whom the Matchless is ideally suited, the principles of the magneto, the carburettor, and the four-stroke engine are fully explained in Chapter III. The expert will find the lubrication, electric lighting, and general overhauling notes of special interest. Numerous sub-headings should enable the reader to lay hands quickly on any special point about which he desires to obtain information

PREFACE

or verify. When such information is not to be found, or when a reader is confronted by some obscure mechanical trouble, the author will be pleased to answer any reasonable queries, provided a stamped addressed envelope is enclosed. Queries should be addressed c/o *Sir Isaac Pitman & Sons, Ltd.*

In conclusion, it should be mentioned that the author has no present or past interest with Matchless Motor-Cycles (Colliers), Ltd., to whom he is, however, greatly indebted for generous assistance in the lending of photographs, and for permission to visit the factory to compile notes in connection with this book, which it is hoped will become a standard reference work for Matchless owners. He would also thank the following for kindly permitting certain illustrations to be reproduced: the Editor, the *Motor-Cycle;* the *Motor-Cyclist Review;* Joseph Lucas, Ltd.; Amalgamated Carburettors, Ltd.; Sturmey-Archer Gears, Ltd.; the Coventry Chain Co., Ltd.

W. C. HAYCRAFT.

CONTENTS

CHAP.		PAGE
	PREFACE	
I.	THE MATCHLESS MODELS	1
II.	DRIVING	58
III.	THE ENGINE AND GEARBOX	67
IV.	LUCAS ELECTRICAL EQUIPMENT	90
V.	MAINTENANCE AND OVERHAULING	104
	INDEX	147
	1933 & 1936 MODELS SUPPLEMENT	151

THE BOOK OF THE MATCHLESS

CHAPTER I

THE MATCHLESS MODELS

IN this chapter the full Matchless programme is described in considerable detail for general reference purposes, and also to assist those contemplating buying a Matchless.

On looking at the table below, the reader will immediately see that there are exactly nine different models listed, and from this range the prospective buyer should have very little difficulty in selecting a model suitable for his own special requirements and marketed at a price within his means. Prices vary from £37 to £75.

THE RANGE AT A GLANCE

Model	c.c.	Bore and Stroke (m.m.)	Valves	No. Cyl.	Lubrication	Gear Ratios (Solo)	Tyres (in.)
A/2	397	54 × 86	S.V.	2	D.S.	17·5, 11·6, 7·8, 5·9	26 × 3·25
B	593	50·8 × 73·02	O.H.C.	4	D.S.	17·0, 12·4, 6·9, 5·7	26 × 3·25
R7	246	62·5 × 80	S.V.	1	D.S.	16·8, 9·4, 6·1	25 × 3
D	347	69 × 93	S.V.	1	D.S.	17·5, 9·3, 5·8	25 × 3
D/S	246	62·5 × 80	O.H.V.	1	D.S.	17·5, 9·3, 5·8	25 × 3
C	586	85·5 × 101·6	S.V.	1	D.S.	14·6, 10·6, 6·5, 4·9	26 × 3·25
C/S	495	85·5 × 85·5	O.H.V.	1	D.S.	14·6, 10·6, 6·5, 4·9	26 × 3·25
X/3	990	85·5 × 85·5	S.V.	2	D.S.	12·8, 9·3, 5·7, 4·3	26 × 3·25
X/R3	990	85·5 × 85·5	S.V.	2	D.S.	11·3, 8·2, 5·0, 3·8	26 × 3·25

The spring frame "Silver Hawk," which is the chief addition to last year's range, has its valves operated by a single overhead camshaft and has *coil ignition*. New type numbers have been allocated to the whole range, but the 246 c.c., 400 c.c., and 990 c.c. side-valve models remain substantially as hitherto, although certain detail alterations have been made. The principal Matchless innovations this year, apart from the introduction of the "Hawk,"

1

are the marketing of four inclined engine models with duplex loop frames, the provision of two-port cylinder heads on two of the new overhead-valve inclined engines, and the fitting of Sturmey-Archer *four-speed* gearboxes to all machines over 350 c.c.

The use of a splined kick-starter shaft and split crank enables the crank to be fixed in alternative positions. The last-mentioned detail improvement is illustrated by Fig. 2.

Deferred Payments. For the benefit of those who do not wish to pay cash down for a new model, a most convenient hire-purchase system has been arranged by The Matchless Motor-Cycles (Colliers), Ltd., in conjunction with The Roadways

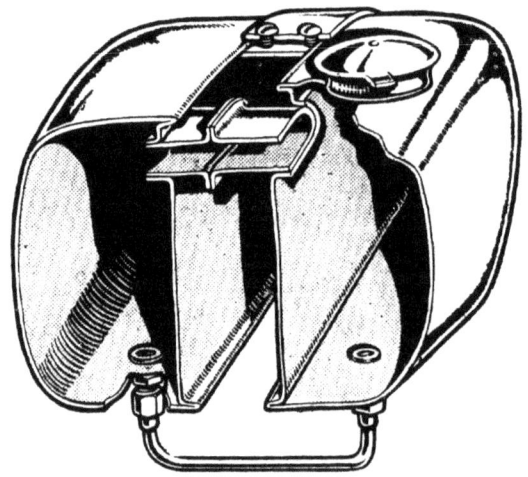

FIG. 1. CUT-AWAY VIEW OF PETROL TANK (ALL MODELS)

Transport Development, Ltd. A deposit of approximately one-quarter of the cash price secures delivery, the balance being payable in twelve equal monthly instalments. Attention is directed to the fact that a Matchless model does not become the property of the purchaser until the absolutely final instalment has been paid off. All Matchless solo motor-cycles or sidecar outfits delivered direct from the factory, or from one of their approved dealers, carry with them a guarantee against defective workmanship or material for a period of six months subject to certain conditions.

Lighting and De Luxe Equipment. For an extra charge of a few pounds, an acetylene gas or electric lighting set can be fitted to most machines, P. & H. and Lucas equipment being used respectively. It is the cheapest and wisest policy to specify a complete electric set, including an electric horn, in the first instance, as this gives infinitely better results.

The six-volt, 20-watt Lucas M-L "Maglita" (type FD), or the latest six-volt, 30-watt "Magdyno" (type MS), with the dynamo portion detachable, are the generators used on all single- and twin-cylinder Matchless machines, and they are driven off the engine camshaft or by chain off the engine mainshaft, according to the type of machine. The equipment used on all de luxe models, i.e. all except R/7, is priced at approximately £9. It comprises, in addition to the Lucas "Magdyno" or "Maglita" in the case of D and D/S, dipping beam headlamp, tail lamp, battery, and Lucas high-frequency "six-volt" electric horn with new mountings, a most handsome improved pattern instrument panel placed immediately above the centre of the handlebars, and housing the gearbox-driven Smith chronometric speedometer, the ammeter, the D.S. lubrication sight-feed opposite, the steering damper knob, and the lighting switch. In the case of some panels this year, a magneto cut-out switch is also included, and on the "Hawk" a tell-tale ignition switch. The sight-feed, ammeter, and speedometer are indirectly illuminated as on modern car instrument panels, the illumination being controlled by a small button switch on the panel.

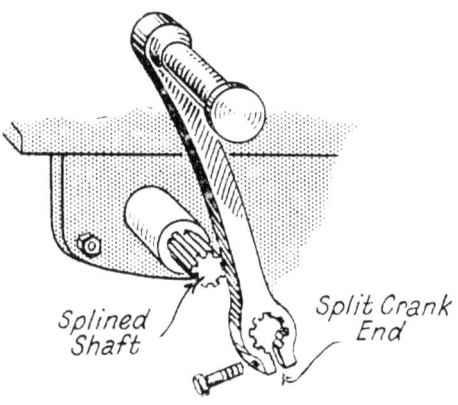

FIG. 2. THE NEW KICK-STARTER CRANK ATTACHMENT

For the sum of five guineas a Lucas M.L. "Maglita" lighting set, with 8 amp.-hr. battery, can be fitted to models R/7, D, and D/S, and a "Magdyno" set alone with 12 amp.-hr. battery to models C and C/S. No instrument panel is provided, the ammeter and switch being mounted on the top and back of the headlamp itself. This is, of course, an alternative to the slightly more expensive de luxe equipment, which cannot, however, be fitted to R/7. Two types of six-volt electric horns are obtainable. The battery is mounted over the gearbox on a raised part of the magneto platform.

No sight-feed can, of course, be provided on standard models without a panel, and when a speedometer is specified it has the usual handlebar clip fixing. All de luxe models, except C, D, and D/S, include an air filter, all have twist-grip throttle control, and models D and D/S de luxe have heavyweight tyres.

The Twin-cylinder S.V. Models. These comprise models A/2 The "Silver Arrow"), X/3, and X/R3, and their prices are £55,

£60, and £62 10s. without de luxe equipment, respectively. All three machines make admirable touring mounts, especially the last two which are designed for carrying two or three persons including the driver.

Model A/2 is a magnificent general purpose utility mount of unusual layout. At the present time this is one of the most popular Matchless models, and mainly for this reason the author has in the following specifications dealt with it in considerable detail. Its very robust construction and design gives it road-holding qualities considerably above the average; the spring frame entirely eliminates rear wheel bounce and spin, in addition to giving a degree of comfort unobtainable with the normal rigid type frame. The provision of a "prop" stand, centrally positioned, enables the machine to be easily jacked up.

Perhaps the most commendable feature of all is the extraordinary ease with which the engine can be started. One gentle depression (with the foot or hand) usually suffices to produce a low-revolution "tick-over." Starting troubles due to a faulty exhaust valve lifter are non-existent, for no lifter is provided. The machine is exceedingly quiet. The only audible sounds being the slight hiss at the air-intake and the swish of the primary chain. Acceleration is very rapid, though somewhat deceptive owing to absence of much exhaust noise. Fuel and oil consumption are good, the former exceeding 75 m.p.g. at a touring speed. There are no appreciable vibration periods above 12 m.p.h., and the interconnected brakes render rapid retardation on treacherous road surfaces both practicable and safe. Fast touring does not "tire" the engine, and a comfortable cruising speed of 40–50 m.p.h. can be maintained over long distances. With the throttle wide open a maximum speed of 65 m.p.h. is attainable—a creditable performance for a 400 c.c. machine weighing just over 3 cwt.

Reliability, low maintenance costs, and general accessibility of this machine are quite above the average, and the monobloc engine can readily be decarbonized.

Models X/3 and X/R3 are the latest versions of the standard Matchless Big Twins, suitable for long distance high speed, solo or sidecar touring, or week-end family runs. Both machines which have duplex loop frames are finished in de luxe style. Their engines, though remarkably quiet and docile are, in some respects, akin to sports engines, acceleration and speed being excellent.

The specification of model X/R3 is identical to that of model X/3, with the exception that a sports engine having polished ports with nickel-plated cylinders is fitted; chromium-plated wheels are standardized, and slightly different gear ratios are used. It is about 5 m.p.h. faster than the standard model.

The Single-cylinder S.V. Models. These are models R/7, D, and C, listed at £37, £38 10s., and £47 10s., respectively. The performance of all the side-valve machines is decidedly snappy. They are, perhaps, a shade more reliable than the overhead-valve type, but there is practically nothing to choose between the two types if the machines be carefully driven and looked after. All have detachable cylinder heads, except model D, and enclosed valve gear.

Model R/7 is the cheapest of the Matchless range. It is a smart looking lightweight qualifying (with complete "Maglita" electric lighting equipment) for the 30s. per annum tax, and embodying all the latest features and refinements of Matchless design. It has ample power for solo or pillion riding, and is a most handy machine for the man who wants economical and efficient motor-cycling with a small initial outlay. Its fuel consumption is remarkably low, and it has a most useful turn of speed. Its specification remains substantially the same as for 1930.

Model D is also a lightweight eligible, with "Maglita" electric lighting but without de luxe equipment, for the 30s. tax, and though

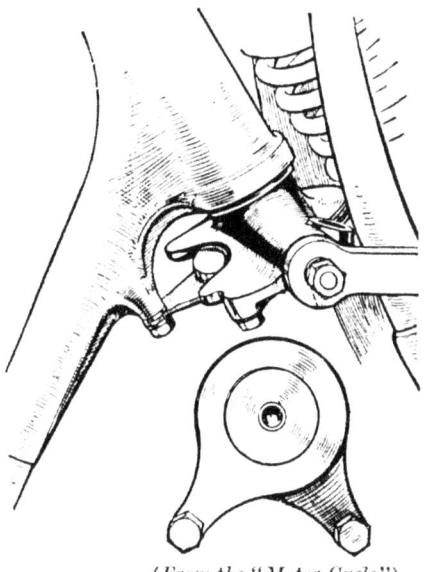

(*From the "Motor Cycle"*)

FIG. 3. STEERING HEAD, FORK STOPS AND STEERING DAMPER

The above type steering damper is fitted as standard to all models over 350 c.c., and control on *de luxe* models is by a knob on the instrument panel (Fig. 45)

costing only a trifle more than R/7, has an extra 100 c.c. engine capacity, and its design is entirely new from stem to stern. With its duplex loop frame and inclined power unit, with decompressor for easy starting, it is a remarkably sturdy and handsome piece of work, with, of course, a somewhat superior performance to Model R/7.

Model C is a new duplex frame machine with a high-powered inclined engine with decompressor, having sufficient stamina to undertake fast solo or sidecar work, and a four-speed gearbox. Its performance should satisfy those who drive really hard, and are in the habit of maintaining more than usually high average speeds, and do not confine their activities to comparatively flat districts.

The Single-cylinder O.H.V. Models. Two models belong to this class, namely, D/S and C/S. Their prices are £42 and £52, respectively. Acceleration, speed, and general liveliness are the characteristics of these mounts, and they will appeal particularly to the sporting type of rider. Numerous detail improvements have been made recently to the overhead-valve engines, and, although they develop a huge brake-horse-power and are capable of almost vicious acceleration, yet they are very silent and, without exception, have a steady, low-revolution " tick-over," a matter of considerable importance. In addition, improved rocker-gear and automatic push-rod and inlet valve guide lubrication renders them absolutely reliable. Both overhead-valve models have decompressors and magnetos mounted behind the engine.

Model D/S is similar to the entirely new Model D design, but this machine has an overhead-valve two-port cylinder head, and automatic inlet valve-guide and rocker-box lubrication. With the inclined overhead-valve engine it is most attractive and a real " hot-stuff " sports model. It qualifies with *acetylene* lighting for the 30s. per annum tax.

Model C/S, also, is an overhead-valve replica of Model C with a two-port sports engine and similar lubrication. As might be expected, this "five-hundred" is phenomenally fast, and can "show its tail" to almost anything on the road. As in the case of the side-valve model, this machine has four speeds and, in consequence, close ratios are available.

The Four-cylinder Overhead Camshaft Model. Model B, or the "Silver Hawk" as it is more usually called, is one of the few " V " fours in existence, and its price is £75. In many respects it resembles the "Arrow," and has a similar spring frame with a 6 in. ground clearance. Its salient features are its coil ignition giving very easy starting, the peculiar arrangement of the monobloc cylinders, the overhead camshaft, and the duplex primary transmission with fixed four speed gearbox. It is a real de luxe solo machine, and a mount *par excellence* for the long distance sidecar tourist and those who travel abroad. Although docile and quiet at touring speeds, it is capable of a speed greater than any other Matchless model, and probably equal to that of any machine on the road.

MODEL A/2 (THE " SILVER ARROW ")

This original, and yet in many ways orthodox, twin has the following specification—

The 3·97 h.p. S.V. Vee-twin Engine. The "A/2" power unit is a narrow angle Vee-twin with a bore and stroke of 54 mm. × 86 mm. respectively, giving a cubic capacity of 397 c.c. It is not so unconventional as might at first be supposed from a casual exterior examination which gives one the impression that there are four cylinders in line. This illusion is caused mainly by the fact that, although the cylinder bores are set at an acute angle to each other, a monobloc car-type cylinder and cylinder head is employed with horizontal finning together with a similarly finned exhaust manifold. The net result is an engine of most pleasing appearance and extreme neatness.

Excellent torque regularity is obtained by the use of a small *firing angle* in the case of a Vee-twin, and in this instance an extraordinarily small angle (26 degrees) is employed, so small indeed that the provision of a monobloc casting becomes imperative. Apart from this practical consideration, a monobloc cylinder casting has been deliberately decided upon as affording the best means of overcoming several inherent disadvantages of the separate cylinder type.

The general arrangement of the engine is well shown by Fig. 4. Although the firing angle is only 26 degrees, the actual angle between the cylinders is but 18 degrees, which means that with the crankpin and connecting rod on top dead centre in the firing position, there is approximately 4 degrees inclination of each piston inwards relative to the connecting rod. This point can be understood by reference to Fig. 4, where the angularity is quite noticeable. Another unusual feature of this engine is the sloping of the piston heads so as to enable the normal form of combustion chamber to be used in spite of the bore angularity. Other noteworthy features are the arrangement of the valves, the longitudinally placed camshaft, the dry sump lubrication system, and the positively driven magneto or "Magdyno."

Dealing with the crankcase first, this is a massive cast aluminium structure of box-like formation split vertically in the usual manner. Separation of the two halves is not recommended to be undertaken by inexperienced amateurs. If complete dismantling is decided upon, care must be taken in regard to the oil pump which is housed in a rectangular crankcase projection immediately below the large rectangular box housing the camshaft and drive, which has a neat and readily removed cover of pressed steel. Right at the base of the crankcase on the offside is a large drain plug. An efficient crankcase pressure release valve of the diaphragm type maintains a uniform pressure within the crankcase, and serves as a means of lubricating the primary chain.

The crankshaft assembly is exceedingly robust, well balanced, and stiff, and the more important parts are clearly shown at Fig. 5. It comprises two webbed flywheels having very heavy rims, closely united by a large diameter, hardened steel crankpin whose gently tapered ends are friction fits in the flywheels. The flywheel mainshafts are also friction fits in the bosses, but are keyed to give extra security. That on the driving side, which is subject to heavy transmission thrusts, has a double row caged

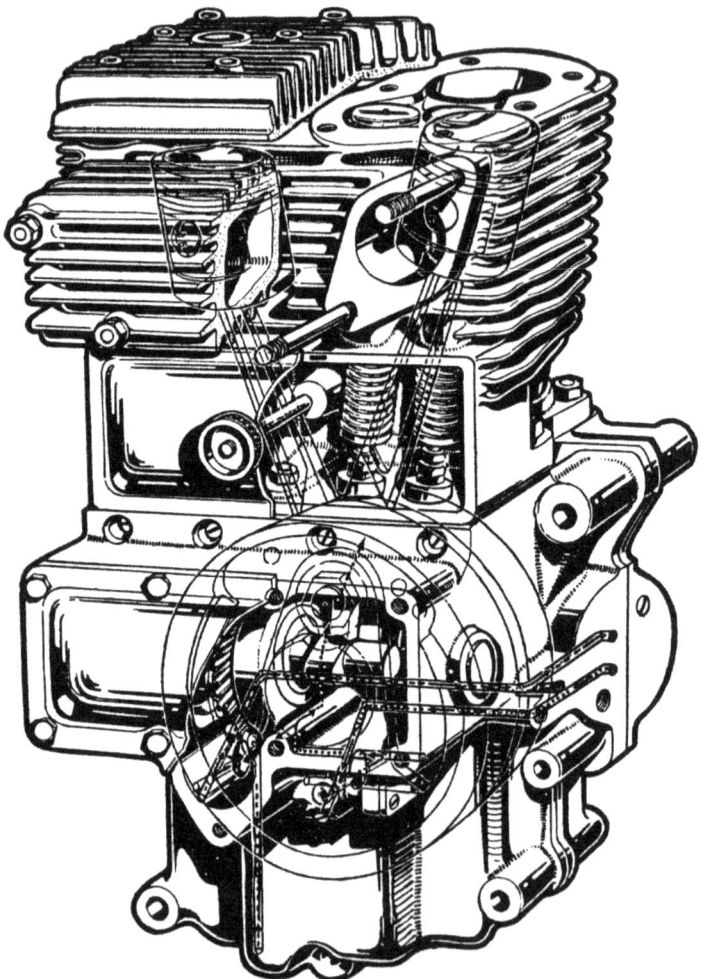

Fig. 4. General Arrangement of the "Silver Arrow" Engine

Various parts have been cut away or sectioned to show the method of construction

roller bearing, while that on the timing side, which incidentally carries the pump driving worm and the skew gear for the camshaft, has a plain phosphor-bronze bush into which the whole oil supply is fed before distribution. These two bearings are capable of withstanding very hard work indeed. Upon the central and enlarged portion of the crankpin are the two double row big-end bearings of the "H" section connecting rods which work side by side. There are no bushes pressed into the slightly eccentric eyes of the connecting rods, but the crankpins can readily be renewed

FIG. 5. THE "SILVER ARROW" CRANKSHAFT ASSEMBLY

A—Connecting rods with small-end bushes
B—Pistons (complete with rings)
C—$\tfrac{11}{16}$-in. dia. gudgeon pins
D—Gudgeon pin circlips
E—Flywheels and mainshafts
F—Crankpin and nuts.

when necessary. The small end bearings are of the usual plain phosphor-bronze bush type, but the fully floating gudgeon pins measure no less than $\tfrac{11}{16}$ in. across their diameters. Such large size pins as these obviously have an excellent life due to their large bearing surfaces. Spring circlips prevent scoring of the cylinder walls.

The pistons themselves (B, Fig. 5) are of aluminium alloy, and of normal construction except in regard to their heads which for reasons already mentioned are sloping. The skirts on one side are split diagonally (see Fig. 30A), so as to allow for the very considerable expansion that occurs with this metal. Two rings only are used, the lower of which acts as a scraper ring, and with a *cold* engine and new rings the correct gap is ·004 in. to ·006 in. A fairly high compression ratio is used (5·6 to 1).

The two pistons reciprocate in a cast-iron monobloc cylinder unit, the general design of which may be gathered by reference to Fig. 4. This unit has a one-piece detachable cast-iron cylinder head, secured in position by twelve small studs with two separate copper-asbestos gaskets inserted between, one for each cylinder. The foremost and rearmost bolts are also used as anchorages for two short steel struts which run to the front and rear frame down-tubes respectively, for the purpose of damping out any tendency for vibration and securing greater rigidity. As on the standard Matchless range, the sparking plugs are located approximately centrally above the semi-turbulent combustion chambers. Removal of the cylinder head bloc (see page 128) exposes to view both valves and pistons, the former having their seatings in the lower cylinder casting. Thus a top overhaul is enormously simplified, and the valves may be ground in and carbon deposits removed without disturbing the cylinder bloc itself. " Heeltite " is recommended as a means of obtaining a perfect joint.

The cylinder bloc is perhaps one of the most interesting features of the whole design. The two cylinders on the driving side of the engine are joined by a web, and on the timing side the casting below the horizontal cylinder finning is shaped to form a rectangular, oil-tight valve chest (Fig. 4) with a pressed steel cover. The valves and their springs thus operate under ideal conditions. The shape of the cylinder bases ensures the bloc being truly located, and a large washer prevents any tendency for oil leakage. The mouths of the cylinder bores are, incidentally, very generously chamfered to allow of safe and easy replacement of the piston rings. On the driving side of the engine bolted in an extraordinarily accessible position is the flanged fitting carburettor. No induction pipe is used, the instrument being attached direct to the cylinder bloc and the vaporized fuel supplied to the two inlet ports via a cored passage running between the cylinders. There is thus no possibility of air leaks or condensation occurring.

On the timing side a large and detachable horizontally-finned exhaust manifold is bolted to two flanges projecting from the cylinder bloc. The products of combustion pass from this manifold into a long sweeping exhaust pipe which is heavily chromium plated and of large diameter with a push-in exhaust pipe connection. Thence the exhaust gases pass through the silencer and fish-tail into the atmosphere. The silencer is of unusual design

THE MATCHLESS MODELS

and highly efficient. With the engine turning over at 4,000 r.p.m., there is no appreciable back-pressure in spite of the fact that a complete reversal of direction of the gas stream is caused by two parallel and diagonally placed sheet metal baffles (see Fig. 6) which, for practical purposes, divide the expansion chamber into three compartments. Before passing through the fish-tail, the gases are compelled to enter a perforated and blind-ended tube. This tubular baffle which further splits up the gas stream, is detachable, but the other baffles obviously cannot and are not required to be disturbed. Owing to the fact that a spring frame is used it is not possible, obviously, to attach the silencer to the

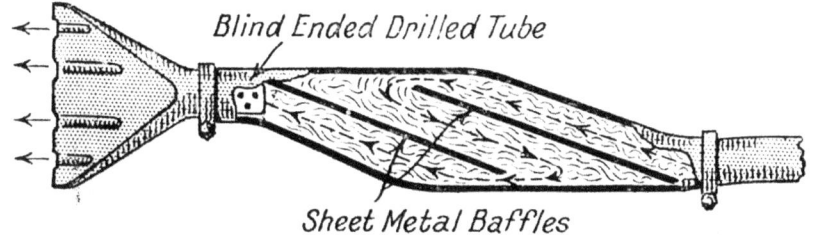

FIG. 6. DIAGRAM SHOWING PRINCIPLE OF MATCHLESS SILENCER

The above type is fitted to all machines and is amazingly efficient. Note the reversal of the gas stream indicated by arrows

offside chain stay in the usual manner, and recourse is had to a kind of triangular outrigger plate bolted to the gearbox cradle.

The valve gear (Figs. 4 and 7) is extremely simple and unusually quiet, due to the use of a single camshaft driven by helical bevels off the mainshaft, and to complete enclosure and adequate lubrication of all working parts. The camshaft, which is a one-piece high tensile steel stamping with the cam profiles accurately ground after hardening, is mounted upon three plain bearings (Fig. 7) across the crankshaft axis, the large centre bush being housed in a vertical crankcase web situated slightly ahead of the mainshaft axis. The two other bushes are fixed at the front and rear of the camshaft, the former being pressed into a housing end cap, and the latter into a special housing cover plate whose removal by undoing four screws enables the complete camshaft to be withdrawn from this end (see page 140). Securely fitted to a slight taper and keyed to the camshaft immediately behind the large centre bush is a large diameter helical bevel drive pinion meshing with the helical bevel fitted in a similar manner, but secured by a locking nut (right-hand thread) to the engine main-shaft. The diameter of the smaller pinion is, of course, exactly half that of the larger one, so as to give the 2 to 1 reduction necessary on a four-stroke engine. Both pinions are marked so that correct replacement and non-interference with the valve timing is ensured. The rear end of the camshaft is made use of to drive the magneto, or "Magdyno," as the case may be, a very simple and most efficient flexible coupling being provided. The design of this coupling is made clear by an examination of the

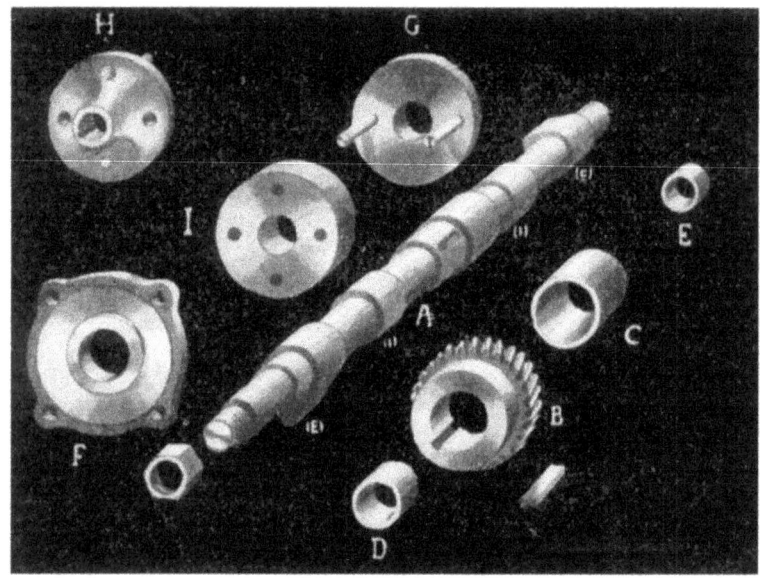

FIG. 7. THE CAMSHAFT, CAMSHAFT BEARINGS AND MAGNETO COUPLING

A—Camshaft
B—Helical bevel-drive pinion and key
C—Large central bush
D—Small bush (rear end)
E—Small bush (front end)
F—Camshaft housing cover plate
G—Camshaft magneto drive disc
H—Magneto armature drive disc
I—Flexible rubber disc.

components shown dismantled in Fig. 7. It will be seen that they comprise two steel pegged discs fitted upon the tapered ends of the camshaft and magneto armature. The magneto disc H is keyed, but the camshaft disc G is a friction fit only (to allow of the magneto timing being altered), and is held firmly in position by a nut (left-hand thread) on the end of the camshaft. The two discs each have two holes spaced at 180 degrees into which two keys on the opposite disc fit. Between the two metal discs is a rubber disc which provides a certain amount of flexibility. The whole camshaft runs submerged in oil, and the life of the bearings and worms is very great indeed.

No valve rockers are provided, the round ends of the non-

THE MATCHLESS MODELS

rotating tappets resting direct upon the cams and reciprocating in chilled cast-iron guides. These tappets are unusual in that they have two flats, and are not of round section. They do not, therefore, rotate in the guides. The guides themselves are light push-fits in the crankcase, and may readily be removed after loosening the four locking screws and wedge-shape collar washers engaging with grooves on the guides (see M in Fig. 8). The tappets have the usual type adjustable heads (H, Fig. 8) secured by lock-nuts. The valves themselves are of the familiar mushroom pattern with very long stems and small heads. The heads are slightly convex, and have the usual slots for screwdriver insertion when valve

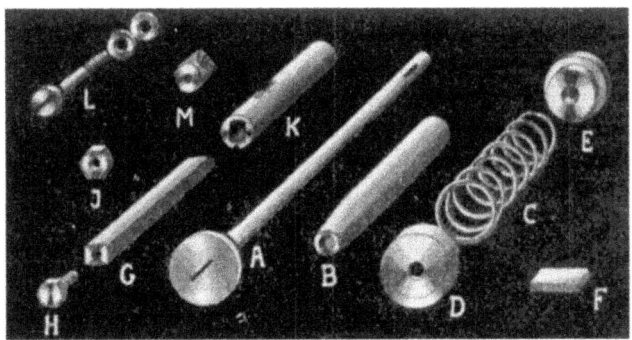

FIG. 8. SHOWING SOME COMPONENTS OF THE VALVE GEAR DISMANTLED

A—Valve (inlet or exhaust)
B—Valve guide (inlet or exhaust)
C—Valve spring (inlet or exhaust)
D—Valve spring cap (upper)
E—Valve spring cap (lower)
F—Cotter
G—Tappet
H—Tappet adjusting head
J—Lock-nut
K—Tappet guide
L—Tappet guide lock screw and washers
M—Tappet guide locking collar.

grinding. Single coil compression springs are used, the lower of the spring caps being anchored to the valve stem by means of a flat cotter passing through a slot in the stem. Inlet and exhaust valves and valve springs are interchangeable, but when the engine has had considerable usage it is very inadvisable to interchange the valves themselves as the faces and seatings wear slightly differently, and a perfect gas-tight seal is of supreme importance. As previously mentioned, there is no exhaust valve lifter.

Lubricating oil recommended (all S.V. engines) . . . . . . Castrol XL
Sparking plugs recommended (all S.V. engines) . . . . . . K-L-G. K.1, or Lodge T.S.3
Tappet clearances (warm) . . . ·004 in. inlet and exhaust
Magneto advance . . . . $\frac{3}{8}$ in. before T.D.C. on full advance, or T.D.C. on full retard

The Dry Sump Lubrication System (**All Models**). The general design of the engine lubrication system is the same for all Matchless models. It is of the force-feed, constant circulation type with dry sump. Briefly its working is as follows: Oil is *sucked* from the tank, distributed throughout the engine, and finally returned to the tank by a duplex internal pump. This comprises a single double-acting, steel plunger (Fig. 51) housed in the crankcase casting below the timing case between two rectangular end caps horizontally and at right angles to the crankshaft axis, and able simultaneously to rotate and reciprocate. This dual action of the plunger is obtained, as is more fully explained on page 73, by the fact that while a positive rotation at one-fifteenth engine speed is effected by direct engagement of a central hobbed portion with a worm cut on the mainshaft, an endwise movement is secured by having an annular cam groove cut in the plunger body in permanent contact with the hardened end of a fixed guide screw. The actual oil circulation is brought about by alternate displacements and suctions at the two ends of the reciprocating plunger, one end being of greater diameter than the other to ensure complete scavenging of the sump and the return of all surplus oil to the tank. Two segments cut in the plunger body constitute the main ports which regulate the circulation. There is no adjustment, however. A point worthy of notice here is that the crankcase cannot safely be split until the pump plunger has first been removed.

With regard to the actual oil distribution, the system adopted is made clear by reference to Fig. 4, and also to Fig. 50. The small end of the plunger (i.e. the front one) forces oil up into the timing case to a predetermined level, such that the camshaft bearings and drive are adequately lubricated. In the case of the "Silver Arrow," the oil level in the timing case is just below the camshaft itself, so that each cam dips into a bath of oil at every revolution. All surplus oil overflows into the flywheel chamber and is eventually returned to the sump, although some of it is caught up by the flywheels and splashed upon the big-ends and the cylinders. Splash lubrication, however, is not relied upon to any extent owing to the small volume of oil remaining at any time in the sump. Oil is forced under pressure direct to the big-end bearings and to the crankshaft bearing on the timing side by means of carefully drilled passages in the flywheel and mainshaft concerned, respectively. Oil is also fed to three points on each of the cylinder walls in such a position that the bulk of the oil is discharged on to that part of the thrust side of the cylinder walls where the maximum cooling effect upon the pistons is required.

The Matchless D.S. lubrication system is simplicity itself, and it guarantees a continual supply of clean, cool oil to the engine whenever the latter is running. The oil circulation should be verified occasionally by removing the oil tank filler cap and noting whether oil is being ejected from the return pipe orifice. This check upon the oil circulation should be made preferably upon starting up the engine from cold. Remember the fact that when the engine has been left stationary for some time, oil from various parts of the engine has drained to the sump and, until this surplus has been cleared, the return to the tank is very positive, whereas normally it is somewhat spasmodic and, perhaps, mixed with air bubbles due partly to the fact that the capacity of the return part of the sump is greater than that of the delivery portion, and partly to the fact that there are considerable variations in the amount of oil held in suspense in the crankcase. For example, upon suddenly accelerating the return flow may decrease entirely for a time only, of course, to resume at a greater rate than before when decellerating. It may be mentioned, however, that on all de luxe models the provision of a sight-feed on the instrument panel, illuminated at night, obviates the necessity for removing the filler cap, the oil supply to the timing-box or rocker-box on the overhead-valve engines being first by-passed up to the panel. It is important that no air leaks occur in this system, the effect of which would tend to cause the sight-feed bowl to fill up even at moderate speeds. Should the sight-feed window be accidentally broken the ends of the two pipes may be connected by a piece of rubber tubing, when the oil will merely flow up one pipe and down the other. All oil returned to the tank is immediately filtered. It is important for several reasons (see page 61) that the oil level in the tank be maintained approximately correct. Beyond this no attention is necessary.

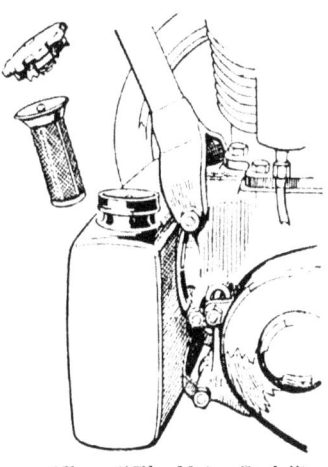

(*From "The Motor-Cycle"*)

FIG. 9. THE OIL TANK BOLTED TO THE ENGINE

A minimum amount of exterior piping is used, and in the case of Models A/2 and B, the oil tank, which is a welded unit of pressed steel and immensely strong, is bolted direct to the front of the crankcase as shown in Fig. 9. A circular face on the tank abuts against a corresponding face on the crankcase, and two holes in the latter coincide with the orifices of the two oil pipes in the tank—the suction and discharge pipes. The former is led nearly to the bottom of the tank, and the latter is visible on removing the filler cap.

Carburettor. A special semi-automatic, two-lever, flange fitting Amal pilot jet instrument is used. Its type number is 4/014, and it has a bottom petrol feed. It is bolted direct on to the near side of the cylinder block at the end of the cored passage between the two cylinders. The usual two-lever control is used, but, if desired, twist-grip control of the throttle may be specified. A throttle stop limits the closing of the throttle slide, and enables a very low revolution tick-over on the pilot jet to be obtained. The main jet fitted as standard is a No. 55, with a 4/4 throttle valve

FIG. 10. MODEL A/2 (THE "SILVER ARROW") DE LUXE

in position 3. This combination provides a low fuel consumption (90-105 m.p.g.), good acceleration, and high maximum speed. On de luxe models a special air cleaner is fitted to the intake. This effectively prevents the ingress of dust and dirt into the cylinder. It should be noticed that when an air filter is fitted to a carburettor, the main jet size may usually advantageously be reduced by 10 to 15 per cent.

Ignition. Lodge type T.S.3, single-point, mica-insulated sparking plugs are standardized on the 1931 side-valve range, and the recommended gap at the electrodes is ·020 in. ($\frac{1}{50}$ in. or, approximately, $\frac{1}{2}$ mm.).

The current is generated, unless a Lucas "Magdyno" unit be specified, by a Lucas type K.L.V. high-tension magneto, secured by four bolts to a platform above the gearbox, and driven by a flexible coupling straight off the camshaft, and, of course, has anti-clockwise rotation (seen from C.B. side). On this machine and on the Big Twins, there are two cams on the cam ring since the armature is driven at one-half engine speed. No. 1 cam, which is responsible for the spark at the plug of the rear firing cylinder,

THE MATCHLESS MODELS

is situated on the right-hand side of the cam ring. Above the contact-breaker is the rotating distributor arm driven by spur gearing off the armature at one-half engine speed. The correct "break" at the contacts should be ·012 in.; a small carbon brush in the bakelite contact-breaker cover enables the primary circuit to be broken by a magneto cut-out switch mounted on the handlebars or instrument panel. Further details and an illustration of a Lucas magneto without distributor will be found on page 79.

Frame and Forks. The Matchless spring frame is one of the

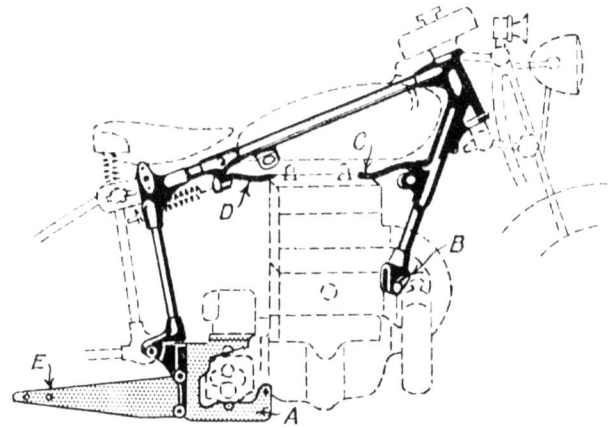

FIG. 11. THE FRONT PORTION OF THE SPRING FRAME
The engine, gearbox, magneto, etc., are shown dotted to indicate their location and method of fixing

most interesting features of the machine, and effectively damps out all road shocks. It also possesses absolute lateral rigidity. It comprises two distinct members—the front main portion and the rear portion which is sprung and pivots at a point just behind the base of the saddle tube.

The front portion of the frame is of the diamond type, and is constructed of three high-grade seamless steel tubes pinned and brazed to two heavy lugs, the steering head lug being particularly massive. Fig. 11 shows how the power unit is installed. A pair of rear engine plates, shown at A, serves the triple purpose of providing a cradle mounting for the engine, housing the four-speed gearbox and supporting the platform for the electrical generator. Forward, the engine crankcase is bolted to a substantial lug B at the end of the front down tube. In addition, two short stays, C and D, run from this tube and the tank tube, respectively, to the cylinder head. At E will be observed the special silencer outrigger plate necessary to counteract the deflection that would otherwise be caused by the sprung portion of the frame.

The design of the rear portion of the frame is made clear by reference to Fig. 12. It consists of what is in effect a triangular girder of immense strength. This portion pivots freely at the point of attachment to the main frame at the base of the saddle tube on two indestructible "Silent-bloc" rubber bearings, which

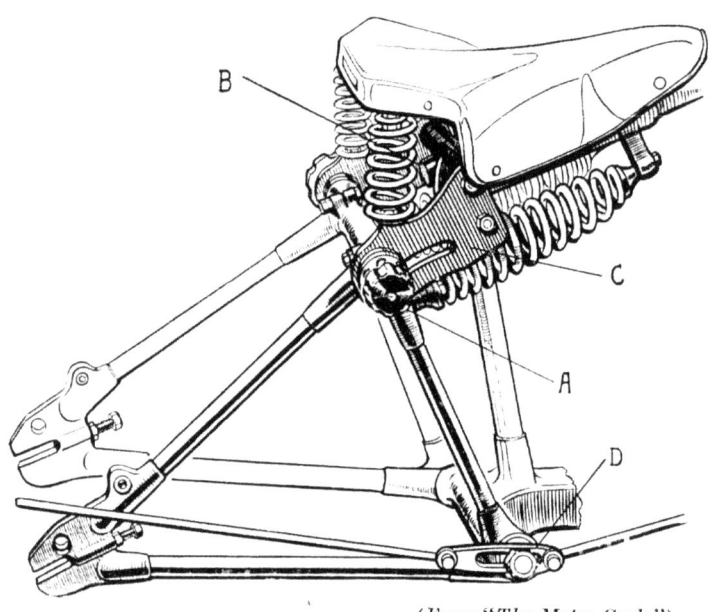

(*From "The Motor Cycle"*)

Fig. 12. THE REAR PORTION OF THE SPRING FRAME

A—Adjustable dampers   C—Damper side plate
B—Rubber buffer stops   D—Brake compensating link

require no lubrication and cannot wear. Three years is regarded as a normal life. Right at the end of the tank tube is a massive "T" lug which carries two rubber buffer stops to prevent the suspension springs closing up solid when negotiating extremely rough ground, and two steel plates bolted to the frame seat lug. These steel plates (C, Fig. 12), which each have a radius slot cut in them, serve as saddle spring anchorages, and the slots themselves act as guides for the two upper transverse spindles which are both clamped so as to enable an adjustment to be made, in the top bridge lug, and at their ends have adjustable shock-absorbing dampers (A, Fig. 12) which can be manipulated by hand from the saddle with the machine in motion. Two fibre friction discs are brought into direct contact with each stationary side plate at the required pressure by rotating the handwheels clockwise the necessary amount to suit varying road conditions. Two metal discs are employed and one spring washer. The main purpose of these friction dampers is to delay the recoil of the two powerful compression springs which take the loading, and which are placed between the rear frame and the tank tube. The rear fork ends are of the usual type with screws between the chain stays for correctly tensioning the secondary chain and aligning the rear wheel. In this connection it is interesting to note that the pivot of the rear frame is not concentric with the rear driving sprocket. In practice, however, the alteration in chain tension consequent upon the movement of the rear portion of the frame is of negligible effect, provided that the chain tension be adjusted with the hinged portion of the frame in its normal position (page 112). In order that the action of the spring frame shall not interfere with the brake mechanism, an extension of the offside "silent-bloc" pin serves as a guide for a slotted link plate which can move in a fore and aft direction only.

The Matchless forks (fitted to all models with slightly different dimensions) comprise a strong brazed up girder assembly of "D" section seamless steel tubes, the two front tubes being of very small section.

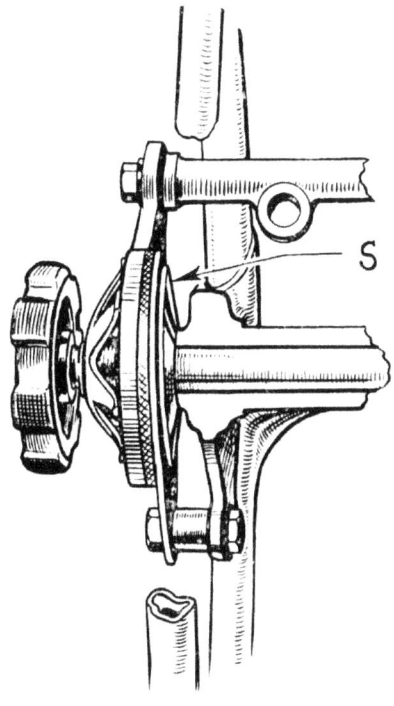

(From "The Motor Cycle")

FIG. 13. PARTLY SECTIONED VIEW OF THE LARGE ADJUSTABLE SHOCK ABSORBERS FITTED TO THE FRONT FORKS

Note the large spherical seating of the back plate S, which remains permanently effective

Suspension is by a single compression spring fitted between the top rear transverse lug and the lower front lug. A good degree of flexibility is thus obtained. Two large adjustable shock absorbers are provided of the type illustrated by Fig. 13. Adjustment may be made, as in the case of the spring frame dampers, with the machine in motion, and this course is the best one. The correct degree of friction is obtained by rotating the ebonite hand adjusting nut on the off-side the required amount.

The back plate of each shock absorber, as may be seen from the illustration, has a spherical seating so that it remains effective throughout the whole life of the machine. Provision is made for correcting lateral play in the fork spindle bearings independently of the damper adjustment and for lubricating the spindles. The fibre washers fitted between the spindle lug ends and the spindle side plates are not intended for frictional purposes, but solely to prevent actual seizure in the event of the hexagon-ended spindles being tightened excessively. Grease-gun nipples are provided for lubrication of the spindle bearings, the lubricants advocated being Tecalemit Grease or Wakefield's "Castrolease Light."

An efficient steering damper with the friction surfaces at the base of the steering head lug (see Fig. 3) is controlled by an ebonite handwheel on the instrument panel or, where this is not fitted, in the centre of the handlebars. Two useful fork stops are also included.

Gearbox and Clutch. The gearbox is the latest four-speed, lightweight Sturmey-Archer, similar in construction and action to the four-speed heavyweight boxes of the same make fitted to the higher powered models. The solo gear ratios are as follows—

First, 17·5 to 1; second, 11·6 to 1; third, 7·8 to 1; fourth, 5·9 to 1. Gear control is by a neat gate-change quadrant bolted to the tank itself, and a straight pattern gear lever connected to the gearbox striker lever by two rods running at right angles to each other, and joined by a neat duplex lever mounted on a shaft just behind the oil tank. The gear lever positions from rear to front are 1st, N, 2nd, 3rd, 4th. The gearbox lubricant recommended is Mobiloil "D" or Mobilgrease. Provision is made in the design of the gearbox for a speedometer drive, which, when fitted, communicates with a Smith chronometric instrument mounted on the panel or on the handlebars.

Further details are given elsewhere. Sufficient it is here to mention its principal characteristics. The lightweight gearbox on Model A/2 is held in place by two bolts between the rear engine plates, which have slotted holes and a draw bolt adjustment for the primary chain. It is of very sturdy construction, embodying a carefully selected series of gear ratios to suit all requirements.

Four pairs of gears are used and of these two are always in mesh. Two of the gears, one on the mainshaft and one on the layshaft, have dog-clutch teeth formed on both faces. They are slidably mounted on splined shafts and engage with four gears which revolve freely on their axles, but do not slide endwise. The two slidable clutch gears are grooved to engage the striking forks which are supported on a separate spindle. The lateral movement of the clutches is obtained by pegs on the striking forks which engage in slots in a cam plate on the periphery of which are cut notches (Fig. 58) to engage a spring-loaded plunger. It will thus be realized that the various gear positions are automatically indexed in the gearbox as well as by the gate-change quadrant notches. The cam plate itself is operated by a lever on the front of the box, and is geared up to reduce the movement of the operating lever.

The kick-starter drive is taken through the low gear train as on the three-speed boxes. An extra long substantial bearing is provided for the kick-starter axle, so that there is no possibility of the layshaft getting out of line with the main axle. A pawl fitted on the axle and engaging with a ratchet on the inside of the layshaft pinion provides the necessary "free-wheel" coupling.

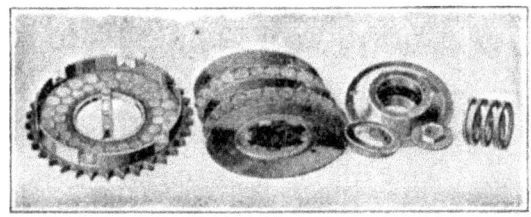

(*Sturmey-Archer Gears, Ltd.*)

Fig. 14. The Three-plate Sturmey-Archer Clutch

A similar type clutch with Ferodo inserts and six springs instead of one is fitted to all other models having 4-speed S.-A. gearboxes

The kick-starter crank is attached to the axle by serrations (Fig. 2), so it can be placed in any desired position.

The clutch used is a single-spring, three-plate type, and is controlled by a lever on the left side of the handlebars which actuates a Bowden cable transmitting its pull to a small upright lever having its fulcrum just above the kick-starter axle housing. When this lever is pulled towards the engine a ball-ended adjustable screw, at its base, pushes a short rod which pushes a long spindle floating in the hollow mainshaft back until its end pushes against the outer clutch boss and so releases the clutch spring pressure. A dual adjustment is provided in the form of a Bowden wire adjustable casing stop, and a pinch-bolt fixing of the small lever to the worm itself. Fig. 4 shows the parts of the three-plate clutch fitted to the "Silver Arrow," and it will be observed that it comprises a main body secured by a nut to the splined mainshaft and three driven plates separated by three cork and Ferodo insert discs, the rearmost of which constitutes the clutch sprocket, and is free to rotate on a brass cage roller bearing. Whenever the clutch sprocket is rotating, the other two friction discs also rotate, since they engage at their peripheries with eight deep tongues and slots in the sprocket. A single coil spring, whose pressure can be adjusted by a nut on the mainshaft, presses the friction discs against the driven discs. Advice on adjustment and dismantling will be found on pages 108 and 144.

Transmission. Coventry "Ultimate" chains are employed for both primary and secondary transmission, the dimensions of the former being $\tfrac{7}{16}$ in. × ·265 in., and of the latter $\tfrac{1}{2}$ in. × ·305 in., and adjustment is by gearbox and rear wheel thrust screws, respectively. The primary chain is automatically lubricated by a short pipe leading from the crankcase disc breather. The secondary chain requires to be lubricated by the rider from time to time. Adequate protection from road dust and mud is given by means of two efficient guards. The rear guard protects the upper half of the chain only, and allows of an eye being kept on chain tension and lubrication. A shock absorber is not fitted owing to the exceptionally even engine torque.

Brakes. Internal expanding brakes of 8 in. diameter × $\tfrac{3}{4}$ in. are fitted to both wheels. They are smooth in action, but very powerful. A special interconnecting gear renders rapid retardation safe when driving in heavy traffic, and little effort is required to exert full pressure. The brake pedal itself is mounted on the off-side on a shaft fixed to the rear engine plates. In addition to the single pedal control of the two brakes, independent handlebar control for the front brake is provided.

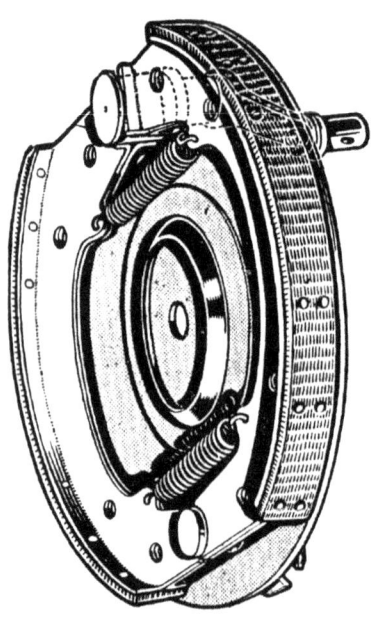

FIG. 15. THE FRONT BRAKE ANCHOR PLATE WITH SHOES IN POSITION

The Matchless brakes do not include separate drums, for these are integral with the hubs, being forced and sweated on. Fig. 15 shows the front anchor plate which is almost identical to the rear one. Two flanged steel brake shoes, to which are riveted the Don friction linings, are pivoted at the top and held together normally out of contact with the drum by two strong tension springs. A "square" type of cam at the opposite side forces the shoes apart when pressure is applied to the brake pedal or handlebar lever. The simple method of interconnecting the two brakes is made clear by reference to Fig. 16, which shows the peculiar shape of the brake pedal mounted on a shaft fixed to the rear engine plates. From the upper end of the pedal lever, a rod with split-pin attachment runs direct to one end of the slotted link mounted on the extremity of the "silent-bloc" bearing spindle (see Fig. 12), and from the other end another rod runs to the lever on the rear brake anchor plate where a spring and knurled nut provide a hand adjustment. From the lower end of the pedal lever a Bowden cable runs to the lever on the front brake anchor plate. Here also a similar hand adjustment is provided. In addition, hand adjustment of the independent handlebar control is

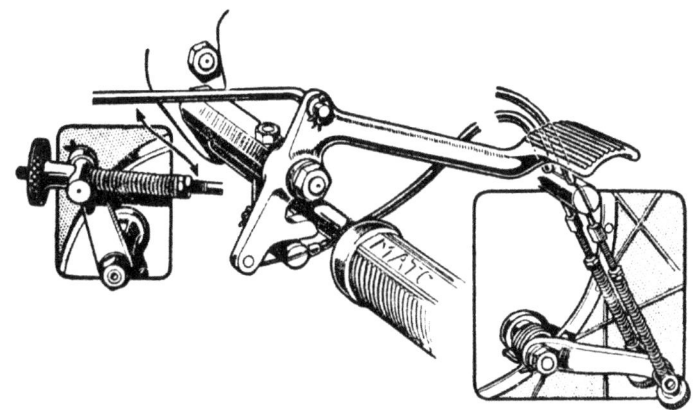

FIG. 16. SHOWING THE MATCHLESS BRAKE INTER-CONNECTING GEAR AND FINGER-TIP ADJUSTMENT
Left inset shows rear brake adjustment and right inset the foot and hand control adjustment for the front brake

also to be found, a common stop for the ends of the two cable casings being used. Considerable care is required in adjusting the brakes to a nicety (see page 115).

Wheels and Tyres. Both wheels are of massive build. Timken taper roller bearings are used throughout, a type of bearing which in order to avoid damage requires exactly the right amount of play (see page 115). Large diameter axles are used and the left-hand cones are adjustable, being secured by thin lock-nuts (Fig. 17).

Dunlop 26 in. × 3·25 in. heavy cord, wired-on tyres are fitted, and they have Schrader valves to enable correct tyre pressures to be maintained. The inflation pressures advised for solo use on the "Silver Arrow" are 15–16 lb. per sq. in., and 21–22 lb. per sq. in. for front and rear tyres, respectively. If a pillion passenger be carried the pressure of the rear tyre should be raised to 26–28 lb. per sq. in. Where a sidecar is used pressures may remain the same as for pillion riding. The sidecar tyre should be inflated to

18 lb. per sq. in. If desired, 27 in. × 4 in. tyres may be specified for an extra 10s.; this applies to all machines over 350 c.c. In this case the solo pressures for front and rear tyres should be 13-14 lb. per sq. in. and 18-20 lb. per sq. in., respectively.

Tanks. The fuel tank (fitted to all models except R/7) is constructionally the same as last year's tank, but it is of vastly improved shape and appearance with a more bulbous nose. It is finished in untarnishable chromium plating with white side panels

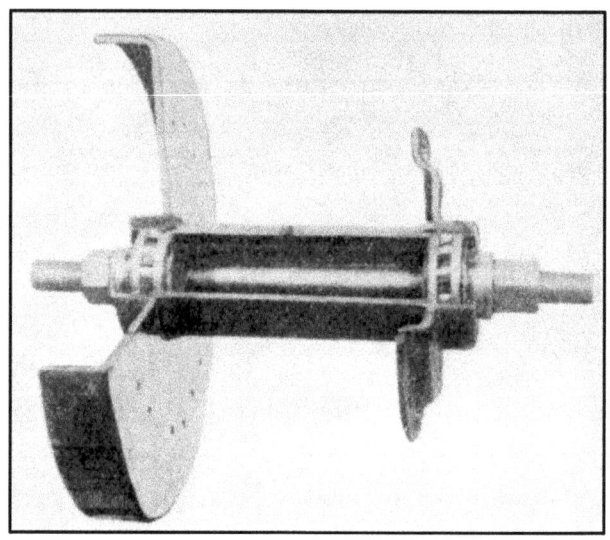

FIG. 17. MATCHLESS FRONT HUB AND BRAKE DRUM PLATE SECTIONED TO SHOW CONSTRUCTION
The adjustable cone for the roller bearings is the one shown on the right of the illustration

and black lining. Right at the front of each panel is a very handsome "M" in chromium plating vividly contrasting with the white background. The word "Matchless" now appears only on the centre tank strips and rear guards. A leak-proof and quickly detachable filler cap is used, and the fuel capacity of the tank is approximately $2\frac{1}{2}$ gal. Two very neat rubber knee grips are provided. The tank is attached to the frame at the base by three bolts, two at the front and one at the rear, with rubber buffers interposed to damp out vibration, and at the top has a strip fixing plate. The tank is immensely strong, being constructed of heavy gauge steel pressings welded together (Fig. 1). Even the petrol pipe union sockets are welded in position, so that there is no danger of the tank developing a leak even after many years service, or after a few minor crashes. A "U" pipe connects the two parts of the tank, thereby balancing the level of petrol therein.

The oil tank also of pressed steel, is bolted direct to the front of the crankcase, there being no exterior piping whatever. This tank, shown at Fig. 9, has a capacity of 6 pints. The oil consumption is 1,600-1,800 m.p.g.

Miscellaneous Equipment. Chromium plated adjustable handlebars of semi-sports type are fitted. The saddle is a large Lycett "Aero." Particularly robust footrests are attached to a square spindle passing right through the two rear engine plates.

Large "D" section mudguards with deep valances are provided. The rear guard is split below the saddle to enable the rear portion, complete with stays, to be quickly detached when tyre repairs are necessary. The rear stays are extended to form a convenient lifting handle by which the machine can be eased back on to its stand, which is a spring-up type fitted below the gearbox, so designed that the machine can be lifted on to it practically without effort. When tyre repairs are undertaken, small extensions to the stand feet can be fitted to give the necessary ground clearance. A carrier is not a standard fitment, but can be had as an extra if desired. A comprehensive tool outfit is contained in one of the two metal pannier bags slung between the mudguard stays. All parts not enamelled or chromium plated are rustless black gun finished.

Maximum speed (solo), 60-66 m.p.h. Weight (without lighting), 320 lb.

MODEL B (THE "SILVER HAWK")

This fascinating machine, which has an astonishingly high road performance and attracted such attention at the 1930 Olympia Show when it was first shown to the public, is, with the exception of the power unit and transmission, an almost exact replica of the popular "Silver Arrow," already described in detail, although most of the dimensions are greater. It has complete de luxe equipment, however, and also a handsome nickel-plated, high-frequency electric horn. The engine and transmission will be dealt with in the following specification—

The 5·93 h.p. O.H.C. Vee-four Engine. As in the case of the A/2 engine, the B power unit is not what it seems on cursory inspection; it is not a vertical "four." Actually it is a very neat and compact monobloc design equivalent to two "Silver Arrow" small-angle Vee twins, set side by side with the crankshaft lying across the frame. Exactly the same firing angle (26 degrees) is employed, and there are many other features in common. The

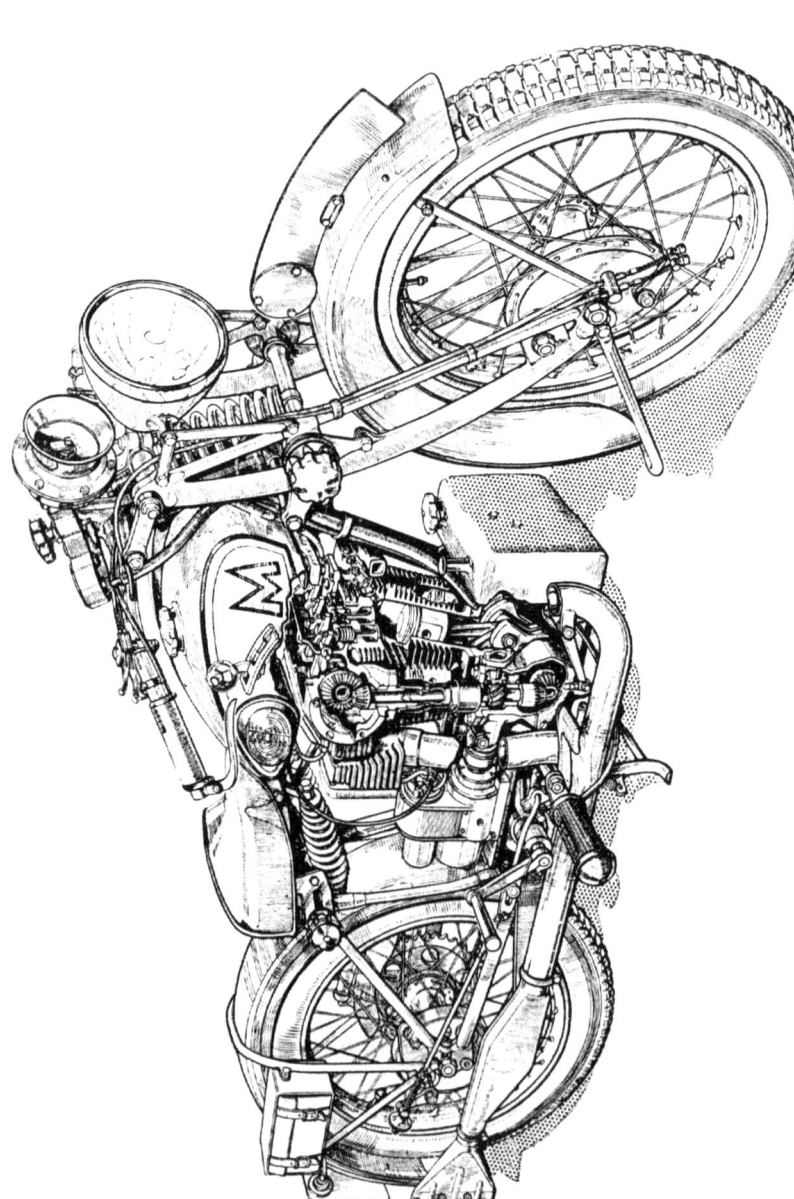

Fig. 18. Partly Sectioned View of the 593 c.c. O.H.C. Narrow Angle Vee-Four Spring Frame Matchless "Silver Hawk"

("The Motor Cycle" copyright)

bore and stroke are 50·8 mm. × 73·02 mm., giving a cubic capacity of 593 c.c.

The crankcase is sturdy but very compact, and houses a built-up, two-throw crankshaft which is carried in three bearings to prevent whip, the centre one being a heavy roller pattern mounted

FIG. 19. CLOSE-UP VIEW OF 5·93 H.P. O.H.C. VEE-FOUR ENGINE
Showing arrangement of the vertical camshaft drive, exhaust manifolds and dynamo-coil-distributor unit

in a large steel plate which forms a partition between the two crankcase halves, by which it is firmly held in position. Phosphor-bronze bushes, pressure fed from the D.S. pump to ensure longevity, are fitted on both the driving and timing side of the crankshaft. Four bobweights and heavy crank cheeks are substituted for flywheels. Fig. 20 illustrates the complete crankshaft assembly, and it may be observed that "Silver Arrow" connecting rods and big-end assembly are used. Aluminium alloy is, of course, used for the pistons, which have unusually long split skirts and have two rings, the lower one acting as a scraper ring. The piston ring gap is ·004 in. to ·006 in. The gudgeon pins are fully floating and of $\frac{11}{16}$ in. diameter. Spring circlips retain them in the piston bosses. In connection with the big-end bearings, it should be mentioned that the eyes of the "H" section connecting rods, as on the "Arrow," are very slightly eccentric and narrowed in depth to permit of slight overlapping. Shouldered

Fig. 20. The "Silver Hawk" Crankshaft Assembly

crankpins are used and a set of rollers (without bush) for each connecting rod.

The angle between each pair of cylinders is 18 degrees, as in the case of the "Arrow" engine, and all four are cast integral in a monobloc casting well finned horizontally and with a large air space between the cylinder banks. This block has a four-bolt attachment to the crankcase, and its upper surface is machined to receive the detachable cylinder head. A gas-tight joint is ensured by the use of a copper-asbestos washer. The compression ratio is 6 to 1. The head itself, which is an intricate monobloc casting containing all four combustion chambers, is held down together with the cam box by twelve bolts. In plan view it is approximately square (Fig. 21), and contains the valve seats, the induction passages, and the exhaust passages. The valves, which have $\frac{5}{16}$ in. stems and $1\frac{1}{16}$ in. heads, reciprocate in chilled cast-iron

THE MATCHLESS MODELS

guides pressed into the cylinder head vertically, and, since the cylinder bores are 2 in. approximately (50·8 mm.), it becomes necessary to use combustion chambers that in plan view are roughly oval. The tops of the cylinder barrels are cut away to conform with this shape. To ensure perfect gas distribution to each cylinder and effective mixture pre-heating, a cored passage leads from the flanged carburettor on the near-side to a central

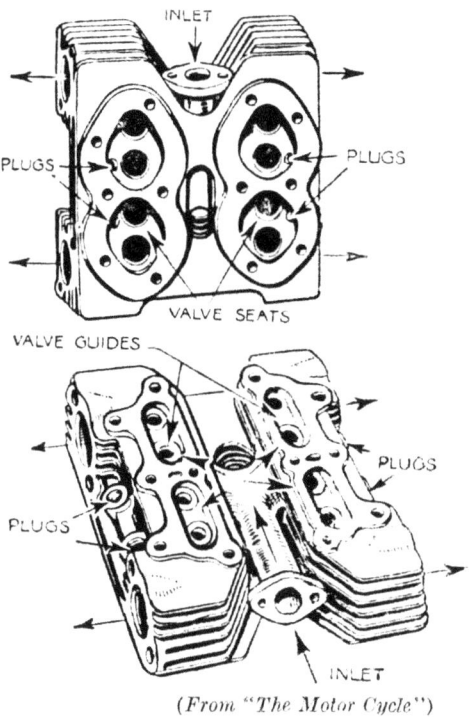

(*From "The Motor Cycle"*)

FIG. 21. SHOWING THE CONSTRUCTION OF THE ONE-PIECE CYLINDER HEAD

position in the head, and from here four passages of *equal length* communicate with the respective combustion chambers. Referring to the upper sketch in Fig. 21, it may be noted that the four valves at the corners of the unit deal with the exhaust, and the four in the centre with the induction. Bolted to the front and rear sides of the cylinder head are two finned cast-iron manifolds, from which the products of combustion from each pair of cylinders are conveyed to two separate large diameter ports, both inclined slightly forward, whence the gases are led by two chromium-plated exhaust pipes to a single large capacity silencer of standard Matchless design.

The top of the cast-iron cylinder head is faced to receive the neat aluminium cam box (Fig. 19) which completely encloses the overhead camshaft and the valves and their rockers, and enables the parts to be well lubricated and kept silent. The aluminium cam box, which is integral with the bevel box, is held down by the same long bolts which retain the cylinder head itself to the main cylinder bloc. Two detachable cover plates give instant access to the valves and their rockers, so that correct valve clearances can readily be maintained. The single piece camshaft runs across the centre of the rocker-box parallel to the crankshaft, and is supported by long plain phosphor-bronze bearings at each end. It is driven clockwise from the vertical shaft by straight bevels which can be adjusted for mesh by shims and are marked for correct replacement. The vertical driving shaft is supported by five plain bearings and has two Oldham couplings.

Each set of four rockers is not mounted on a single bearing spindle in the usual manner. Instead, what might be termed "floating" fulcrums are used. For each rocker there is a small steel barrel with a square hole across its axis (see Figs. 18 and 22) in which the rocker fits. There are thus four such "floating fulcrums" on each side of the camshaft, and they are mounted on a long $\tfrac{3}{16}$ in. steel bolt running across the cam-box, and they are spaced out with springs. Valve clearances are adjusted in the usual way by grub screws and lock-nuts. The valves themselves are of nickel-chrome steel and have mushroom heads. Single springs of normal pressure are used and these have a split collet anchorage for the lower caps. No exhaust valve lifter is fitted.

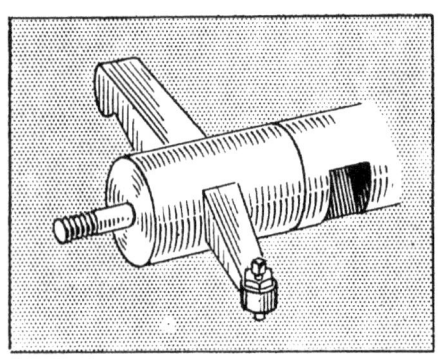

FIG. 22
A "FLOATING" ROCKER FULCRUM

With regard to lubrication, the system closely follows "Arrow" practice. Some of the oil is sucked from the tank at the front of the engine by the double-acting pump housed in the base of the crankcase and driven by skew gears off the crankshaft, and *forced* through drilled oil passages to the main bearings, big-ends, and piston skirts, while the remainder passes, via a sight-feed in the instrument panel, to the top of the bevel-box. Incidentally, the oil return may be verified, as on the "Arrow," by removing the oil tank filler cap. At a predetermined level the oil in the bevel-box overflows into the cam-box, and thoroughly lubricates the camshaft, rocker gear, and inlet valve guide. Both sets of bevels and the vertical shaft are entirely submerged in oil which makes for long life and quiet running. There is a separate drain passage from the cam-box down through the cylinder block casting to the crankcase whence all oil is returned to the tank. A

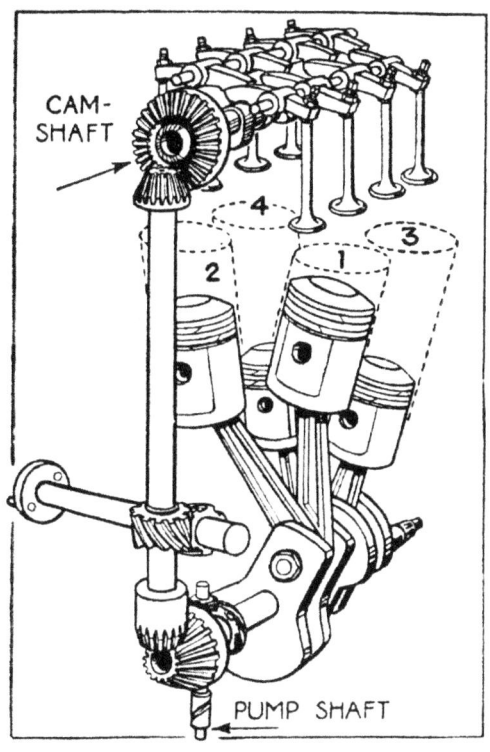

(*From "The Motor Cycle"*)

FIG. 22A. SEMI-DIAGRAMMATIC VIEW SHOWING THE CYLINDER ARRANGEMENT OF THE "HAWK" AND THE CAMSHAFT, PUMP, AND MAGNETO DRIVES. THE FIRING ORDER IS 1, 4, 2, 3

crankcase pressure-release disc valve serves to lubricate the primary chain.

Sparking plugs recommended (all O.H.V.
    and O.H.C. engines) . . . . Lodge, H.1. or K.L.G., K.5
Valve clearances (cold) . . . As near nil as possible
Magneto advance . . . . 9/16 in. before T.D.C. on
                                            full advance

Carburettor. A special semi-automatic, twist-grip control, flange-fitting, pilot jet Amal instrument is used of very similar design to that fitted to the "Silver Arrow," except that a top petrol feed is used. Its type number is 4/004, and it is bolted direct to the near side of the cylinder head between the finning (Fig. 21). Twist-grip control is standard, but lever control is obtainable. A throttle stop for slow running is included. The jet fitted as standard is a No. 75, with a 4/5 throttle valve in position 2. The pilot outlet measures ·020 in. An Amal air cleaner is fitted.

Ignition. Lodge H.1 sparking plugs, which are pocketed, are fitted as standard, while the current for ignition and lighting is generated by a special Lucas D.F.V.4 dynamo-coil-distributor unit, mounted on a platform above the gearbox with the dynamo itself, driven clockwise (from distributor end) at engine speed by helical bevels indirectly off the vertical shaft (Fig. 19) with a

FIG. 23. MODEL B (THE "SILVER HAWK")

flexible rubber coupling similar to the A/2 coupling (Fig. 7) interposed between a metal disc on the dynamo armature and one on the horizontal driving shaft. The dynamo, above which is mounted the coil, includes an enclosed electro-magnetic cut-out to prevent overcharging of the battery or discharge through the dynamo, whilst the timing is advanced by cable control from the handlebars which rotates the contact-breaker rocker arm and distributor moulding, from whose four terminals heavily insulated high-tension cables lead up to the plugs. The distributor shaft, whose bearings require periodic lubrication, is driven anti-clockwise at half engine speed by helical bevel gearing off the dynamo shaft, and has a four-lobe cam operating the single-lever contact-breaker housed in the lower half of the distributor body (Fig. 55). The correct gap at the contacts is ·015 in. To the top of the distributor shaft is fixed the rotating distributor arm, whose outer tip has a metal electrode which passes sufficiently close to the four metal segments in the distributor moulding to enable the high-tension current to jump the gaps and fire each plug consecutively. The recommended gap at the plugs is approximately

·027 in. A ballast resistance is incorporated in the primary circuit to limit the flow of current from the battery to the coil when the engine is running slowly or is stationary; of course, when the ignition is switched off no current can flow through the primary coil. To guard against the possibility of the battery being allowed to exhaust itself when the machine is left stationary with the switch "on," a tell-tale warning lamp is fixed on the instrument panel and in such circumstances gives a red light. It will also light, however, when the engine is running very slowly, due to

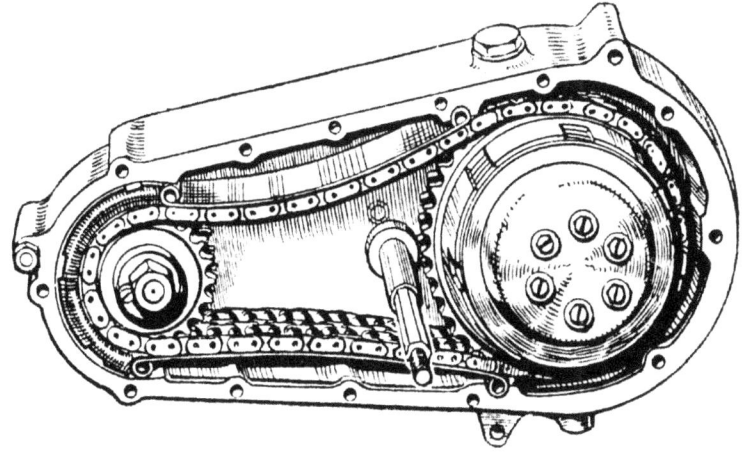

(*From "The Motor Cycle"*)

FIG. 24. THE DUPLEX PRIMARY CHAIN AND AUTOMATIC TENSIONING DEVICE

The chain is shown slack to illustrate more clearly the action of the two steel springs

the fact that the dynamo is generating a current of insufficient voltage to actuate the cut-out. The battery itself which supplies low-tension current to the coil of this very compact lighting-ignition unit, and also to the lamps, is mounted adjacent to this unit and held by a strap.

Gearbox and Clutch. A four-speed, heavyweight Sturmey-Archer gearbox is mounted *rigidly* between the rear engine plates and a three-plate clutch is used in conjunction with it. This clutch closely resembles the lighter pattern employed on the "Silver Arrow," but it is of heavier design in order to bear the greater transmission loads on this higher powered machine. The complete clutch runs in oil, including all the friction plates, which are tongued and slotted and rotate as one with the clutch sprocket. For the same reason, six coil springs instead of one are used to press the three driving plates against the friction insert plates. The pressure of these springs which are spaced radially is adjustable by means of bolts whose slotted heads are countersunk in the outer clutch boss. A lever type of hollow mainshaft plunger spring release control is used. The solo gear ratios are as follows—

Solo: first, 17·0 to 1; second, 12·4 to 1; third, 6·9 to 1; fourth, 5·7 to 1

The gear lever positions, rear to front, are 1st, N, 2nd, 3rd, 4th.

Transmission. There is considerable novelty displayed in regard to the primary transmission which is at once apparent on removing the front chain case (see Fig. 24). A special ⅜ in. × ·250 duplex Coventry "Ultimate" chain is used, necessitating the use of extra wide sprocket teeth. This chain runs in an oil bath, and is kept automatically tensioned by a very clever form of spring loading produced under Weller patents. It comprises two spring steel strips on each side of the chain. These keep the chain permanently taut even when a considerable degree of stretch develops. The chain case may be replenished with oil from time to time by pouring it through the plug hole at the rear. The dimensions of the secondary chain are ⅝ in. × ·380 in. There is, of course, no shock absorber. Tyre pressures for sidecar use are the same as for the "Arrow." When running solo, 18, 24 lb. per sq. in. are recommended for front and rear, respectively.

Maximum speed (solo), 80-85 m.p.h. Weight, 370 lb.

MODEL X/3

The standard Matchless Big Twin has the following specification—

The 9·90 h.p. S.V. Vee-twin Engine. This engine has a bore and stroke of 85·5 mm. × 85·5 mm., giving a cubic capacity of 990 c.c. The two cylinders are set at 50 degrees to each other, and the bores, being "square" with the cylinder castings, the firing angle is also 50 degrees. Fig. 25 shows the general design and construction of the power unit.

The crankcase itself is a very neat aluminium casting split longitudinally in the usual manner. An extension immediately below the annular timing case, which has a readily detachable cover, houses the D.S. pump plunger, and if separation of the crankcase halves is contemplated care is necessary in respect of this unit. A disc breather maintains atmospheric pressure in the crankcase, and also serves to lubricate the primary chain. The crankshaft assembly is an ordinary single-throw type built up of two flywheels, to which are keyed the friction fitting mainshafts, and a shouldered crankpin upon which with two sets of rollers interposed, but no bushes, are mounted a pair of "H" section

THE MATCHLESS MODELS

connecting rods having $\frac{7}{8}$ in. (I-D) phosphor-bronze small end bearings. With regard to the crankshaft bearings, that on the driving side has a heavy double-row caged roller bearing, while the other one is of the plain bush type. The pistons themselves are of aluminium alloy and have two rings each, the lower acting

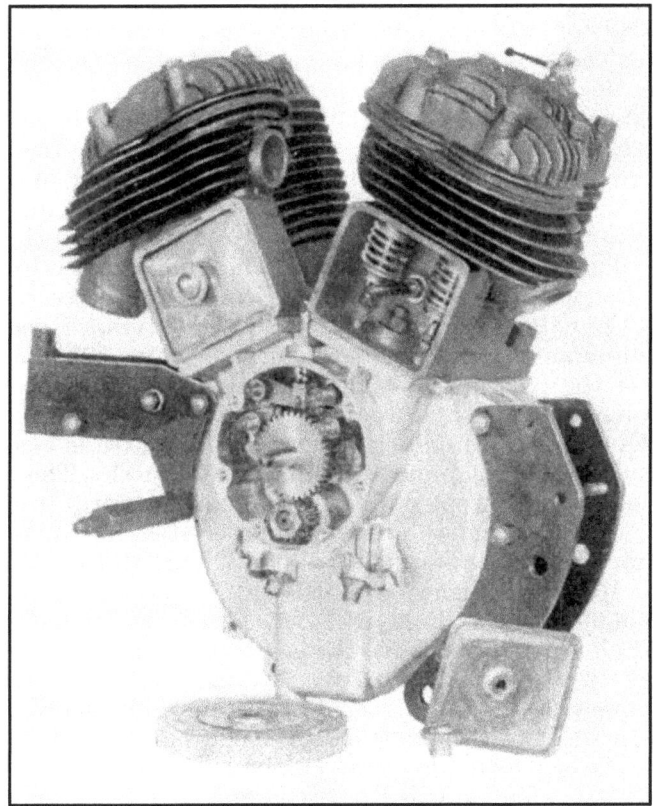

FIG. 25. CLOSE-UP VIEW OF THE 9·90 H.P. S.V. VEE-TWIN ENGINE

The timing case cover and one valve cover plate have been removed to show the valves and timing gear

as a scraper ring. They are split diagonally across the skirts to allow for expansion, and they have fully floating gudgeon pins secured by small spring circlips to prevent scoring. With a *cold* engine, the correct gap at the piston ring slots is ·006 in. to ·010 in.

The cylinders, which have a compression ratio of 4·8 to 1, have cast-iron detachable heads, and the cylinder barrels are cast integral with two very neat valve chests which entirely enclose and protect the valves and their springs, two pressed steel cover plates held firm by centrally placed knurled nuts giving instant access to the valves. The barrels are deeply spigoted at their bases and paper washers are used; C. and A. gaskets are fitted between the barrels and heads which are of semi-turbulent design. The sparking plugs are centrally located, and a useful compression cock is provided for each cylinder head for priming purposes in cold weather. The two cylinders are interconnected by a horizontal induction manifold with screw-in unions.

The valves themselves are of large diameter and of the mushroom type with single springs and slotted valve stems for the flat cotters used for anchorage. They reciprocate in chilled cast-iron guides which are readily detached for renewal. Round section tappets are used, and the adjustable heads screw into the tappet bodies and are secured by lock-nuts. The timing gear is extremely simple. It comprises a single cam wheel having three cams, one each for the exhaust and one for the inlet valves, driven off the engine pinion, and four rockers mounted on pivot pins and separated from the back of the timing case by $\frac{29}{64}$ in. distance collars. The arrangement of these rockers is shown by Fig. 25, and the neat exhaust valve lifter mechanism in the centre is also clearly illustrated; the timing pinions are marked for mesh. The products of combustion are swept out from the exhaust ports into an imposing and exceedingly quiet exhaust system comprising two $1\frac{3}{4}$ in. diameter chromium plated pipes, each terminating in a standard Matchless silencer and fish-tail.

The magneto, or "Magdyno," as the case may be, which is mounted on a platform above the gearbox, is driven by chain and sprockets direct off the camshaft. The camshaft sprocket fits on a slight taper, is keyed, and held firmly by a nut screwed to the threaded end of the shaft. Chain tension is adjusted by sliding the magneto platform along the engine cradle plates by a special adjuster. A black-enamelled pressed steel chain case protects the chain.

The lubrication of the engine is carried out by a D.S. system similar to that described on page 14. The double-acting oil pump forces oil under pressure to the big ends of the connecting rods, the mainshaft bearings and the camshaft bearings, while the whole of the timing gear runs submerged in oil, and oil mist penetrates into the valve chests, the surplus being returned to the timing case via grooves cut in the tappet guides longitudinally.

Tappet clearances (all S.V. engines except A/2)	·004 in. inlet and ·006 exhaust (warm)
Magneto Advance (X/3 and X/R3)	$\frac{7}{16}$ in. before T.D.C. on full advance

Carburettor. This is a two-lever, semi-automatic clip-fitting, pilot jet Amal instrument, having a top petrol feed and fitted with a slow running throttle stop. The type number of the carburettor is 6/012. A size 110 jet is used in conjunction with a 6/4 throttle valve in position 3. This combination, which provides a fuel consumption of 70-80 m.p.g., is found to give very satisfactory running for general purposes. On Model X/3 an Amal air cleaner is fitted. Twist-grip control of the throttle is optional, but standard on Model X/3 de luxe.

Ignition. Lucas equipment is used throughout, the K.L.V. magneto, as stated above, being driven from the camshaft. It has, therefore, a clockwise rotation, seen from the contact-breaker

FIG. 26. MODEL X/3

side. The contact-breaker, incidentally, has two cams, No. 1 cam being nearest to the rear firing cylinder. Lodge T.S.3 plugs are used.

Frame and Forks. The frame used on the 9·90 h.p. models is immensely strong. It is of the trussed loop pattern with duplex torque stays. Four large engine plates and a pair of torque tubes constitute a rigid and inflexible cradle mounting for the power unit. The two rear plates, incidentally, form a bracket for the four-speed gearbox which has the usual drawbolt for primary chain adjustment and a two-bolt fixing. The forks are of the standard Matchless pattern, with a single central compression spring, fork stops, and hand-adjusted shock absorbers.

Gearbox and Clutch. The gearbox is the latest heavyweight, four-speed Sturmey-Archer as fitted to the "Silver Hawk," mention of which is made on page 33, and a sectional view of which appears on page 84. It has a bottom bracket and stud type of mounting, and a very similar type of four-plate clutch with Ferodo inserts and multiple springs. In this case, however, the arrangement of the gear lever control results in a reversal of the gear lever positions. From rear to front they are: 4th, 3rd, 2nd, N., 1st. The gear ratios are as follows—

Solo X/3, sidecar X/R3   First, 12·8 to 1; second, 9·3 to 1; third, 5·7 to 1; fourth, 4·3 to 1.
Sidecar X/R3   First, 14·2 to 1; second, 10·4 to 1; third, 6·4 to 1; fourth, 4·8 to 1.

A Smith chronometric speedometer with 80 m.p.h. dial is driven by gearing from the near side of the gearbox.

Transmission. The dimensions of the primary and secondary chains, which are both Coventry "Ultimates," are $\frac{1}{2}$ in. × ·305 in. and $\frac{5}{8}$ in. × ·380 in., respectively. Both are adequately protected by steel guards, the primary chain being totally enclosed and lubricated from the crankcase disc breather. There is no shock absorber.

Brakes. 8 in. × $\frac{3}{4}$ in. brakes are used on both wheels, and they are coupled together by the special interconnecting gear (page 23). There is, of course, no slotted link as on the spring frame models. Separate control by handlebar lever is retained for the front brake, and finger tip adjustment for both brakes is provided.

Wheels and Tyres. Both wheels have Timken roller bearings, with adjustable cones on the near side (Fig. 17). On Model X/R3 chromium-plated wheels are standard. The tyres used are 26 in. × 3·25 in. heavy cord, wired-on Dunlops, with Schrader valves. Oversize covers measuring 27 in. × 4 in. are available. The recommended inflation pressures for solo use with standard covers are: front, 18 lb. per sq. in., rear, 24 lb. per sq. in. When a sidecar is used the pressure of the rear tyre should be increased to 26 lb. per sq. in. The tyre on the sidecar wheel itself should be inflated to 20 lb. per sq. in.

Tanks. The new type fuel tank has a capacity of $2\frac{1}{2}$ gal., and with its chromium "M" and rubber knee grips is exceedingly handsome. The oil tank which has a capacity of 4 pints is strapped to the saddle tube and has a quick release filler cap, on removal of which may be observed the return pipe from the D.S. pump situated just above the filter as on the "Silver Arrow" tank. The oil consumption is 1,000–1,200 m.p.g. solo.

Miscellaneous Equipment. Standard equipment includes a detachable rear mudguard, adjustable handlebars, a Lycette "Aero" spring seat, stands to both wheels, rubber-covered footrests (foot boards optional), a steering damper, lifting handle, pannier tool bags, and a complete set of tools with pump attached to the front forks.

Maximum speed (Solo) . . . . 70–75 m.p.h.
Maximum speed (Sidecar) . . . 60–65 m.p.h.
Weight (without lighting) . . . 360 lb.

MODEL R/7

The specification of the smallest lightweight side-valve Matchless is as follows —

The 2·46 h.p. S.V. Engine. The power unit is practically identical to the 1930 version. It has a bore and stroke of 62·5 mm. × 80 mm., giving a cubic capacity of 246 c.c. A crankcase of similar design to that used on all single cylinder side-valve models is used. The crankshaft assembly comprises two flywheels, a shouldered crankpin, and two mainshafts, all of similar pattern to those used on the 9·90 h.p. engine already described. A caged roller bearing is fitted on the transmission side, and a plain phosphor-bronze bearing on the timing side. The connecting rod of " H " section, and a set of 30 hardened rollers is placed between the crankpin shoulder and the eye of the rod. No connecting rod bush is used. The small-end bearing is of the plain bush type with fully floating $\frac{11}{16}$ in. diameter gudgeon pin secured by circlips. The piston which is of aluminium alloy has a split skirt and two rings. The compression ratio is 4·43 to 1.

The design of the well finned cylinder and cylinder head may be gathered from Fig. 27; the barrel, spigoted at the base and held down by three bolts, is cast integral with the valve chest, and the detachable turbulent cylinder head, which has a gasket, is secured to the upper face by four bolts. The sparking plug is located centrally over the combustion chamber behind the valves which are totally enclosed and lubricated, a quickly detachable valve chest cover giving immediate access to them. Mushroom valves with single compression springs and flat cotters for spring cap anchorage are used.

With regard to the timing gear (Fig. 27), this is the essence of simplicity. A single cam wheel, marked for mesh and having two cams, is driven off the small engine pinion and transmits the necessary reciprocating motion to the tappets and valves by two rockers mounted on a single shaft. The tappet bodies have the usual screwed-in adjustable heads and lock-nuts. An exhaust valve lifter is provided. The whole of the timing gear runs submerged in oil at a level automatically built up by the oil pump, which cannot be exceeded or reduced. The exhaust noise is negligible.

The magneto on this engine is bolted on a platform at the front of the engine and protected by a shield; it is driven off the engine shaft at half engine speed in a clockwise (C.B. side) direction by a $\frac{1}{2}$ in. × $\frac{3}{16}$ in. chain and sprockets in the manner shown by Fig. 28. The chain is totally enclosed and runs in an oil-bath. The magneto can be slid on its platform for chain tensioning purposes. When a " Maglita " is fitted, it is driven at *engine* speed.

A dry sump lubrication system is used, as described on pages 14 and 73. Oil is force fed by the duplex horizontal reciprocating rotary plunger pump to three points on the cylinder wall, the big-end bearing, mainshaft bearings, and camshaft bearings. Surplus oil is sucked from the crankcase sump and returned to the

Fig. 27. The 2·46 h.p. S.V. Engine with Timing Cover and Valve Cover Plate Removed

oil tank. Its return can be verified at the return pipe orifice. No sight feed can be fitted.

Magneto advance: $\frac{29}{64}$ in. before T.D.C. on full advance, or T.D.C. on full retard

Carburettor. The carburettor used is a semi-automatic, two-lever, pilot jet Amal, with top petrol feed and a screw-in connection. Its type number is 4/114. A size 70 jet is used in conjunction with a 4/4 throttle valve in position 3, giving a fuel consumption of approximately 125 m.p.g. solo. Good slow

THE MATCHLESS MODELS

running is ensured by the use of a throttle stop. Twist-grip throttle control is extra.

Ignition. The forwardly placed magneto is a type M.A.1. Lucas, and it runs at half engine speed. Where electric lighting is specified, an F.D. type "Maglita" set only can be fitted. A "Magdyno" lighting set cannot be specified. The sparking plug fitted as standard is a Lodge T.S.3.

Frame and Forks. The frame is a strong welded-up structure

FIG. 28. VIEW OF 2·46 H.P. S.V. ENGINE FROM TRANSMISSION SIDE SHOWING MAGNETO DRIVE
It will be observed that the magneto is driven at half engine speed off a sprocket on the engine main shaft.

of the diamond type arranged to give a low C.G. and a low and comfortable saddle position. The wheelbase is only 4 ft. 4½ in. Standard Matchless forks with shock absorbers and forkstops are specified, but no steering damper is included.

Gearbox and Clutch. The three-speed gearbox used is an F.W. (featherweight) type, constant mesh Sturmey-Archer, specially designed for engines up to 250 c.c. This gearbox has the same gearing arrangement as the B.S. type box fitted last year, and control is by a neat elliptical quadrant fixed at the front of the fuel tank with the adjustable connecting rod running diagonally

at about 45 degrees to the gearbox striker lever. The gearbox has a two-stud fixing, and can be slid fore and aft between the rear engine plates by a thrust screw. The gear lever positions, front to rear, are 1st, N., 2nd, 3rd, and the ratios are—
    First, 16·8 to 1. Second, 9·4 to 1. Third, 6·1 to 1.
The gearbox lubricant recommended is Wakefield's "Castrolease Light," or Speedwell "Crimsangre Light." Provision is not made for a speedometer drive.

The gearbox is a constant-mesh, countershaft gear, having a totally enclosed kickstarter mechanism, and three pairs of pinions only are used. The low gear wheel on the layshaft includes a "free wheel" ratchet operated by a pawl on the kickstarter.

Fig. 29. Model R/7

which has a steel shaft, having as its bearing the layshaft axle bush. When the kickstarter return spring brings the crank back to its normal vertical position, a projection on the pawl engages with a fixed cam in the gearbox cover, and positively depresses the pawl out of action. All gear changes are effected by dogs and two sliding pinions simultaneously moved by a striker plate at the end of a horizontal rack which receives lateral movement from a rocking segment.

The clutch used in conjunction with the gearbox is a single plate type with cork inserts and the usual plunger type control. A single compression spring is used to provide the necessary degree of friction.

Transmission. A $\frac{1}{2}$ in. × ·205 in. Coventry "Ultimate" chain is used for both primary and secondary transmission with efficient steel guards. There is no shock absorber. The primary chain is lubricated from the engine breather.

Brakes. $6\frac{1}{2}$ in. internal expanding brakes with the special Matchless interconnecting gear, finger tip adjustment, and dual control of the front brake, are specified.

THE MATCHLESS MODELS

Wheels and Tyres. "Timken" roller bearings with adjustable cones (page 24) are used for both wheels, which are shod with 25 in. × 3 in. Dunlop cord tyres. Oversize covers *cannot* be fitted. The correct inflation pressures are 16 lb. per sq. in. and 20 lb. per sq. in. for front and rear tyres, respectively.

Tanks. The fuel tank is made of pressed steel sections welded together (Fig. 1), and has a capacity of $2\frac{1}{4}$ gal. which is sufficient for about 250 miles at normal speeds. It is handsomely finished with the new panel and chromium "M." The oil tank strapped to the saddle tube holds 3 pints, sufficient for about 500 miles, the consumption being 1,800-2,000 m.p.g.

Miscellaneous Equipment. This includes sports or semi-sports adjustable handlebars at option. A Lycett "Aero" spring seat, knee-grips, strong non-valanced mudguards, a spring-up rear stand and a front one also, lifting handle, rubber-covered foot rests, two pannier toolbags, and a pump inflator.

Maximum speed (Solo)	48-52 m.p.h.
Weight (with "Maglita")	218 lb.

MODEL C

The specification of the larger of the two entirely new side-valve inclined engine models is as follows—

The 5·86 h.p. S.V. Engine. This inclined power unit, although embodying a large number of standard Matchless features, is an entirely new design. The bore and stroke are 85·5 mm. × 101·6 mm., giving a cubic capacity of 586 c.c. The compression ratio is 4·8 to 1. As may be seen in Fig. 30, the crankcase differs from previous side-valve models chiefly in respect of the housing for the timing gear. The crankshaft itself, which comprises two heavy rimmed flywheels, a shouldered crank pin, and two sturdy mainshafts, has a roller bearing on the transmission side and a plain bush bearing on the timing side. A needle roller bearing is also used for the "H" section connecting rod big-end. The small-end receives a $\frac{7}{8}$ in. gudgeon pin, which is fully floating and is prevented from moving in the piston boss excessively by spring circlips. The piston itself (see Fig. 30A) is of aluminium alloy, with two rings and the usual diagonal split in the skirt. A high degree of finish is noticeable throughout the engine. The usual Matchless design of cylinder with the valve chest cast integral is used. The head itself is detachable. The large diameter valves and the adjustable mushroom tappets both have detachable press-fit, cast-iron guides and work under ideal conditions, the detachable valve chest cover plate precluding all dirt and noise and enabling the parts to be well lubricated. The exploded gases after ignition by a plug placed over the middle of the combustion chamber, are conveyed to a standard silencer and fish-tail by a chromium-plated exhaust pipe. In spite of the fact that the engine has a stroke of just 4 in., there is practically no back-pressure.

The valve gear (see Fig. 30) departs from usual single-cylinder Matchless practice in that, instead of employing a single camshaft having two cams, two separate camshafts are used, and both cam wheels which run submerged in oil are driven off the engine

Fig. 30. The 5·86 h.p. S.V. Engine
The timing and valve covers have been removed to show the valve gear of this new inclined power unit

pinion. No rockers are interposed between the cams and mushroom tappets and, to facilitate starting, a decompressor lever acting direct on the tappet is made to lift the exhaust valve slightly off its seat during the compression strokes. It is controlled by a small lever on the timing case. The magneto or magneto-dynamo unit is mounted at the back of the engine, and is driven at half engine speed by chain and sprockets off the inlet camshaft. The chain is enclosed in an oil-tight chain case and lubricated from the timing case. Lubrication throughout the engine is effected by the Matchless dry sump system (page 14), and all working parts, in addition to three points on the cylinder wall, are pressure fed. On de luxe models an oil indicator on the instrument panel enables the oil circulation at all times to be observed. On standard models removal of the oil tank filler cap enables a momentary inspection to be made at the oil return pipe orifice.

Magneto advance (C, C/S): $\frac{1}{2}$ in. before T.D.C. on full advance
(or $\frac{1}{16}$ in. before T.D.C., full retard)

Carburettor. A two-lever, semi-automatic pilot jet Amal is used with a top petrol feed and flange fixing to the induction pipe. An air cleaner cannot be fitted. The instrument has the usual throttle stop for "tick-over" adjustment. Twist grip for the throttle is optional, but standard on the de luxe model. The type number of the carburettor is 6/014, and it differs only slightly from the standard Amal described on page 76. The jet size is 150, with a throttle valve 6/5 in position 3. This combination should give a fuel consumption of about 85–95 m.p.g.

(*From "The Motor Cycle"*)

Fig. 30A
STANDARD MATCHLESS PISTON
Note the split skirt and the thick section at the crown

Ignition. A Lucas type KSA1 magneto placed behind the engine is driven clockwise off the inlet camshaft at half engine speed. The sparking plug is a Lodge T.S.3.

Frame and Forks. The frame is an entirely new design, having exceptional structural strength and possessing with its duplicated tubes perfect lateral rigidity. It is a welded-up job of high grade steel tubing, and has a single tank tube and twin front down tubes which are trapped at the bottom ends, where they are bolted to two tubes running on either side of the crankcase to the rear fork ends. Only two engine plates are used, and the neat manner in which the power unit is bolted parallel to the front down tubes may be gathered from Fig. 32. The rear portion of the plates, it will be observed, form with the aid of two transverse spindles a pivot mounting for the four-speed gearbox, which can be slid backwards or forwards by turning a small thrust-screw located at the top of the off-side plate. The forks themselves show no differentiation from the standard type, and adjustable shock absorbers are included.

Gearbox and Clutch. The gearbox is a pivot-mounted, four-speed, heavyweight Sturmey-Archer, semi-constant mesh type, as fitted to the "Silver Hawk," with totally-enclosed kickstarter mechanism. It provides the following gear ratios—

Solo (C and C/S): First, 14·6 to 1; second, 10·6 to 1; third, 6·5 to 1; fourth, 4·9 to 1.
Side-car (C and C/S): First, 16·0 to 1; second, 11·7 to 1; third, 7·2 to 1; fourth, 5·4 to 1.

The speedometer drive is included within the gearbox, a sectional view of which appears on page 84. The clutch is a dry three-plate, multiple spring type with Ferodo inserts, and has a Bowden

Fig. 31. Model C de Luxe

control giving a straight pull on the plunger in the hollow mainshaft.

Transmission. Coventry "Ultimate" chains are used front and rear, and the respective dimensions are $\frac{1}{2}$ in. × ·305 in. and $\frac{5}{8}$ in. × ·380 in. Both chains are well protected, and the front one is lubricated by the disc type engine breather.

Brakes. 8 in. × $\frac{3}{4}$ in. internal expanding brakes with special interconnecting gear are fitted to both wheels, so arranged that application of the pedal puts a braking effect on both wheels simultaneously and uniformly. A handlebar lever provides independent control of the front brake. Finger tip adjustment is used for all controls.

Wheels and Tyres. Timken adjustable roller bearings and heavy gauge butted spokes are used for both wheels, and the tyres are 26 in. × 3·25 in. wired-on heavy cord Dunlops with Schrader valves. Oversize 27 in. × 4 in. tyres may be obtained

THE MATCHLESS MODELS

for an extra charge. The correct inflation pressures for the standard tyres are 15-16 lb. per sq. in. for the front tyre, and 21-22 lb. per sq. in. for the rear tyre when driving solo, and 26 lb. per sq. in. for the rear and 18 lb. per sq. in. for the side wheel when a sidecar is used.

Tanks. The new design bulbous fuel tank is used, and has a capacity of $2\frac{1}{2}$ gal., sufficient for at least 200 miles. The oil tank

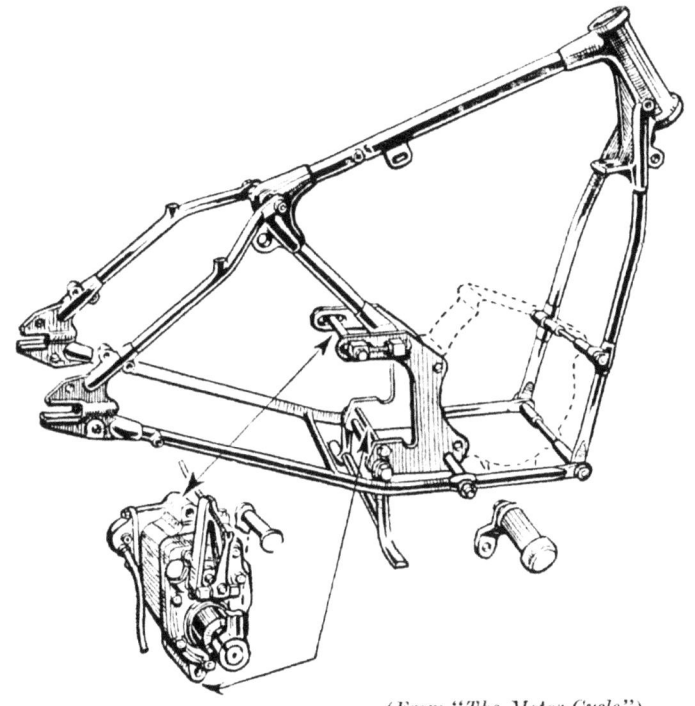

(*From "The Motor Cycle"*)

FIG. 32. THE NEW DUPLEX CRADLE FRAME USED FOR THE INCLINED ENGINE MODELS

is of new design also, and is almost rectangular in shape. It is mounted vertically above the gearbox and holds 4 pints. A large cylindrical filter is included. The oil consumption is 1,200-1,400 m.p.g.

Miscellaneous Equipment. Semi-sports handlebars, adjustable for angle, and a large Lycett "Aero" spring seat ensure a comfortable riding position, while large "D" section mudguards protect the rider from all dirt. The front guard is deeply valanced, while the rear one is hinged to facilitate rear wheel removal and tyre repairs. Included also in the specification are fork stops, kneegrips, an adjustable steering damper, comfortable footrests, a spring-up central stand with ordinary front stand, lifting handle, pump inflator, and two large pannier tool bags placed between the top and bottom chain stays.

Maximum speed (Solo)	60-65 m.p.h.
Weight (without lighting)	330 lb.

MODEL D

The specification of the smaller side-valve inclined engine model, which is eligible for the 30s. per annum tax with "Maglita" electric lighting, is very similar to that of model C, the chief differences being as follows—

The 3·47 h.p. Inclined S.V. Engine. This closely resembles the 5·86 h.p. engine, but there are some important variations in its

Fig. 33. Model D

design. The bore and stroke are 69 mm. × 93 mm., giving a cubic capacity of 347 c.c., and a similar decompressor is fitted.

In order to save weight the cylinder head and barrel are cast integral on this engine only. The magneto drive is taken by chain and sprockets off the transmission side mainshaft. The engine, which has a compression ratio of 4·7 to 1, develops roughly 10 b.h.p. at 5,000 r.p.m. on the bench. A road speed of 60 m.p.h. is equivalent to about 4,500 r.p.m.

Carburettor. A two-lever, type 4/024 Amal, semi-automatic, pilot jet instrument is used. It has a flange fixing and a top petrol feed. A size 80 jet is used in conjunction with a 4/5 throttle valve in position 3. This combination gives good slow running (a throttle stop is included) and a fuel consumption of 95-115 m.p.g. An air cleaner cannot be fitted.

Ignition (D and D/S). Unless an F.D. type "Maglita" lighting set is installed, the current is generated by a Lucas M-L type

NA1 magneto with laminated pole shoes and a pair of arched-shape cobalt steel magnets. It weighs about $4\frac{1}{2}$ lb., and differs from most well-known types in regard to the contact-breaker mechanism (Fig. 54), where the action of a face cam and vertical plunger causes the contacts to open and close in a direction at right angles to the usual motion. The timing is variable to the extent of about 20 degrees from full retard and a self-contained spring control is provided. The magneto setting (D and D/S) is T.D.C. on full retard, or $\frac{3}{8}$ in. before T.D.C., full advance.

Gearbox and Clutch. The gearbox used is a B.W. type three-speed Sturmey-Archer with a special swivel fixing and special design of casing. It gives the gear positions, rear to front, in this order: 1st. N., 2nd, 3rd; and the gear ratios are—

First, 17·5 to 1; second, 9·3 to 1; third, 5·8 to 1

The B.W. gear, which is specially designed for engines up to 350 c.c., follows standard Sturmey-Archer practice in that only six pinions are used to provide three speeds and a kickstarter. The gears are constantly in mesh for the full width of the teeth.

The special feature of this gear consists in the design of the control mechanism. The various gear positions are automatically indexed inside the box, and the whole mechanism completely enclosed. The gear operating spindle is placed on the front of the cover, and a short lever to which the long rod is attached is fixed to this by serrations. An internal stop is provided for arresting the return stroke of the kickstarter crank.

The clutch is a dry, two-plate type with cork inserts and a hollow mainshaft and plunger type control. It has a single compression spring.

Transmission. $\frac{7}{16}$ in. $\times$ ·265 in. and $\frac{1}{2}$ in. $\times$ ·205 in. Coventry "Ultimate" chains are used for primary and secondary transmission, respectively. There is no shock absorber. The primary chain is automatically lubricated.

Tanks. The capacity of the fuel tank is 2 gal., and the capacity of the oil tank 3 pints. The oil consumption is 1,800-2,000 m.p.g.

Wheels and Tyres. The wheels which have $6\frac{1}{2}$ in. non-coupled brakes are shod with 25 in. $\times$ 3 in. wired-on Dunlop cord tyres, and the recommended inflation pressures (solo) are 15–16 lb. per sq. in. and 21–22 lb. per sq. in. for front and rear tyres, respectively. Oversize tyres are fitted to Model D de luxe.

Maximum speed (Solo) . . . . 55–60 m.p.h.
Weight (with "Maglita" set) . . . Approx. 215 lb.

MODEL C/S

This model, illustrated by Fig. 34, has a specification identical to Model C except in regard to the engine, which has overhead valves and a decompressor and, of course, a dual exhaust system.

The 4·95 h.p. O.H.V. Two-port Engine. Only in so far as that part of the engine above the crankcase is concerned, does this inclined power unit differ from the 5·86 h.p. side-valve version to any extent. The bore and stroke are 85·5 mm. × 85·5 mm., giving a capacity of 495 c.c. The compression ratio is 6·6 to 1.

For racing purposes a special high compression piston giving a ratio of 11·5 to 1 is available.

The two-port cylinder head (Fig. 35) is very neat, and forms a hemi-spherical combustion chamber with the sparking plug dead

Fig. 34. Model C/S de Luxe

in the centre. A spigot on the barrel face provides a gas-tight joint. The exhaust ports into the outlets of which the exhaust pipes are a push-in fit, converge on Model C/S at an angle of 46 degrees to a point just above the inlet valve. On the opposite side of the head is a flange for carburettor attachment. Hollow headed, tulip pattern valves with detachable hardened end caps are used, and they reciprocate in detachable cast-iron guides pressed into the head at 70 degrees to each other. These valves are quickly removed by a special tool as shown on page 131. Duplex valve springs with split collet anchorages are used. The entire rocker gear is of new design as illustrated by Fig. 36, where the rectangular-shaped, two-piece aluminium rocker box is shown divided. It is raised clear of the cylinder head finning, and secured by three stout bolts arranged triangular about the rocker axes thrust centre, the two outer ones screwing into special distance sleeve bolts fixed to the cylinder head extensions, and the centre one to a cylinder head retaining sleeve bolt. There is in addition a small tiebar connecting the front support bolt to the frame. A rigid mounting is thus provided. The upper half of the rocker-box is secured to the lower by four bolts, in addition to the three special bolts already mentioned which pass right through the rocker-box. One-piece rockers are used and they are each housed in two pairs of roller bearings (*E*, Fig. 36), which can readily be removed with the rockers after removing the upper half of the rocker-box, and their races afterwards slipped off the rocker arms if necessary. Grease-gun lubrication of the rocker bearings is provided, a special chamber *F* to which is attached a grease-gun

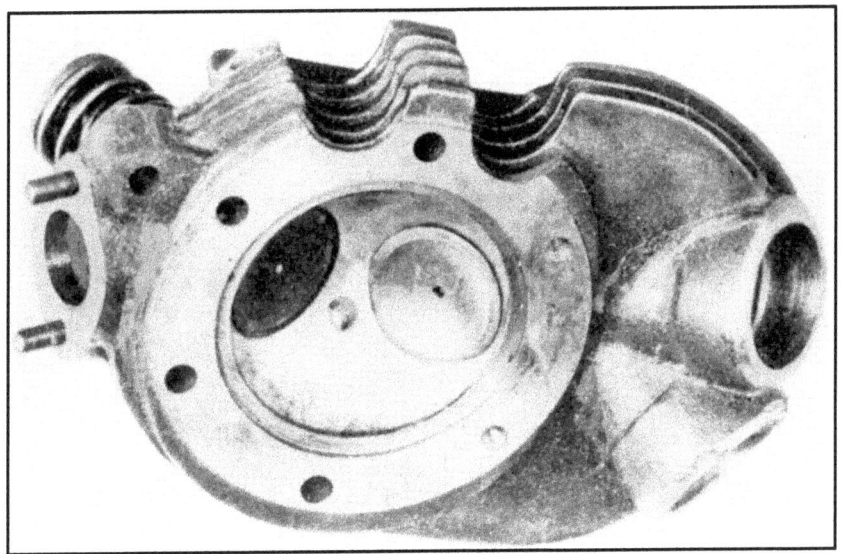

FIG. 35. UNDERNEATH VIEW OF TWO-PORT CYLINDER HEAD SHOWING HEMI-SPHERICAL COMBUSTION CHAMBER AND VALVES

nipple *G* communicating with the two pairs of roller bearings by small channels cut in the lower housing. Oil is fed from the sight-feed chamber on de luxe models, or direct from the pump on standard models to a "T" piece on the top of the rocker-box and filling up the two smaller chambers *H*, positively lubricates the cupped ends of the push rods, and also the inlet valve guide, the supply to which may be regulated by a pointed screw in the "T" piece. Clockwise rotation cuts down the supply, and adjustment should only be made in the event of any shortage or excess being made apparent by inlet valve squeaking or, alternatively, excessive leakage of oil. All surplus oil afterwards drains to the timing case down through the telescopic push-rod covers which have internal springs and fit closely into the rocker-box at their upper ends. These covers may be kept raised for tappet inspection by means of a small spring plunger at the top engaging a hole at the bottom of each cover.

The push-rods themselves are of steel tubing with hardened steel ball ends fitting into the cupped rocker arm ends at the top and resting upon the adjustable tappet heads at the bottom.

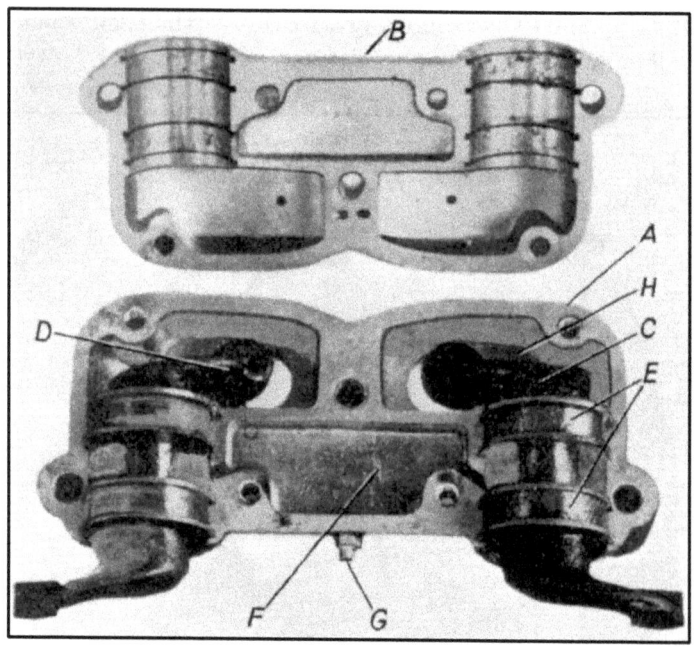

FIG. 36. THE O.H.V. ROCKER BOX WITH COVER REMOVED

A—Lower half of rocker box
B—Upper half of rocker box
C—Inlet valve rocker
D—Exhaust valve rocker
E—Roller bearings
F—Grease chamber
G—Grease-gun nipple
H—Oil compartments

The tappets are of the mushroom pattern, and rest direct upon the cams as on the 5·86 h.p. side-valve engine.

Lubrication is by the D.S. system. (Page 14.)

Carburettor. A two-lever, semi-automatic pilot jet Amal, type 6/024, is used, and it has a flange fixing, is provided with a top petrol feed, and has twist-grip throttle control and an air filter as standard on the de luxe model. The jet size is 120 with a throttle valve 6/4 in position 3. The fuel consumption is 85-100 m.p.g. For further details see page 76.

Lubricating oil recommended (C/S and D/S)   Touring: Castrol XL. Racing: Castrol R

Sparking plugs recommended (C/S and D/S)   Lodge H.1. or K.L.G. K.5.

THE MATCHLESS MODELS

Tappet clearances (C/S and D/S) . .	·002 in. inlet and ·004 in. exhaust (warm)
Weight (without lighting) . . .	330 lb.
Tyre pressures (Solo)	Front, 18; rear, 24 lb. per sq. in.
Maximum speed (Solo) . . .	Approx. 75 m.p.h.

MODEL D/S

As in the case of Model C/S, this model differs from Model D in regard to the engine valve gear and the gear ratios, cubic capacity and exhaust system only. It has a similar type decompressor on the timing case.

The 2·46 h.p. O.H.V. Two-port Engine. The bore and stroke

FIG. 37. MODEL D/S

of this inclined engine are 62·5 mm. × 80 mm., giving a capacity of 246 c.c. The compression ratio is 5·5 to 1. The power unit is identical to the 3·47 h.p. side-valve engine but for the fact that a detachable two-port cylinder head with overhead-valve gear, including telescopic push-rod covers and aluminium rocker-box with adjustable, automatic inlet valve guide lubrication, replaces the non-detachable side-valve cylinder head, and the cylinder capacity is less. The overhead valve gear is fully described in the C/S specification, and on this engine is the same except that the valves are placed at 68 degrees to each other and that some of the dimensions are less.

Carburettor. This is a two-lever, semi-automatic pilot jet, type 4/014 Amal with flange fixing and top petrol feed; an air filter is included on the de luxe model. A size 70 jet is used in conjunc with a 4/4 throttle valve in position 3. The fuel consumption is 100–120 m.p.g.

Weight (without lighting) . . .	215 lb.
Tyre pressures	Front, 16; rear, 22 lb. per sq. in
Maximum speed (Solo) . . .	60–65 m.p.h.

THE MATCHLESS SIDECARS

A very handsome range of sidecars is marketed, and Matchless owners and prospective owners should have little difficulty in selecting a sidecar suitable for their requirements. Of the present range, six are designed for private purposes and seven for commercial use. The private sidecars are designed for attachment to all except Models R/7, D, D/S. Prices vary from £15 to £32. A

FIG. 38. NO. 1 SIDECAR

FIG. 39. NO. 2 SPORTS SIDECAR

special spring frame chassis for use with the "Arrow" or "Hawk" is available.

No. 1 Sidecar. This is the standard touring sidecar, fitted with a body giving an exceptional amount of accommodation and of sporting appearance. A large locker at the rear has a lift-up lid, which is covered with aluminium matting and adapted for use as a luggage grid. The sidecar is finished in stoved black enamel with white lines and aluminium beading, and has a 26 in. × 3·25 in. Dunlop cord tyre. A 27 in. × 4 in. tyre is extra for all sidecars.

No. 2 Sports Sidecar. This very attractive sports sidecar is fitted with a handsome body with black nose panel with white lines and polished aluminium side panels with black lines. A six-foot passenger can readily be accommodated. Equipment includes a hammock seat with spring upholstered cushion and a fixed luggage grid. It is fitted with a 26 in. × 3·25 in. Dunlop cord tyre.

No. 4a Sunshine Saloon Two-seater. This sidecar is suitable for two adults, and is built on the lines of a sunshine saloon car with sloping windscreen, fixed side windows, one of which opens with the door, and a fabric-covered back panel in which is a

FIG. 40. NO. 4A SUNSHINE SALOON TWO-SEATER

spacious window. When the roof is in position (as shown in Fig. 40), the body is absolutely weatherproof. In fine weather the roof can instantly be rolled up. The whole roof is then open, but the passengers are protected from draughts by the fixed windows. The finish throughout is black with white lines, and the chassis has a 26 in. × 3·25 in. Dunlop tyre.

No. 4 Two-seater. This is similar to the above model but minus the all-weather equipment.

No. 13 Occasional Two-seater. The "occasional" type of body is designed for those who require accommodation for two adults only occasionally. When only one passenger is carried, the back of the sidecar folds up, hiding the rear seat, and the body then has the appearance of a luxurious single-seater. The windscreen shown (see page 56) is extra.

Fig. 41. No. 13, Occasional Two-seater

Fig. 42. No. 16, Special Sports Sidecar

Fig. 43. "Air Mail" Box Sidecar

No. 16 Special Sports Sidecar. This sidecar is a real de luxe sports type with a deep well seat and remarkably comfortable upholstery, including arm-rests. The body is finished throughout in aluminium. The windscreen is mounted on a hinged scuttle-dash, providing exceptional weather protection. The luggage grid at the rear is chromium plated.

Commercial Sidecars (C, X/3, X/R3, and B). The same high quality of material and finish noticeable in the private sidecar bodies and chassis is here in evidence also. Fig. 43 illustrates a typical example. The illustration shows the well-known "Air-Mail" type, first introduced for carrying urgent mails between the G.P.O. and Croydon aerodrome. Shelves can be fitted to order in the rear part of the body. Another commercial type is a truck sidecar intended for the carriage of agricultural produce. It is also suitable for dairymen, since it will carry two churns. The normal load is 3 cwt. The body is 3 ft. 10 in. long and 2 ft. 2 in. wide. Besides the type illustrated there are five others which are modifications of this type. In short, a remarkably fine range of sidecars as well as solo machines is offered to the public at very moderate prices.

CHAPTER II

DRIVING

Driving Licence. It is unlawful to drive any motor vehicle on the road without a driving licence bearing the rider's signature, which may at any time be demanded by a police officer, together with a "certificate of insurance." Five days' grace is now allowed, however. If after this period the licence cannot be produced a summons will follow. The fee for a licence is 5s., and it is valid for one year from the day it is issued. Applications should be made to the licences department of the county council in whose area the motor-cyclist normally resides. If the applicant is 16 years of age he can, subject to a certain standard of physical fitness, obtain a licence to drive a motor-cycle only, but if he be 17 or over, a licence enabling him to drive a car or motor-cycle is, subject to the same condition, obtainable. For forging or altering a licence, the offender makes himself liable to two years' imprisonment.

With regard to physical fitness, no test is *compulsory*, but a driver is required to make a declaration on form DF1 that he suffers from *"no such physical infirmity" as to render him a source of danger to the public.* A "source of danger" includes a man having abnormal eyesight to the extent that he cannot *read a car number plate at a distance of* 25 *yd.*, has lost a limb, has muscular paralysis, is liable to fainting or giddiness, or suffers from any form of epilepsy. It should be stated, however, that if after the licence application form has been filled up, the licensing authorities are doubtful as to the driver's fitness, they may decline to issue a licence, but the would-be motor-cyclist can demand an official test for driving fitness, the fee for which is 10s. Defective eyesight,* epilepsy, or giddiness definitely bars a man from obtaining a licence. The penalty for making a false declaration is a fine not exceeding £50, and if done deliberately may incur imprisonment.

Registration. At present all motor-cycles are taxed on a weight basis, a tax at the rate of 30s. per annum being imposed on lightweight machines weighing not more than 224 lb. All medium and heavyweight machines are subject to taxation at the rate of £3 per annum, and where a sidecar is attached an additional £1 per annum is required. All Matchless models except three (R/7, D, D/S) have a £3 tax.

* Defective eyesight is no bar if it can be proved that the licence applicant has been driving satisfactorily for six months prior to application.

DRIVING

In connection with the tax paid for a motor-cycle, a registration licence is issued, a circular disc that the law requires to be mounted on the near-side of the machine in certain definite places, such as the front number plate or the handlebars. Unless this disc, which is in effect a receipt for the tax, be fixed on the machine, it is unlawful to use it. A licence application form (R.F.1/2) may be obtained from any head post office, from which renewals for the same type and period may be obtained. It should be very carefully filled in and posted to the licences department of the county council in whose area the machine is normally kept, together with the cost of the licence and a certificate of insurance, without which a licence cannot be obtained. They will send along the necessary licence and also a registration book, in which all particulars of the machine, such as engine number,* frame number, horse-power, etc., and its history are entered. Application for annual licence renewal should be made between the 1st and 15th of January each year. An annual licence expires, of course, on 31st December; but in addition to the annual licence there are the quarterly licences expiring on 24th March, 30th June, 30th September, and 31st December. The cost of a quarterly licence is 16s. 6d. for machines over 224 lb., and, of course, licences are available for any period from three to twelve months. A rebate can be obtained for the unexpired portion of a licence if surrendered, conditional upon the unexpired portion being not less than one month.

The Registration Book. The registration book must be kept in a safe place by the owner, except in the following four cases when it must immediately be returned to the authorities for amendment—

(a) On change of address.
(b) On change of ownership or on sale.
(c) When substantial alterations are made (s/c attachment).
(d) On the machine being destroyed, broken up, or exported.

Number Plates. Definite regulations are laid down concerning the size of motor-cycle number plates and their identification numbers. Up till 6th October, 1930, both number plates were permitted to be in accordance with the dimensions given at A, Fig. 44. This still holds good in respect to the *front* number plate, but as regards the rear plate new dimensions are now specified. They must be as shown at B, Fig. 44. All letters and figures must be $2\frac{1}{2}$ in. high, with a total width for each letter or number of $1\frac{3}{4}$ in., except in the case of the figure 1. Every part of every letter and figure must be $\frac{3}{8}$ in. broad. The space between adjoining

---

* On every Matchless the engine number is stamped on the transmission side of the crank case directly below the cylinder base (see Fig. 28), while the frame No. is on the right side of the saddle lug.

letters and between adjoining figures must be ½ in., and there must be a margin between the nearest part of any letter or figure, and the top, bottom, and sides of the black background, of at least ½ in. The lettering if placed above the numbers need not be centralized, but the letters themselves cannot be separated more than the prescribed ½ in., and there must be ½ in. space between

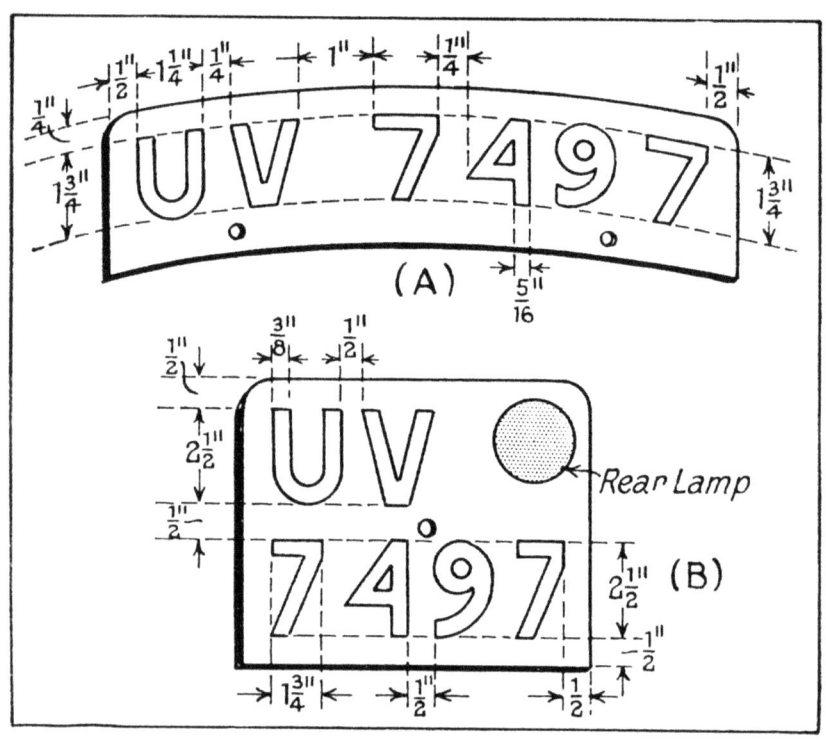

Fig. 44. Number Plate Dimensions

At *A* are shown the old dimensions still used for a front plate and at *B* the new dimensions required for rear plates

the bottom of the lettering and the top of the numbers. The rear plate must be illuminated after dark by a suitable tail light.

Lamps. During the period between one hour after sunset and one hour before dawn (summer time) it is compulsory to show a white light to the front and a red light to the rear. In the case of a sidecar machine, an additional front lamp must be provided so as to indicate the entire width of the vehicle.

Horn. An "audible warning of approach" is required by law, and in the case of some of the Matchless models which are phenomenally quiet, a Lucas "Altette" high frequency electric horn

DRIVING

is perhaps the most effective type, although a bulb is very satisfactory and has the considerable advantage that in the event of the battery becoming exhausted or the dynamo failing to charge, the rider is not suddenly left helpless. It is a good plan to fit a bulb horn for emergency use.

ON THE ROAD

The Matchless Controls. An excellent view of the Matchless control lay-out is shown at Fig. 45, where the de luxe instrument panel is also shown. It will be observed that it is extremely neat and comprises nine controls, all of which have provision for making adjustments. The four engine controls are: (a) the throttle lever or twist-grip, opening inwards; (b) the air lever, also opening inwards; (c) the ignition lever, similarly advanced; (d) the decompressor or exhaust valve lifter. The five cycle controls are: (e) the gear-lever; (f) the clutch; (g) the rear brake pedal (interconnected with the front brake except on D, D/S); (h) the front brake lever; (i) the steering damper. Before attempting to start up the engine the novice is advised to become thoroughly acquainted with the controls and their action, and to remember that the gear lever and clutch lever must always be used simultaneously, and that physical force must on no account be used on the gear lever, especially on the four-speed models where the gears are not all in constant mesh. The ignition lever should be three-quarters advanced for starting-up, and afterwards kept as far advanced as possible.

Fuel and Oil Replenishment. Any well-known brand of petrol or petrol-benzole mixture is suitable for Matchless engines. Petrol-benzole mixture gives good results particularly with the overhead-valve and overhead-camshaft engines. Although a large gauze filter is included in the petrol tank itself it is, nevertheless, advisable when refueling from cans to see that a funnel with a filter is used.

As regards lubricating oil, it is sound policy to follow the manufacturer's recommendations closely both as regards the brand and grade, and not to change over except under extenuating circumstances. The mixing of lubricants is to be strongly deprecated. To be careless in regard to engine lubricating oil is to be "penny wise and pound foolish" in the strongest sense. On no account buy loose oil from unsealed tins.

No attention to the lubrication system is required other than occasional cleaning of the cylindrical gauze filter below the filler cap, and the maintenance of oil at the correct level which should be *above the half full mark but not higher than 1 in. below the return pipe orifice* when the engine is cold. No immediate ill-effects are likely to follow temporary running of the engine with the oil tank almost exhausted so long as the oil is not diluted, since whatever remains is constantly circulated, but it should be borne in mind that the more oil there is in circulation, the cooler it will keep, with therefore less risk of engine overheating taking place.

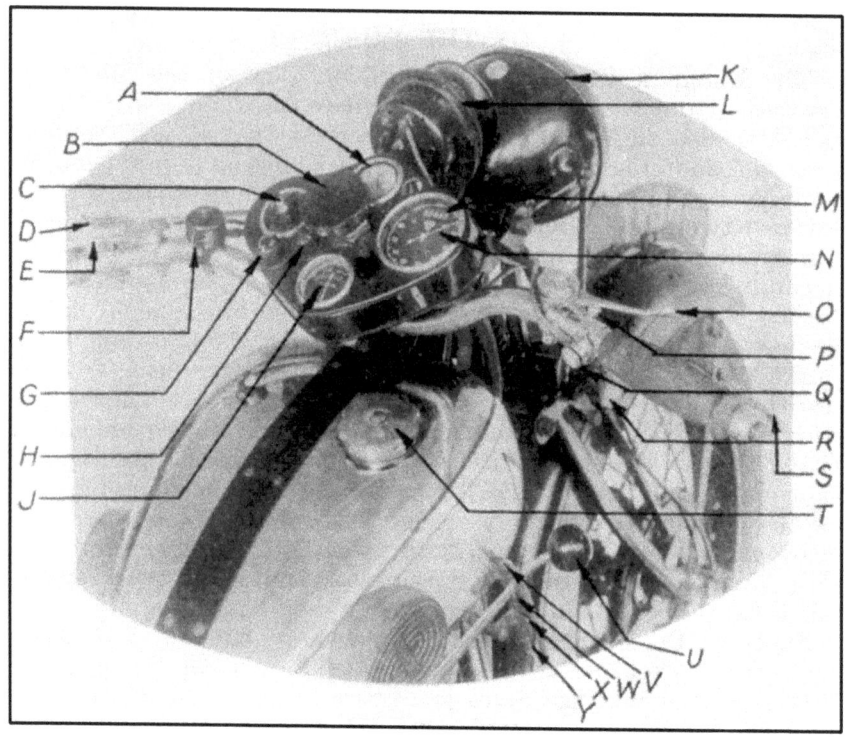

FIG. 45. THE MATCHLESS CONTROLS AND INSTRUMENT PANEL

A—Oil sight-feed
B—Steering damper knob
C—Lamp switch
D—Clutch lever
E—Ignition lever
F—Dipping switch
G—Ignition switch
H—Panel light switch
J—Ammeter
K—Head lamp
L—Electric horn
M—Mileage recorder
N—Speed indicator
O—Throttle lever
P—Air lever
Q—Horn switch
R—Fork damper knob
S—Brake lever
T—Petrol tank cap
U—Gear lever
V—1st gear notch
W—2nd ,, ,,
X—3rd ,, ,,
Y—Top ,, ,,

On all models except A/2 and B, where no exterior oil piping other than that for the sight-feed is used, it is advisable to keep an eye on the pipe unions as a loose or broken union may interfere with the oil circulation. This would, of course, be indicated by extensive oil leakages. On Model B and all de luxe models,

DRIVING

the supply of oil to the engine may be observed at the sight-feed on the instrument panel. On other models it is advisable, before setting out on a run, to remove the oil filler cap immediately after starting-up and note whether regular ejection of oil from the return pipe (proof of correct functioning) is occurring. Should the inlet valve on an overhead-valve machine commence squeaking, increase the oil supply by anti-clockwise rotation of the rocker-box "T" piece screw. Always see that the grease in the gearbox is maintained at the correct level by occasionally removing the filling plug.

Tyre Inflation. If the maximum mileage from the covers, the greatest degree of comfort, and the best steering are to be obtained it is essential to run with the tyres correctly inflated. The inflation pressures (see specifications) can quickly be verified by using a Schrader tyre pressure gauge, obtainable for a trifling sum. Incorrectly inflated tyres wear, due to rolling and flexion, far more quickly than is generally supposed, and motor-cycle tyres are by no means cheap articles.

Starting Up. Having turned on the petrol, flooded the carburettor, and turned on the ignition switch (where fitted), proceed as follows: Place gear lever in neutral; open the throttle lever or twist grip to about one-sixth of its total movement and completely close the air lever, unless the engine be warm, when it may be opened very slightly; move the ignition lever to the three-quarter advance position. The correct settings of the Bowden controls are dependent, of course, upon there being no backlash, and if there is any it should be rectified at once by means of the small adjusting stops. On all present models an adjustable carburettor throttle stop gives a slow-running "tick-over" position, and prevents the throttle slide closing entirely, so that once the engine has been started up it can be stopped only by choking it with the air lever or by switching off the ignition. Difficult engine starting is often due to faulty setting of the carburettor controls, and the importance of *keeping the throttle nearly closed* cannot be too strongly emphasized. Only by doing this can a sufficiently high velocity air current be induced over the pilot jet, as may be understood by reference to Fig. 52. The main jet plays no part in starting, but as the throttle slide is opened so the suction on the pilot lessens and increases on the main jet, until finally the pilot goes right out of action. A small milled edge screw at the mixing chamber base controls the air supply to the pilot jet. This screw is accurately adjusted by the manufacturers and, as a general rule, is best not tampered with.

In the case of the 990 c.c. side-valve models it may in exceedingly cold weather be advisable to prime the engines by means of the compression cocks to overcome piston gumminess, although, with split skirt aluminium pistons having a large working clearance, this procedure is seldom necessary. Then, after bringing the decompressor into action where fitted, by moving the lever on the side of the timing case, stand astride the machine and smartly kick the engine over several times with the kickstarter, when the engine should fire with little difficulty. In the case of the "Silver Arrow" and "Silver Hawk," where neither decompressor nor valve lifter is fitted, one or two gentle depressions is usually sufficient, and these small bore engines may, in fact, be started by using *hand* pressure on the starter crank. With regard to Models R/7, X/3, and X/R3, a valve lifter enables the compression to be overcome, and the lifter should be dropped instantaneously when the kickstarter crank is half way down. Only a few kicks should be necessary. Failure to start with the controls properly adjusted and tappet or rocker clearances correct is usually due to ignition trouble, and the sparking plug or plugs should be removed, inspected, and, if necessary, cleaned and the points adjusted. A common source of engine-starting difficulties is an over-rich mixture caused by excessive flooding of the carburettor, or by numerous ineffectual attempts with the kickstarter, accentuated, perhaps, by exorbitant priming. This trouble is generally accompanied by continuous banging in the exhaust system with the ignition lever fully retarded. To clear the combustion chamber, or chambers, open the throttle and air levers fully and revolve the engine (with ignition off, preferably) several times.

Once the engine has started, put the decompressor out of action and ease back the throttle slightly, or close entirely to give a low revolution "tick-over." Do not make an attempt to race the engine until it has thoroughly warmed up and the oil is circulating freely. Sudden engine racing from cold is liable to cause a semi-engine seizure with possibly slight cylinder scoring and smearing of the aluminium piston. Avoid running an engine idle for long periods, especially the single-cylinder type where a somewhat high speed is required to give uniform running. When running the engine in a garage do not keep the doors closed, or a dangerous quantity of odourless carbon monoxide gas from the exhaust may accumulate.

Moving Off. Lift the clutch (when both gearbox mainshaft and layshaft become stationary), place gear lever in first gear, and with the engine running at a moderate speed, gently re-engage the clutch when the machine will slowly move off. As it picks up speed, advance the ignition lever fully and give full air and slightly more gas.

Gear Changing. On a motor-cycle the process of gear changing is simple and rapidly mastered. There are two important points to remember: (1) never employ brute force on the gear lever, (2)

DRIVING

never change gear without first de-clutching. Another point to remember having regard to the engine is to *make full use of the gearbox*, and always keep the engine running under load at a good speed. If the machine is driven slowly under load there is a tendency for "knocking," and this is exceedingly injurious. A change to a lower gear should be made instantly the engine shows symptoms of labouring, and do not slip the clutch as an alternative except occasionally when rounding sharp corners or travelling slowly on top gear.

All gear changes should be made gently but firmly. Practice alone will enable the rider to become proficient. When changing-up, the machine should be accelerated to a speed some 10 m.p.h. faster than it is already travelling, the throttle momentarily eased back, the clutch raised for the fraction of a second only, and the gear lever smartly pressed home into the necessary quadrant notch, the throttle afterwards being opened up again to take the increased load; sometimes it may be advisable to retard the ignition a trifle or slightly close the air lever. When travelling on a gentle down grade, or even on the level, if care be taken and the machine be given sufficient momentum, a change from bottom to top gear may be made direct by passing the gear lever right through the gate. This method of changing-up, however, is not recommended on the level even to the expert rider with plenty of experience, for it usually entails racing the engine unduly and this is neither good for engine nor gearbox.

When changing-down, reduce speed until the machine is travelling at a rate at which it normally does on the gear to be engaged, lift the clutch and push the gear lever home. The throttle meanwhile may be closed or nearly closed. When the clutch is again engaged let it in gently or a rear wheel skid may ensue, which is bad for both tyres and transmission. Always keep the gear control properly adjusted.

Although in general driving it is always advisable to advance the ignition as far as possible without causing knocking, when ascending a steep gradient, care should be taken to retard the ignition as the engine revolutions fall, just sufficiently to prevent knocking, and if a change down is made the ignition should again be advanced with increase of engine revolutions. When descending very steep hills the middle gear may be engaged enabling the engine compression to assist in reducing speed, but do not use the bottom gear for this purpose as this sometimes severely stresses the transmission.

Use of Brakes. The Matchless brakes have unusually good stopping power and for this reason are liable to abuse. Harsh brake application results in heavy tyre wear and is bad for the transmission. Do not, except in an emergency, apply the brakes sufficiently strongly to cause either wheel to stop revolving or to extract a squeak of protest from the tyres. *Always drive on the throttle.* On wet and greasy roads special care is necessary to minimize the danger of skidding.

Running-in. After buying a brand new Matchless, special caution must be exercised for a certain period of driving, in order to allow all moving parts to become bedded down and bearing surfaces to harden. Any attempt to expedite matters is doomed to failure and may permanently spoil the engine. *Until* 500 *miles have been covered a speed in excess of* 25 *m.p.h. should not be attained*, and large throttle openings should not be used. The first 500 miles of an engine's existence is far more important than the next five thousand.

Hand Signals. Cultivate a habit of giving clear signals to following traffic some little distance before turning off into a side road. Failure to give clear signals *in plenty of time* is responsible for many mix-ups on the road. When turning left or right, extend the left or right arms, respectively, full out.

Pillion Riding. It is now compulsory for a proper pillion seat to be used when a passenger is carried, and where a sidecar is not attached it is unlawful to carry more than one passenger. The passenger, moreover, is required to ride *astride* and not aside the machine, and must be covered by insurance.

" Dangerous " and " Careless " Driving. Although the general 20 m.p.h. speed limit, honoured more in the breach than the observance, has now disappeared, a vigilant police watch on driving is kept by the new mobile police force, and woe to the motor-cyclist or motorist caught driving to the public danger. "Dangerous driving," now heavily punished, means driving at a speed or manner *dangerous having regard to all the circumstances* actual or hypothetical, i.e. having regard to other traffic or pedestrians that are in the vicinity or might reasonably be expected to be there.

In order to meet cases of negligent driving of an unpremeditated nature, such as failure to give hand signals, "careless driving" is made an offence with which a motorist may be charged, and the penalties for this are not quite so severe as for "dangerous driving." Passing on corners and cutting in would come under the first heading, however. "Drunk in charge" usually means imprisonment and automatic suspension of the driving licence. A summons must be served within fourteen days of an alleged offence, and the driver must be notified at the time of committing it of intended prosecution.

CHAPTER III

THE ENGINE AND GEARBOX

THIS chapter is divided into two main sections, the first part, intended for novices, consisting of a brief theoretical explanation of the four-stroke internal combustion engine, and the second part constituting a description of the design and action of some of the Matchless engine features.

FOUR-STROKE ENGINE PRINCIPLES

General Principles. In the internal combustion (I.C.) engine the gases are made to expand within a cylinder closed at one end and containing a piston free to reciprocate, with a gas-tight fit within the cylinder. When an explosion occurs, the piston is driven downwards and, by employing a crank connected by a connecting rod to the piston, this downward thrust can be converted into rotary motion of a flywheel and sprocket, and it is then a simple matter to transmit this to a road driving wheel by employing suitable transmission. This is the simplest explanation of the internal combustion engine possible. The devices used for supplying and firing the explosive mixture are known as the *carburettor* and *magneto* respectively. Through the carburettor, air and petrol are fed to the combustion chamber after being mixed in certain definite proportions. Air consists of oxygen and nitrogen, while petrol consists of carbon and hydrogen; and, on combustion, the residual gases are nitrogen, carbon dioxide, and water (steam). They are expelled on the upward stroke of the piston via an exhaust port into the atmosphere. When too much petrol is supplied, carbon-monoxide is also formed, and this is a highly dangerous gas, capable of producing death if absorbed into the respiratory system to any large extent.

Considering the construction of a single-cylinder internal combustion engine, it will be noticed that the principal parts are the cylinder, bolted to the crankcase which houses the flywheels (necessary to ensure continual rotation) and their interconnecting crank; the piston, complete with gas-sealing rings and connected to the crank of the crankshaft by the connecting rod; the magneto and carburettor; and the mechanism which enables the magneto and carburettor to do their work in unison with the reciprocating piston. This mechanism is known as the *valves* and *timing gear*. Obviously two valves are necessary, one to allow the mixture to be sucked in on the downward piston strokes, and one to permit of the combusted or exhaust gases to be ejected on the upward piston strokes. These two valves are the *inlet* and *exhaust* valves, and it is a *sine qua non* that both must be shut on the power strokes to enable the force of explosion to react upon the piston head. In the case of the four-stroke engine, which is more efficient than the two-stroke engine and which will alone be considered, the valves are metal, cone-headed bodies capable of being lifted by *cams* and suitable gearing off their seats at the necessary intervals, which will be considered later. The timing gear comprises

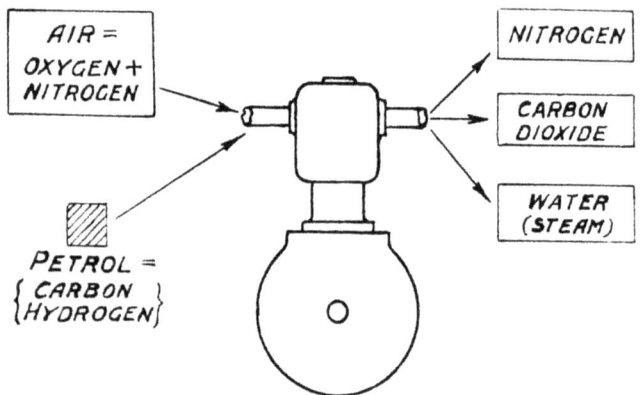

FIG. 46. DIAGRAM ILLUSTRATING THE PROCESS OF COMBUSTION IN A PETROL ENGINE

the valve-lifting cams and camshaft or shafts driven by suitable gearing from the engine mainshaft.

The Four-stroke Cycle. The explosive mixture has to be sucked in, compressed, exploded, and the products of combustion exhausted. For the purpose of elementary considerations, we may assume that a complete piston stroke is required to effect each of these requirements. Hence the term "four-stroke" or "Otto" cycle, for only one power stroke is delivered in every four piston strokes. Each piston stroke corresponds to half an engine revolution, and thus for a complete cycle the engine rotates only two revolutions, and accordingly the valve cams and magneto are driven at *half engine speed*.

We will now suppose that the piston has just reached the top of its stroke after sweeping out through the open exhaust valve the products of combustion after a firing stroke. During the upward stroke the inlet valve is closed.

1. INDUCTION STROKE. The exhaust valve has now closed, and the inlet valve has opened. The downwardly moving piston has

to fill the space behind it with air. This produces an intense draught or suction through the induction pipe and carburettor. The blast of air sweeping over the small aperture, or "jet," to

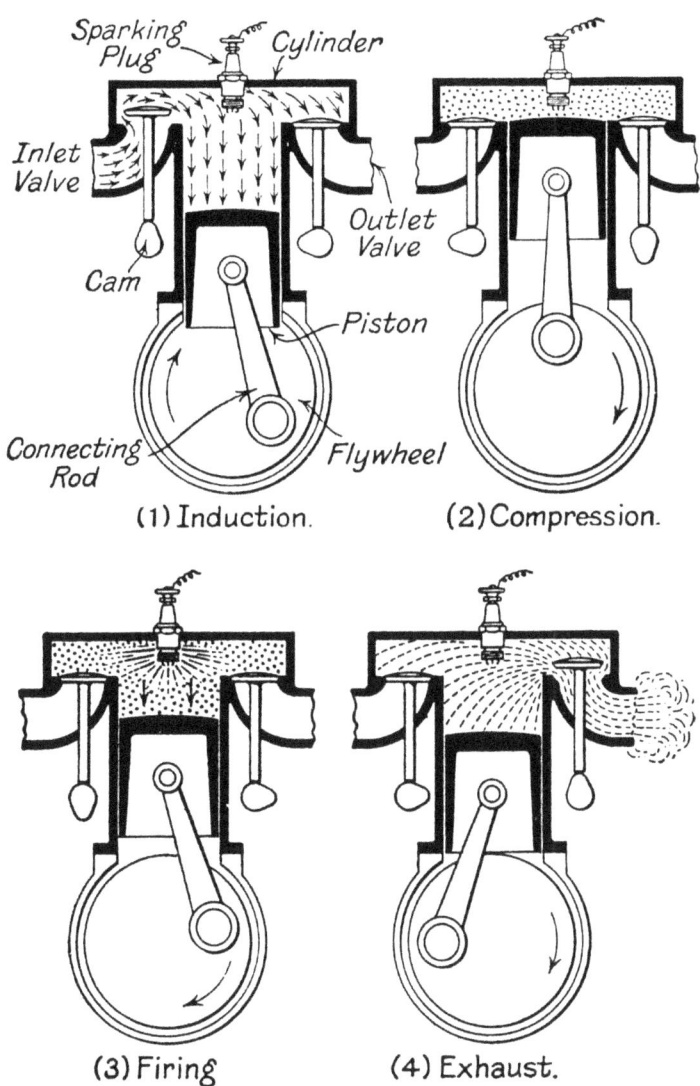

FIG. 47. THE FOUR-STROKE CYCLE

which a supply of petrol is constantly fed, causes a fine jet of petrol to rise like a fountain in the carburettor. The fountain resolves itself into spray, or is "atomized," and the "mixture," consisting as it were of air converted into a fog by the tiny petrol particles, passing along the induction pipe into the cylinder. At the end of the downward stroke of the piston the inlet valve closes, and the cylinder becomes a sealed chamber containing the explosive mixture.

2. COMPRESSION STROKE. The crank on the engine shaft, assisted by the flywheels, passes over its dead point, and the piston commences its upward stroke. The well-fitting piston rings prevent the escape of the mixture on charge into the crankcase chambers, and the charge undergoes compression.

3. FIRING STROKE. We have now reached the moment at which the charge is to be fired. The inlet and exhaust valves are closed, the charge is fully compressed, and all is ready for the explosion. This, of course, is brought about the properly timed passage of an electric spark between the *electrodes*, or points, of the sparking plug. The correct time for the spark depends upon the speed at which the engine is running. The reason for this is that in the case of an explosive mixture of air and petrol vapour, the explosion takes quite an appreciable time, and there is a lag, so to speak, between the passage of the spark and the moment when the exploded charge reaches its maximum temperature and pressure (approx. 450 lb. per sq. in.).

4. EXHAUST STROKE. The exhaust valve now opens, and the products of combustion are ejected from the cylinder into the exhaust pipe and silencer by the ascending piston. After undergoing cooling, the burnt gases are now finally allowed to escape into the atmosphere.

In the case of a twin-cylinder engine with single-throw crankshaft, the cycle is exactly the same for each cylinder, but two cams are used in the magneto cam ring to provide two sparks for every two engine revolutions, one for each cylinder, and the two cycles are overlapped so that while the front cylinder is beginning a firing stroke, the rear one is commencing an induction stroke. Similarly on the four-cylinder machines, still greater overlapping prevails, and a firing stroke occurs every half engine revolution (for sequence of firing see Fig. 22A), thus requiring the generation of four sparks for a complete cycle. This is accomplished on the "Silver Hawk" by using two cams in the contact-breaker and driving the latter at *engine* speed.

THE PRINCIPLE OF THE CARBURETTOR

It has been found by experiment that the most satisfactory way of encouraging petrol to evaporate is to drive it under pressure through a very tiny hole, called a jet, and the process is assisted by heating the spraying device. Fig. 48 shows the salient features of a simple carburettor. It will be observed that the petrol level in the jet must be below the orifice at the top; otherwise the petrol

THE ENGINE AND GEARBOX

will overflow and cause *flooding* of the carburettor. The level is automatically regulated by the action of a *float* attached to a spindle, which operates a needle valve, thereby cutting off the petrol supply immediately the level in the chamber reaches the height of the jet orifice. On the downward stroke of the piston, air is sucked in through the air intake; past the partially open throttle, which is a closely-fitting hand-controlled slide, operating up and down in a barrel; past the jet; past the inlet valve; and thence into the cylinder. The extremely high velocity air current

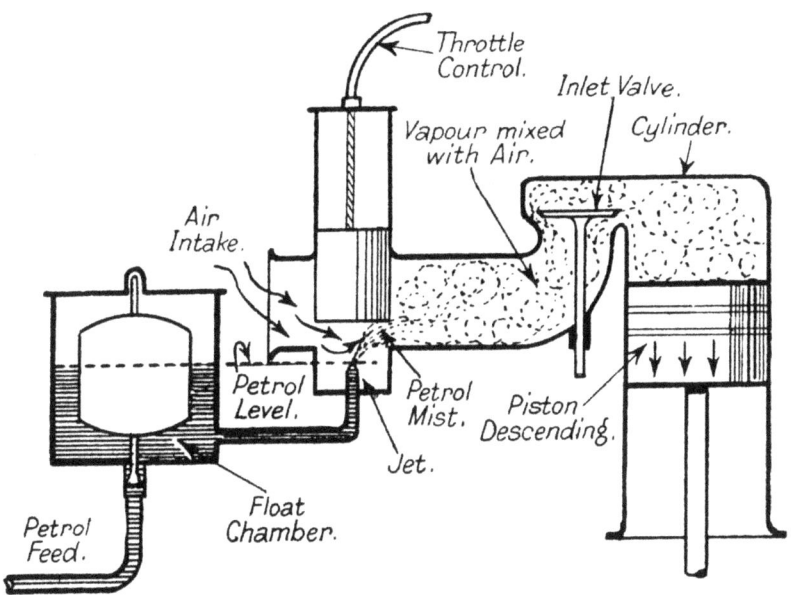

FIG. 48. THE PRINCIPLE OF THE CARBURETTOR

that must obviously sweep over the jet causes the fuel to issue in a small fountain, and simultaneously causes the spirit to be atomized and mixed in definite proportions with the air rushing in towards the combustion chamber.

THE PRINCIPLE OF THE MAGNETO

The magneto primarily consists of three parts: (1) the *armature*; (2) a U-shaped *magnet*; (3) the *contact-breaker*.

The armature comprises an iron core or bobbin of "H" section, on which are two *windings*: firstly, a short winding of fairly heavy gauge wire; and, secondly, on top of the former, a very big winding of fine wire. The first winding is known as the *primary*, and the second as the *secondary*. The armature, which can rotate on ball bearings, is placed such that on rotation it periodically cuts across the *magnetic field* of the magnet, and creates a current in the primary winding. Incidentally, the contact-breaker forms part of the primary circuit. This current, however, is at a very low voltage—far and away too small to produce anything in the nature of a spark. But if a *break* is suddenly caused in the primary by separating the platinum contacts when the current is at its maximum flow, a high voltage or tension current will be instantly *induced* in the secondary winding—sufficient to jump a small space, if the circuit be incomplete. In this circuit the sparking plug is included, and things are so arranged that, in order for the secondary circuit to be complete, the current must jump across the electrodes of the plug, or, in other words, a spark must occur. Now in the case of a single-cylinder engine, the points in the rotating contact-breaker separate once in every armature revolution (there being one cam only), and the armature to which the contact-breaker is fitted being driven off the camshaft runs at half engine speed; that is to say, a "break" takes place once every two engine revolutions, i.e. four strokes of the piston. Hence if the initial "break" be timed to occur when the piston is at the top of the compression stroke, all the other "breaks" (and therefore sparks) will occur at this point also, and thus the engine will go on firing correctly.

The *cam ring*, against which the cam of the contact-breaker works, can be rotated by handlebar control through about 15 degrees, thereby giving means of advancing and retarding the spark.

The *condenser* is a device for the purpose of eliminating "arcing" at the contacts, and the *pick-up* is a small carbon brush kept in continual contact with the *slip-ring*, in order to collect or pick up the high tension current for the sparking plug lead.

The distributor is a rotating brush mechanism fitted to multi-cylinder engines only, and driven by gearing off the armature. Its purpose is to see that the high tension current at each "break" is distributed to the right sparking plug.

THE PRINCIPLE OF COIL IGNITION

Coil ignition has many features in common with magneto ignition, but there are certain very distinct variations. Its principal characteristic is that it generates a high tension current of practically *constant voltage*, and is thus admirably suited for easy starting and efficiency at low engine speeds. On the magneto the high tension current is induced in the secondary winding by the interruption of the primary circuit, which depends for its voltage upon the speed at which the armature is rotating. With coil ignition a low tension current is generated by a *dynamo* and led

THE ENGINE AND GEARBOX

straight to a *battery*, from which the current is supplied at a practically fixed voltage to the primary coil, and the high tension current is generated in the secondary coil by induction as on the magneto, a contact-breaker driven at half engine speed interrupting the primary circuit at predetermined intervals. Coil ignition is used only on the four-cylinder Matchless, and, in consequence, the contact-breaker, which is of different design to that on a magneto (Fig. 55), has four cams. Immediately above the contact-breaker and fixed to the same shaft as the four-lobe cam

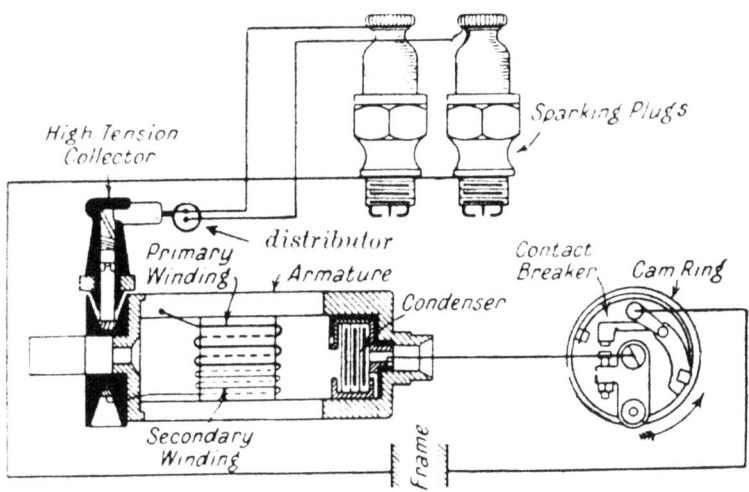

FIG. 49. HIGH TENSION MAGNETO IGNITION WIRING DIAGRAM
(TWIN CYLINDER ENGINE)

is the *distributor*, a rotating arm mechanism providing small "jump-spark" gaps from the rotating electrode to metal segments in the distributor cover where the high tension current is led to the respective sparking plugs.

SOME MATCHLESS FEATURES

The Double-acting Oil Pump. A general description of the Matchless dry sump lubrication system has already been given on page 14, and Fig. 50 shows how the oil is circulated in a single-cylinder Matchless engine. It remains to deal with the action of the pump itself. As already mentioned on page 14, the pump has only one moving part—a steel plunger driven at $\frac{1}{15}$ engine speed by a worm cut on the engine mainshaft. This plunger slowly oscillates to and fro, its precise travel being determined by the relieved end of a guide screw (*b*, Fig. 51) screwed into the rear of the pump housing and engaging with a profiled cam groove at the large return end of the plunger. This groove plays an all important part. In addition to causing the plunger to oscillate and thereby obtain a pumping action at each end (for the plunger is completely enclosed by its housing and end caps), its carefully planned contour enables the pumping impulses to be synchronized with the opening and closing of two main ports and a small auxiliary port, thus definitely regulating the oil circulation and

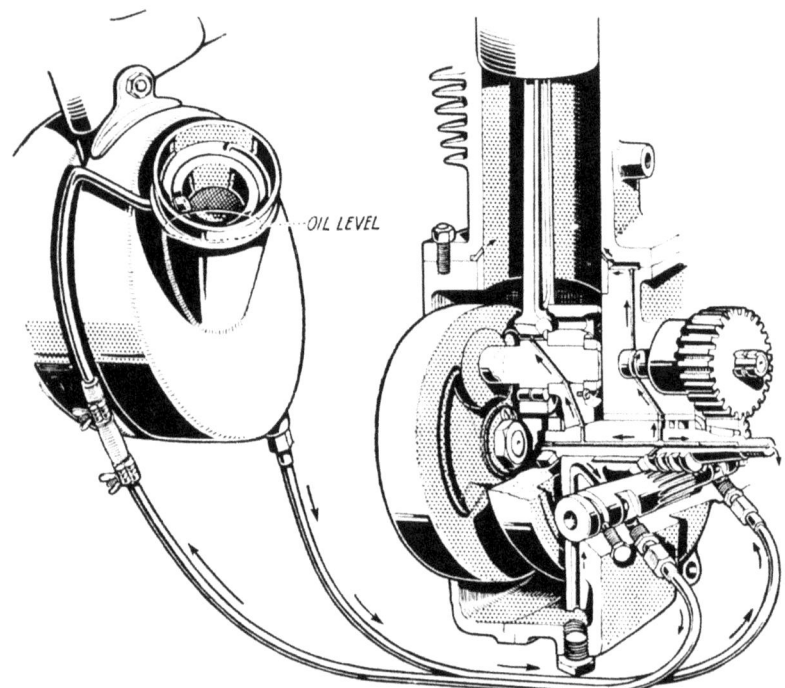

Fig. 50. Diagram showing the Oil Circulation in the Dry Sump Lubrication System

controlling the supply of oil to the engine and the return of oil to the tank.

The two main ports are shown at D and C, and the small auxiliary port at E, Fig. 51. The main ports are known as the *delivery* port and the *return* port respectively. They comprise two shallow segments cut in the pump plunger body and communicating with the hollowed ends of the plunger by two holes. The auxiliary port comprises simply an $\frac{1}{8}$ in. diameter hole drilled at the back of the main delivery port segment. The plunger itself, as mentioned on page 14, has two diameters and, therefore, the capacity of the return portion of the pump is greater than that of the delivery portion, so that the sump is always kept clear of

THE ENGINE AND GEARBOX

oil. Fig. 50 enables the action of the pump to be understood. Oil flows by gravity, assisted by suction, from the tank to a point in the pump housing, such that no further passage can take place until the plunger has moved to a point, approximately, as shown when oil flows into the hollowed end *via* the cut-away segment constituting the delivery port. Then as the plunger continues to advance with simultaneous reciprocation, the oil which has completely filled the hollowed end is momentarily retained and the bulk of it finally ejected by displacement from this port into an oil passage opposite the point of entry, and forced to the cylinder walls and main engine bearings. During the advance of the plunger culminating in the automatic injection of fresh oil into the engine, the receding of the large end of the plunger causes a strong vacuum directly opposite an oil passage leading from the sump base, and communicating with the plunger interior only when the return port is in a suitable position. All surplus oil in the sump is, therefore, sucked up as the plunger advances, and retained when the port closes until the plunger begins to reverse its motion when, the return port coming into line with the return pipe passage, the oil is forcibly ejected by displacement into this pipe and so to the oil tank where its intermittent emergence can, if a sight-feed is not provided, be observed. (See page 63.)

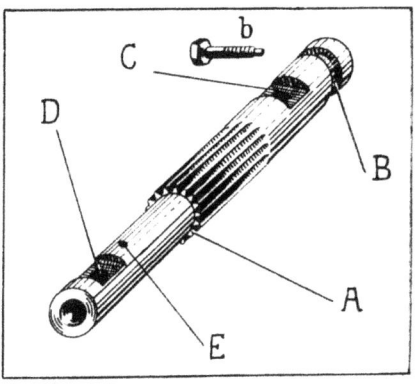

FIG. 51. THE OIL-PUMP PLUNGER.
A—Hobbed portion of plunger
B—Annular cam groove
b—Guide screw (crank case)
C—Plunger return port
D—Plunger delivery port
E—Small auxiliary port

Thus it will be seen that so long as the engine is running, fresh oil is being constantly fed to it and then, after circulation, sucked from the sump and forced up back into the tank to be recirculated *ad infinitum*. Coincident with the ejection of oil from the main delivery port, a supply of oil is forced out of the auxiliary port to the timing box on the side-valve engines, and the rocker-box "T" piece or bevel-box on the overhead-valve and overhead-camshaft engines, and where de luxe equipment is provided is first forced up into the panel sight-feed, whence it flows by gravity to the respective parts requiring lubrication. Only a small portion of the total oil feed to the engine is diverted in this manner, but this portion is important and a definite index as to the correct functioning of the whole D.S. lubrication system, for only when the pump is forcing oil into the engine at a certain pressure can the oil flow at the drip-feed be observed.

The action of the pump plunger is almost fool-proof, but care must be taken to remove the plunger before separating the crankcase (see page 144), and the guide screw must always be kept fully tightened. A point worthy of note is that with the plunger stationary no oil can possibly enter the engine.

The Two-lever Semi-automatic Amal Carburettor (Fitted to all Models). Referring to Fig. 52, showing a sectional view of the instrument, A is the carburettor body or mixing chamber, the upper part of which has a throttle valve B, with taper needle C attached by the needle clip. The throttle valve regulates the quantity of mixture supplied to the engine. Passing through the throttle valve is the air valve D, independently operated, and serving the purpose of obstructing the main air passage for starting and mixture regulation. Fixed to the underside of the mixing chamber by the union nut E is the jet block F, and interposed between them is a fibre washer to ensure a petrol-tight joint. On the upper part of the jet block is the adaptor body H, forming a clear through-way. Integral with the jet block is the pilot jet J, supplied through the passage K. The adjustable pilot air intake L communicates with a chamber, from which issues the pilot outlet M and the by-pass N. It is undesirable, except in special circumstances, to interfere with the pilot jet screw as the volume of air admitted is accurately determined by the makers. An adjusting screw (TS, Fig. 52A) is provided on the mixing chamber, by which the position of the throttle valve for tick-over is regulated independently of the cable adjustment. The needle jet O is screwed in the underside of the jet block, and carries at its bottom end the main jet P. Both these jets are removable when the jet plug Q, which bolts the mixing chamber and the float chamber together, is removed. The float chamber, which has bottom feed, consists of a cup R suitably mounted on a platform S containing the float T, and the needle valve U attached by the clip V. The float chamber cover W has a lock-screw X for security.

The petrol tap having been turned on, petrol will flow past the needle valve U until the quantity of petrol in the chamber R is sufficient to raise the float T, when the needle valve U will prevent a further supply entering the float chamber until some in the chamber has already been used up by the engine. The float chamber having filled to its correct level, the fuel passes along the passages through the diagonal holes in the jet plug Q, when it will be in communication with the main jet P and the pilot feed hole K; the level in these jets being, obviously, the same as that maintained in the float chamber.

THE ENGINE AND GEARBOX

Imagine the throttle valve *B* very slightly open. As the piston descends, a partial vacuum is created in the carburettor, causing

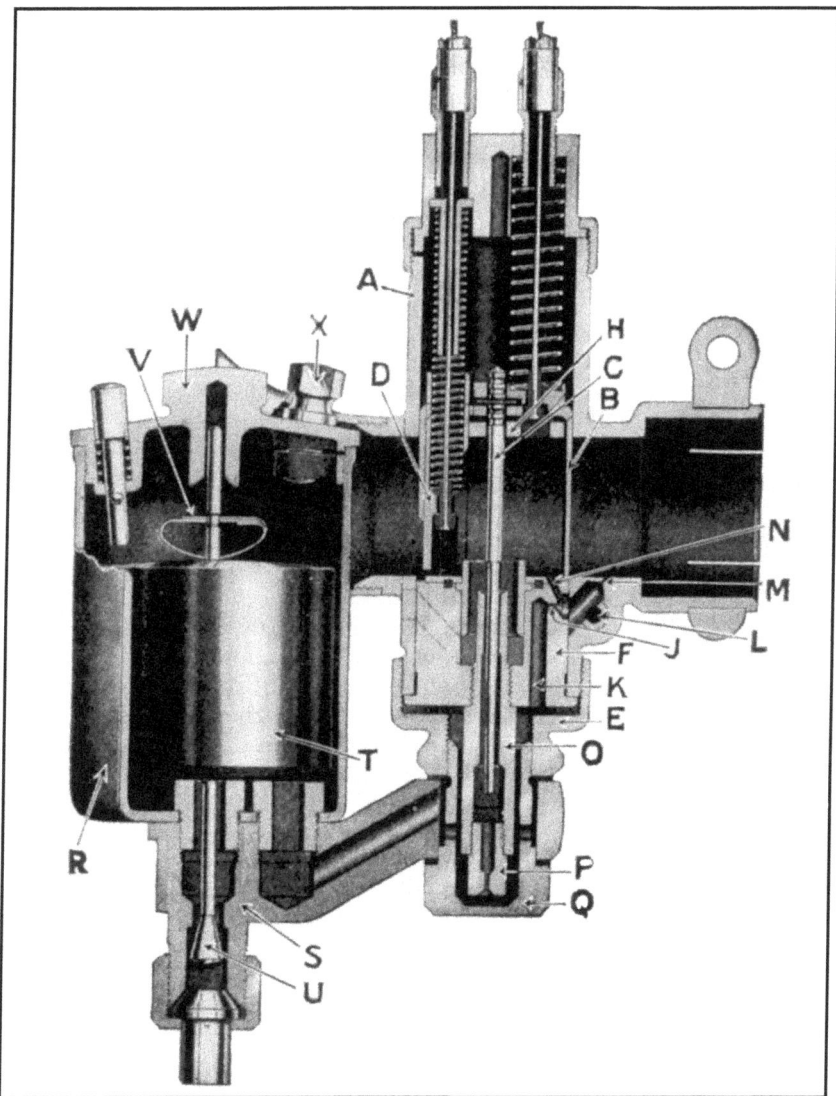

Fig. 52. Sectional View of Semi-automatic Pilot Jet, Amal Carburettor

The pilot jet adjusting screw is not shown

a rush of air through the pilot air hole *L*, and drawing fuel from the pilot jet *J*. The mixture of air and fuel is admitted to the engine through the pilot outlet *M*. The quantity of mixture capable of being passed by the pilot outlet M is insufficient to run the engine. This mixture also carries excess of fuel. Consequently, before a combustible mixture is admitted, throttle valve B must be slightly raised, admitting a further supply of air from the main air intake. The farther the throttle valve is opened, the less will be the depression on the outlet M, but, in turn, a higher depression will be created on the by-pass N, and the pilot mixture will flow from this passage as well as from the outlet M. As the throttle valve is farther opened the fuel passes the main jet P, and this jet governs the mixture strength from seven-eighths to full throttle. For intermediate throttle positions the taper needle C working in the needle jet O is the governing factor.

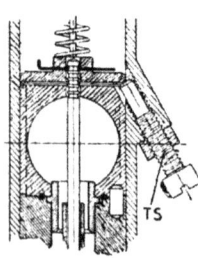

Fig. 52a. Amal Throttle Stop

The farther the throttle valve is lifted, the greater the quantity of air admitted to the engine, and a suitable graduation of fuel supply is maintained by means of the taper needle. The air valve D, which is cable-operated on the two-lever carburettor, has the effect of obstructing the main through-way and, in consequence, increasing the depression on the main jet, enriching the mixture.

Tuning and maintenance hints will be found on pages 116 and 134 respectively.

The Lucas H.T. Magnetos. All Lucas magnetos manufactured during and since 1926 carry a two years' guarantee, and before being sent out from the works are subjected to a high speed test at which they are required to function satisfactorily. The high tension mouldings are tested before assembly at about 40,000 volts, i.e. at least three times the maximum possible operating voltage as limited by the safety gap.

Fig. 53 shows a KSA1 magneto fitted to Models C, C/S, and from this the salient features may be observed. The magneto, which is waterproofed throughout, has a standard timing range of about 30 degrees, the cam ring being moved by a spring-controlled rack giving a smooth action.

The contact-breaker (Figs. 53 and 75), which is secured to the tapered end of the armature shaft and rotates with it at half engine speed in a clockwise direction (C.B. side), has the usual type rocker arm with a fibre heel bearing against the cam ring. To prevent excessive wear of the rocker arm, automatic lubrica-on is provided in the form of an oil-soaked piece of felt in the C.B. housing and a wick leading to the cam ring surface. The contacts, whose correct "break" is ·012 in., are of platinum with the inner one adjustable. A spring carbon button in the centre of the C.B. cover makes contact with the C.B. fixing bolt, and

THE ENGINE AND GEARBOX

enables the low tension current to be earthed by the ignition switch. The high tension current is picked-up by a spring carbon brush from the slip-ring and conveyed to the plug by 7 mm. cable.

The MA1 magneto fitted to Model R/7 is very similar to the KSA1 type, and the above details are applicable. In the case of the KLV magnetos fitted to all the twin-cylinder models there is also very little difference, and the contact-breaker is exactly

(*Joseph Lucas, Ltd.*)

FIG. 53. LUCAS KSA1 SINGLE-CYLINDER MAGNETO WITH CONTACT-BREAKER COVER REMOVED

A—Pick-up
B—Carbon brush
C—Contact-breaker cover securing spring
D—Contact-breaker fixing bolt
E—Contact points
F—Locking nut
G—Locating spring
H—Contact-breaker cover

the same. The high tension current is taken from the secondary winding by means of an ordinary slip-ring and two pick-up carbon brushes kept in contact with metal segments. No separate distributor is used. The whole instrument is very robust, the body being a one-piece die casting.

The magneto armature rotates in ball bearings, and there is a renewable grease-soaked washer in the driving-end bearing. (For maintenance and timing advice, see pages 135 and 137 respectively.)

The Lucas M-L NA1 H.T. Magneto (Fitted to D, D/S). This magneto, which has laminated pole shoes and cobalt steel magnets, is a small and compact machine, having an excellent electrical performance. The magnet and pole shoes are covered by a light aluminium cover, which serves to exclude dirt, dust, and water. The terminal and contact-breaker are accessible, and adjustment of the contact-breaker points can be readily carried out. (See page 107.) The contact-breaker mechanism on this instrument is of unique construction. Tungsten steel and not platinum is used for the contacts. Referring to Fig. 54, the face cam *B* causes movement of a fibre rod to separate the contacts *A*, by lifting the outer spring and contact *G*; ·010 in. is the correct "break."

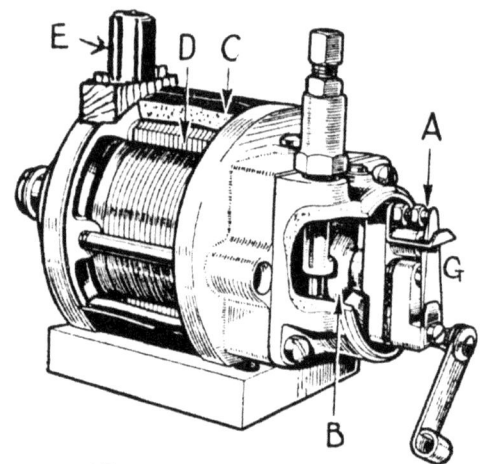

(*From the "Motor-Cyclist's Review"*)

FIG. 54. THE LUCAS M-L MAGNETO

Above is shown partly cut-away a racing type CMAK. The NA1 type used on the Matchless is very similar

The illustration also shows the laminated pole shoes *D* and the position of one of the two part-circular magnets *C*.

Self-contained spring control to the timing lever is provided, and the whole mechanism is adequately waterproofed. A rubber sleeve is fitted to the Bowden cable and adjustable stop. This rubber sleeve should not be omitted, as if this is done there is a possibility, in wet weather, of water running down the Bowden cable and getting access to the interior of the machine.

The pick-up terminal *E* for the high tension current is now of the flanged type, and is secured by two small screws as shown; 7·5 mm. cable is used, and is held firm by the terminal screw entering the stranded core of the cable and expanding the rubber insulation. For general maintenance and similar information, see page 136.

The Lucas DFV4 Dynamo-coil-Distributor Unit. The principle of coil ignition has already been described on page 72, and it

THE ENGINE AND GEARBOX

remains to enlarge upon the special Lucas DFV4 features and construction. Fig. 55 shows a view of the distributor and contact-breaker, and Fig. 19 the unit housed in the "Silver Hawk." The principal components are (*a*) the battery, (*b*) the dynamo, (*c*) the coil, (*d*) the resistance "tell-tale" lamp and ignition switch, (*e*) the contact-breaker, (*f*) the distributor.

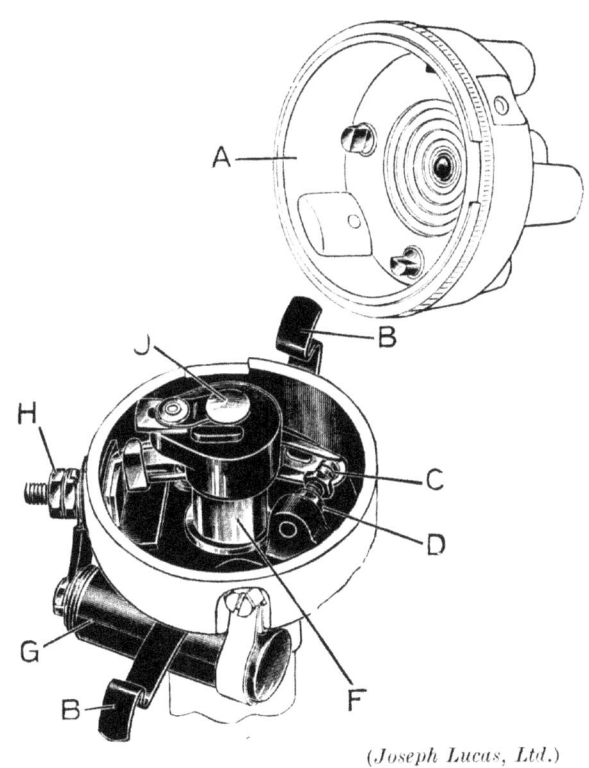

(*Joseph Lucas, Ltd.*)

FIG. 55. THE DISTRIBUTOR AND CONTACT-BREAKER ON THE LUCAS 4-CYLINDER DFV4 COIL IGNITION SYSTEM

A—Distributor moulding
B—Moulding securing springs
C—Contacts
D—Locking-nut
F—Rotating four-lobe cam
G—Condenser
H—Low tension terminal
J—Spring contact

The battery which supplies current to the coil and lighting equipment is the PUW7E type, as used on all except the light-weight Matchless models, and it gives 6 volts with a capacity of 12 amp.-hours. For maintenace, see page 100. The dynamo is a 6-volt generator of the wound pole type, with a maximum output of 4-5 amp. Regulation is effected, as on the "Magdyno," by the well-known three-brush method, the two main brushes lying across a horizontal diameter with the positive insulated, and the negative earthed to the frame of the machine. In construction, this dynamo, which has clockwise rotation (seen from distributor side), closely resembles the dynamo portion of the "Magdyno," and its maintenance instructions are exactly the same. (See page 97.)

The ignition coil comprises a laminated iron core wound firstly with a primary winding of a few hundred turns, and secondly with a secondary winding of several thousand turns, in which the high tension current is induced at each collapse of the magnetic fields caused by interruption of the primary circuit by the contact-breaker. The ends of the two windings are brought to the low tension and high tension terminals on the outside of the casing. Connected in series with the primary winding between the battery and coil is a panel-mounted ignition switch and "tell-tale" lamp, and a ballast resistance (a coil of very fine wire) with automatic cut-out, whose function it is to minimize wastage of current in the event of the ignition switch being left "on" with the contacts closed.

The automatic cut-out acting on the solenoid principle diverts the current through the ballast resistance immediately the dynamo stops, or its speed falls below a certain number of revolutions per minute. One of the coil low tension terminals is connected direct to the contact-breaker, while the high tension terminal is connected to the centre terminal of the distributor moulding.

The distributor and contact-breaker comprise a single unit, illustrated by Fig. 55. Considering the contact-breaker first, this comprises a make-and-break mechanism somewhat similar to that on a magneto with two platinum contacts, one of which is adjustable, actuated by a rocker arm with its fibre heel sprung against a four-lobe cam fixed to and rotating with a central shaft helical bevel driven off the dynamo at half engine speed in an anti-clockwise direction. Connected in parallel with the contacts, clipped to the outside of the housing, is the usual type of tin-foil condenser providing an alternative path to the low tension current and preventing arcing when the primary voltage reaches its maximum at each "break." The surfaces of the cams are lubricated by a wick which requires occasional oiling, and wear on the fibre heel is thus negligible. With regard to the distributor, this comprises the distributor shaft, which is an extension of the contact-breaker camshaft with its bearing lubricated by means of a greaser on the housing exterior; the distributor arm, a metal lever fixed to the top of the distributor shaft carrying on the outside the metal electrode, and in the centre a spring contact which picks up the high tension current from a carbon brush connected to the terminal in the centre of the distributor moulding; the distributor nickel

THE ENGINE AND GEARBOX

segments spaced round the inside of the moulding at 90 degrees to each other, and providing jump-spark gaps of about ·012 in. consecutively for each "break." These segments are connected directly to the four sparking plug terminals. The "jump-spark" system ensures a really "fat" spark at the plugs. Variable ignition timing is arranged for by simultaneous rotation by a Bowden cable of the distributor moulding and also the contact-breaker case, so that the rocker arm heel moves relatively to the quadruple cam. It is, of course, imperative always to keep the contacts, the segments, and electrode absolutely clean. Notes on contact-breaker and distributor maintenance will be found on pages 108 and 121 respectively.

The Sturmey-Archer Gearboxes. There are four types of gearboxes fitted to Matchless machines—the new heavyweight and lightweight four-speed, and the B.W. and F.W. lightweight three-speed boxes.* In each case the layshaft is placed immediately below the mainshaft with a totally-enclosed kickstarter drive taken through the low gear pinions. The heavyweight and lightweight four-speed gearboxes differ as regards dimensions and structural strength. The clutch-operating control on both lightweight and heavyweight boxes comprises a lever-actuating mechanism, but the lightweight box (fitted to the Silver Arrow only) is mounted horizontally so that the layshaft operates *behind* the mainshaft.

The Heavyweight Four-speed Gearbox (Fitted to all except A/2, D, D/S, R/7). Referring to Fig. 56, the clutch body (14A) is keyed and held by a nut to the end of the mainshaft (1). Rigidly fixed to the clutch body and moving with it are four driven plates (14) kept in contact by the clutch springs (15) with three friction insert plates (13), of which the rearmost constitutes the clutch sprocket (3) driven by chain from the engine sprocket. These friction plates, owing to their construction (see page 21), rotate when the engine is running as a single unit, and the driven plates also rotate with them except when the clutch spring pressure is released by the lever (17) through the plunger (16). It will thus be seen that with the clutch engaged, the engine always drives the gearbox mainshaft at a speed equal to the ratio of the engine sprocket diameter to the clutch sprocket diameter (i.e. at about half engine speed).

The mainshaft itself is carried in two bearings, that on the clutch side where the secondary transmission thrust is received being a heavy single-row, self-aligning ball bearing, and that on the opposite side a light double-row ball bearing. The mainshaft, however, is not carried direct on the large bearing for the gear-

*Detailed overhaul information for Sturmey Archer 3 speed gearboxes and clutches can also be found in our '1930's British Motorcycle Gearboxes & Clutches' publication ISBN 9781588501813

box sprocket (4), which is connected to the rear wheel sprocket by chain, is rigidly attached to a sleeve (5A) which also carries the top gear dog wheel (5), and the whole is free to revolve on the mainshaft with a phosphor-bronze bush as a bearing. It is the sleeve itself which is carried by the thrust ball bearing, and, consequently, the loading of both primary and secondary transmission is taken through this bearing. The top gear dog wheel is in permanent engagement with a small fixed layshaft driving pinion (9), and so the gearbox sprocket rotates whenever the

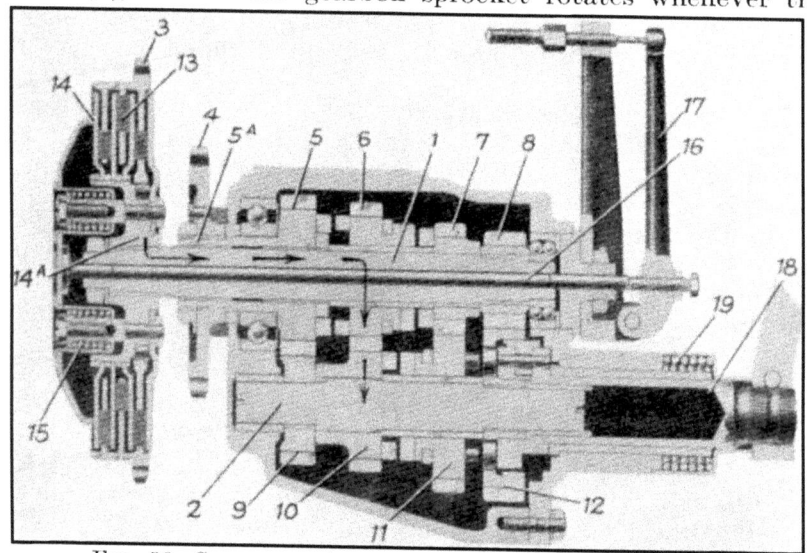

FIG. 56. SECTIONAL ARRANGEMENT OF STURMEY-ARCHER HEAVYWEIGHT 4-SPEED GEARBOX AND 3-PLATE CLUTCH

1—Main shaft
2—Layshaft
3—Clutch sprocket
4—Gearbox sprocket
5—Top gear dog wheel
5A—Top gear dog wheel sleeve
6—Mainshaft sliding dog wheel
7—Second gear dog wheel
8—First gear pinion
9—Layshaft driving pinion
10—Layshaft third gear dog wheel
11—Layshaft sliding dog wheel
12—Layshaft driven k.s. dog wheel
13—Clutch friction plates
14—Clutch-driven plates
14A—Clutch body
15—Clutch springs
16—Clutch plunger
17—Clutch actuating lever
18—Kick-starter axle

layshaft is in motion and *vice versa*. Adjacent to this small layshaft pinion is another slightly larger pinion (10), free to rotate on the layshaft and dogged on its inner side. This pinion provides third gear. At the end of the mainshaft opposite the clutch are two small pinions, the second gear dog wheel (7) free to revolve on the mainshaft, and the low gear pinion (8) which is not dogged, but is fixed to the mainshaft and in constant mesh with the large layshaft kickstarter driven dog wheel (12) which can revolve freely on the layshaft. As may be seen from Fig. 56, with the gears in neutral, the kickstarter axle, when rotated anti-clockwise,

THE ENGINE AND GEARBOX

drives by means of the pawl and ratchet the large layshaft k.s. pinion (12) which, in turn, rotates the first gear pinion and thus drives the mainshaft and clutch sprocket clockwise. Taking the engine sprocket into consideration, a total gear reduction of about 4:1 occurs. Between the top gear and the second gear mainshaft dog wheels on a splined portion of the mainshaft is one of the two sliding pinions (6). Below this on a splined portion of the layshaft is the second sliding pinion (11). Both these sliding

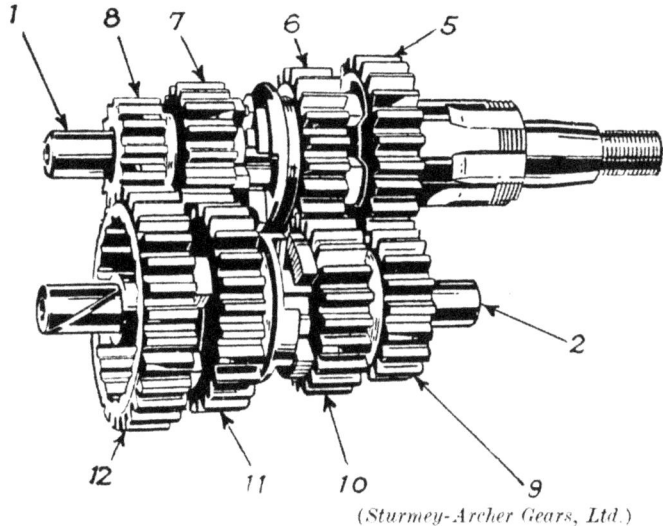

(*Sturmey-Archer Gears, Ltd.*)

FIG. 57. THE STURMEY-ARCHER 4-SPEED TRAIN OF PINIONS
This illustration should be studied in conjunction with Fig. 56

pinions are dogged on each side, and together are capable of engaging four dog wheels.

A very clever cam operating mechanism whose design is made clear by Fig. 58, co-ordinates and controls the horizontal motion of the two sliding pinions which have grooves into which the striker forks A fit. The cylindrical bases of the striker forks can slide endwise on a fixed shaft B mounted parallel to the mainshaft, and the necessary and somewhat complex movement of the two strikers is obtained by partial rotation of a cam plate G into whose curiously shaped grooves C fit closely two small studs on the striker fork bases. The cam plate itself has a central stub spindle bearing, and is caused to rotate by the gearbox lever F through the agency of a toothed quadrant E engaging a pinion fixed to the back of the cam plate. To prevent the possibility of the gears being missed, the periphery of the cam plate has five notches *G* which are engaged by the end of a spring-loaded plunger *H*.

Briefly the action of the gearbox is as follows—

Fourth Gear. The upper sliding pinion is moved to the extreme left (Fig. 70) until the dogs of the mainshaft sliding pinion engage with those of the top gear dog wheel, when the mainshaft and top gear dog wheel sleeve become locked together and rotate as one. There is thus no gear reduction within the gearbox and the

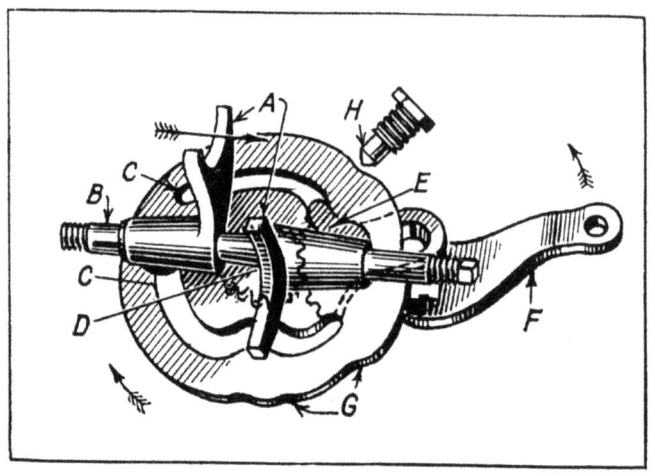

Fig. 58. The Cam Gear Operating Mechanism and Striking Forks on the 4-speed Gearbox

A—Striking forks
B—Fork shaft (fixed)
C—Cam grooves
D—Cam plate and pinion bearing
E—Actuating quadrant (shown dotted)
F—Gearbox lever
G—Cam plate index notches
H—Spring-loaded plunger

layshaft simply idles, while the clutch and gearbox sprockets rotate together at the same speed.

Third Gear. The mainshaft sliding pinion is moved to the right into the position shown at Fig. 56, while the layshaft sliding pinion is interlocked with the third gear layshaft dog wheel which is in mesh with the mainshaft sliding pinion. Here the drive is taken from the clutch sprocket, transmitted through these two pinions, the lower of which is now locked to the layshaft, and then back to the sliding sleeve and gearbox sprocket through the layshaft driving pinion and top gear dog wheel which are in constant mesh. Only a small gear reduction, equal to the resultant ratio of the diameter of the four pinions, occurs.

Second Gear. The upper sliding pinion is moved across farther to the right until the dogs on the mainshaft sliding pinion interlock with those of the second gear mainshaft pinion, thus

THE ENGINE AND GEARBOX

locking the latter to the mainshaft. The drive is here taken from the clutch sprocket, transmitted along the mainshaft, and passed to the layshaft through the second gear and layshaft sliding pinions to the layshaft, and then back to the gearbox sprocket sleeve through the layshaft driven pinion and top gear dog wheel. Two separate gear reductions of considerable magnitude occur.

Neutral. *Neutral* is obtained by positioning the sliding pinions as shown in Fig. 56, when, as may be seen, the pinions on either side of them run idly and no motion is imparted to the layshaft whatsoever. One of the sliding pinions is always in *neutral*.

First Gear. The layshaft sliding pinion is moved across to the extreme right until it interlocks with the layshaft driven kick-starter dog wheel. Here again two considerable gear reductions occur, the drive being transmitted to the gearbox sprocket in the usual manner after transmission via the low gear pinion and kick-starter dog wheel.

The Sturmey-Archer Three-speed B.W. Type Gearbox (Fitted to Models D, D/S). Referring to the sectional view at Fig. 59, the clutch body (51) is keyed to the tapered end of the mainshaft, and the clutch sprocket which becomes locked to the body by the spring (12) pressing the driven plates (19) against the friction inserts of the clutch sprocket. Thus so long as the engine is running and the clutch lever (23) is not causing the mainshaft thrust plunger (10) to release the spring pressure, the mainshaft (20) rotates on its ball bearings. In the clutch lever side a double-row ball bearing is used, while on the sprocket side a heavy single-row thrust ball bearing is used. Interposed between this and the mainshaft is a sleeve (26) to which are fixed the top gear dog wheel (16) and the gearbox sprocket (17). This sleeve is free to rotate on the mainshaft. The top gear dog wheel is in constant mesh with the layshaft driving pinion (29) keyed to the layshaft, so that whenever the layshaft is in motion (top gear excepted), the sleeve and gearbox sprocket transmitting the drive also rotate at a speed equal to layshaft speed $\times$ ratio of the diameters of the two meshing pinions. Keyed to the end of the mainshaft opposite the clutch is the bottom gear pinion (22), and free to rotate upon the layshaft, and in constant mesh with it is the layshaft driven dog wheel (31) which has a ratchet on its outer face with which the kickstarter pawl engages, thus rotating the clutch sprocket direct via the fixed low gear pinion and this dog wheel. The mainshaft is splined for a considerable portion of its length, the unsplined half being that adjacent to the low gear pinion. Similarly, the layshaft is splined except adjacent to the driving pinion. Two sliding dog wheels—one on the mainshaft and one on the layshaft—are simultaneously moved by a single striking plate (75, Fig. 60) and two forks (S, Fig. 61), whose endwise

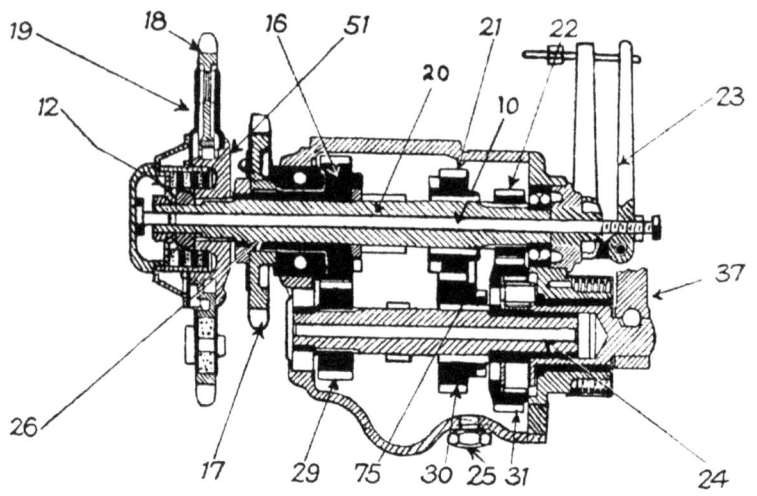

FIG. 59. SECTIONAL ARRANGEMENT OF STURMEY-ARCHER 3-SPEED B.W., F.W. GEARBOX AND SINGLE PLATE CLUTCH

10—Clutch operating plunger
12—Clutch spring
16—Top gear dog wheel
17—Gearbox sprocket
18—Clutch sprocket
19—Clutch driven plates
20—Mainshaft
21—Mainshaft sliding dog wheel
22—Bottom gear pinion
23—Clutch operating lever
24—Layshaft
25—Drain plug
26—Top gear dog wheel sleeve
29—Layshaft driving pinion
30—Layshaft sliding dog wheel
31—Layshaft kick-starter driven dog wheel
37—Kick-starter crank
51—Clutch body
75—Striking plate

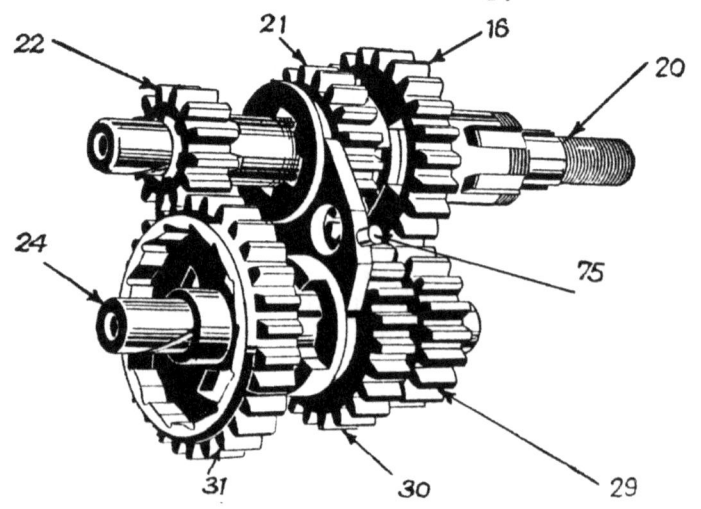

(*Sturmey-Archer Gears, Ltd.*)

FIG. 60. THE STURMEY-ARCHER 3-SPEED TRAIN OF PINIONS

This illustration should be studied in conjunction with Fig. 59
Also see footnote on page 83 regarding Sturmey-Archer 3 speed gearboxes.

THE ENGINE AND GEARBOX

movement is controlled by a lever arm engaging a ball end; positive indexing of the gear positions is provided by a spring-loaded plunger engaging four small circular recesses in one of the fork sides as may be observed. The two sliding dog wheels are responsible for connecting the primary and secondary drives, and providing the three speeds which are obtained as follows—

Top Gear (Third). The mainshaft and layshaft sliding dog wheels are moved to the extreme left (Fig. 59), until the mainshaft sliding dog wheel interlocks with the top gear dog wheel. The layshaft sliding dog wheel thus automatically becomes free to idle on the layshaft non-splined portion, while the top gear dog wheel, gearbox sprocket, and clutch sprocket rotate as a single unit giving a direct or top gear drive.

Middle Gear (Second). The sliding dog wheels are moved slightly to the left of the half-way position, thus allowing the layshaft splines to engage with the corresponding keyways on the lower sliding dog wheel. The drive is then transmitted from the mainshaft via the two sliding dog-wheels, layshaft, and layshaft-driven pinion back to the top gear dog wheel sleeve and gearbox sprocket. The resultant gear ratio obtained* (about 1·5 to 1) depends upon the relative diameters of the two pairs of gear wheels involved.

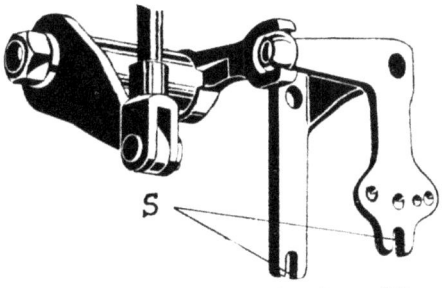

(*Sturmey-Archer Gears, Ltd.*)

FIG. 61. GEAR-OPERATING MECHANISM ON THE B.W. TYPE GEARBOX

Neutral. The sliding dog wheels are moved a trifle farther to the right until the mainshaft sliding dog wheel leaves the mainshaft splines and simply idles on the mainshaft, causing no rotation whatever of the layshaft. Fig. 59 shows neutral position.

Bottom Gear (First). The sliding dog wheels are moved to the extreme right until the layshaft sliding dog wheel engages with the dogs of the layshaft kickstarter-driven pinion. The mainshaft sliding dog wheel has now left the mainshaft splines, and idles while the mainshaft drive is transmitted to the layshaft by the bottom gear pinion and layshaft kickstarter-driven dog wheel, and thence to the gearbox sprocket and secondary transmission via the layshaft driving pinion and top gear dog wheel. Two separate gear reductions occur, giving bottom gear.

The Sturmey-Archer Three-speed F.W. Type Gearbox (Fitted to Model R/7). This gearbox, while of the same general design and construction as the B.W. type, has an entirely different gear-operating mechanism, comprising a rocking segment and rack.

* I.e. within the gearbox, excluding the sprocket ratio.

CHAPTER IV

LUCAS ELECTRIC LIGHTING EQUIPMENT

LUCAS equipment is used on all present Matchless machines, and in this chapter the reader will find most essential information relating to its care and maintenance. Two distinct generator units, each comprising a combined dynamo and magneto, the dynamo portion alone being primarily dealt with in this chapter, are used on all single- and twin-cylinder models. The generators concerned are the new Lucas M.S. "Magdyno," used on all heavyweight models, and the Lucas F.D. "Maglita," used on the three lightweight machines. As explained on page 3, a plain generator and lamp, or a generator with complete de luxe panel equipment, may be fitted. In the case of the four-cylinder Matchless, the dynamo portion of the dynamo-coil-distributor unit closely resembles that of the "Magdyno," and the maintenance instructions following later in this chapter are applicable. Three different types of Lucas headlamps are used, type S.51 on "Magdyno" and "Maglita" de luxe models, type H.52 on plain "Magdyno" models, and type M.40 on plain "Maglita" models. An S.51 headlamp is also used on the four-cylinder Matchless.

THE "MAGDYNO" TYPE M.S.

The type M.S. "Magdyno" (Fig. 62) is similar in design to the M.D. type used prior to 1931, except that the dynamo unit is detachable. A suitable fitment can be supplied which protects the gears when it is desired to run the machine without the dynamo unit for racing or trials purposes. This complete generator, which weighs but 12 lb., has a 30-watt dynamo (i.e. the output is 5 amp. at 6 volts) of the wound pole type, operating on the third brush principle, housed above the magneto for battery charging, and driven by gearing at about half magneto speed.

A special feature of the dynamo is the method of output control. During daytime running the dynamo is arranged to give an ample output which ensures that the battery is charged at a suitable rate without liability to excessive overcharging, and is thus kept in good condition. At night when the lamps are switched on the dynamo automatically gives an increased output, which compensates for the lamp load and prevents the battery from being

LUCAS ELECTRIC LIGHTING EQUIPMENT

unduly run down. This method of control is obtained by inserting a resistance in the dynamo field circuit which is automatically cut out whenever the lamps are switched on. A two-brush commutator transforming alternating current into direct current is used, and above it is an electro-magnetic cut-out which prevents

(Joseph Lucas, Ltd.)

FIG. 62. THE LUCAS M.S. "MAGDYNO" PARTLY SECTIONED SHOWING CONSTRUCTION

A—Dynamo armature
B—Dynamo pole piece
C—Dynamo magnet
D—Dynamo retaining strap
E—Strap tensioning screw
F—Dynamo cover
G—Cover fixing screw
H—Carbon commutator brush
J—Brush retaining spring lever
K—Socket for + headlamp switch cable terminal
L—Electro-magnetic cut-out
M—Dynamo gearing
N—Magneto armature
O—Magneto magnet
P—Slip ring
Q—Contact-breaker fixing screw
R—Contact-breaker cover
S—Cover retaining spring
T—Cam ring

the battery discharging to the dynamo when the dynamo voltage falls below that of the battery.

The stationary parts of the "Magdyno," the dynamo yoke, and the magnetic pole laminations are cast in the aluminium housings. Both dynamo and magneto armatures rotate on ball bearings. The magneto, which has two arched cobalt steel magnets, is of

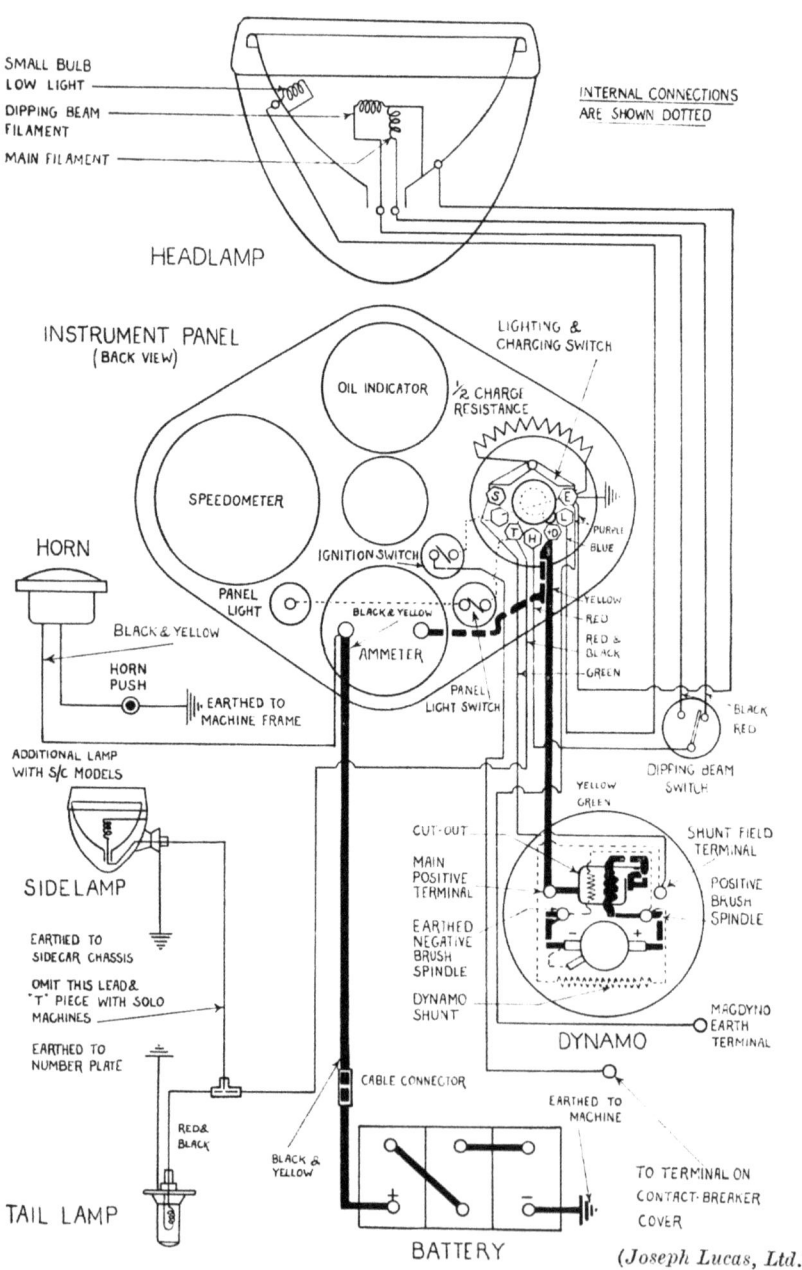

FIG. 62A. WIRING DIAGRAM FOR LUCAS M.S. "MAGDYNO" WITH S.51 HEADLAMP

The diagram shows switch in *L* position, proving full dynamo charge, low, panel, sidecar and tail lights. With switch in *H* position, + *D* is connected to *H*, giving full dynamo charge, high light sidecar and tail lights, with control of main and dipped beam filament bulb by operating handlebar switch. With switch in *C* position, the resistance is inserted in the dynamo field circuit, giving half dynamo charge and lights off. With switch in "off" position, the dynamo field is broken, giving dynamo not charging and lights off.

the usual Lucas design with a contact-breaker similar to that on the K.S.A.1 magneto illustrated on page 79. In the case of twin-cylinder "Magdynos," two carbon pick-up brushes are provided on the driving side of the magneto, and these conduct the high tension current from two metal segments on the slip-ring. There is no electrical connection between the dynamo and magneto units, so that a dynamo defect cannot interfere with ignition. For maintenance of the magneto portion, see page 135.

THE " MAGLITA " TYPE F.D.

The Lucas M-L. "Maglita" is a single armature machine, the armature serving the dual purpose of providing current for the

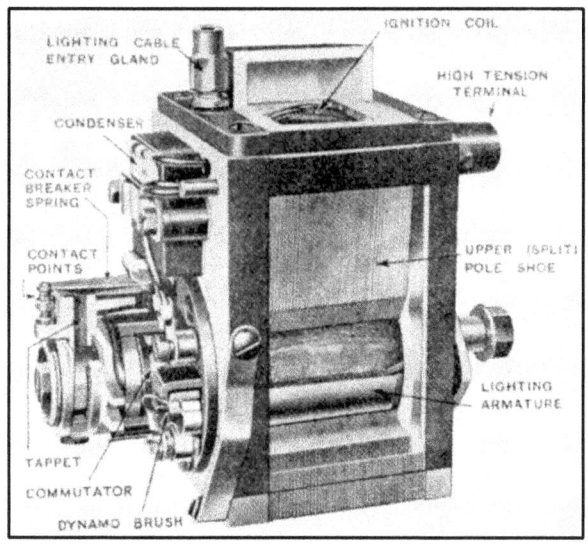

FIG. 63. VIEW OF LUCAS "MAGLITA" WITH COVERS REMOVED SHOWING CONSTRUCTION

lighting circuit, and acting as an inductor for a stationary ignition coil. Its salient features are shown by Fig. 63. It has an output of approximately 16 watts at 6 volts at 2,000 r.p.m., with a maximum output of 20 watts. The armature, which carries a low tension winding only, rotates between laminated pole pieces, the upper pole being split and bridged by the ignition core. Two straight cobalt steel magnets provide the magnetic flux, and, as the "H" armature rotates, the direction of the lines of force in the bridge portion is alternately reversed. This magnetic flux reversal provides the ignition spark. A high tension current being generated in the stationary ignition coil immediately the primary circuit is interrupted by the contact-breaker. As in the case of the M-L. magneto, a contact-breaker of special design is provided and a condenser used in conjunction with it. The end of the secondary winding is conveyed to an insulated terminal on one of the end plates. A commutator is provided on the rotating armature for rectification. Carbon pick-up brushes are used.

The automatic dynamo cut-out is contained in a circular case carried on the end of the armature. It comprises two suitably mounted contact points, one connected to the end of the armature winding, and the other to the commutator, one brush of which is earthed and the other connected to the battery. These are closed when the engine is running by the movement, due to centrifugal force, of a pivoted rocker-arm. To prevent the cut-out contacts closing when the "Maglita" is rotated in the reverse direction, as the result of a back-fire, a sliding locking weight is provided. In the event of the engine back-firing, the inertia of the weight causes it to move into such a position as to lock the contacts in the open position. Both lighting and ignition circuits are independent of each other; a resistance in the dynamo field circuit prevents the battery being overcharged with the switch in the C position. Fig. 64 shows a wiring diagram of the two circuits.

LAMPS AND BATTERIES

The H.52 Headlamp. This lamp is fitted with a double filament bulb, the one filament providing the normal driving light, while the second one gives an anti-dazzle dipped beam. The change over from the normal driving light to the dipped beam is made by a handlebar switch. A small pilot bulb is provided for use when the machine is stationary or when driving in towns.

A centre zero ammeter is incorporated in the lamp, which gives the driver an indication of the amount of current in amperes by which the battery is being charged or discharged under the various conditions governed by the particular position of the switch. When the lamp is switched on, the ammeter is illuminated by indirect lighting.

The rotary switch housed at the back of the lamp has the following positions—

"Off"—Lamps off, and dynamo not charging.

C—Lamps off and dynamo giving half its normal output ($2\frac{1}{2}$ amp.).

H—Headlamp (driving light), tail lamp, and sidecar lamp (when fitted) on; dynamo giving maximum output (4-5 amp.).

L—With the exception that the pilot light is in the place of the driving light, the conditions are exactly the same as in position H.

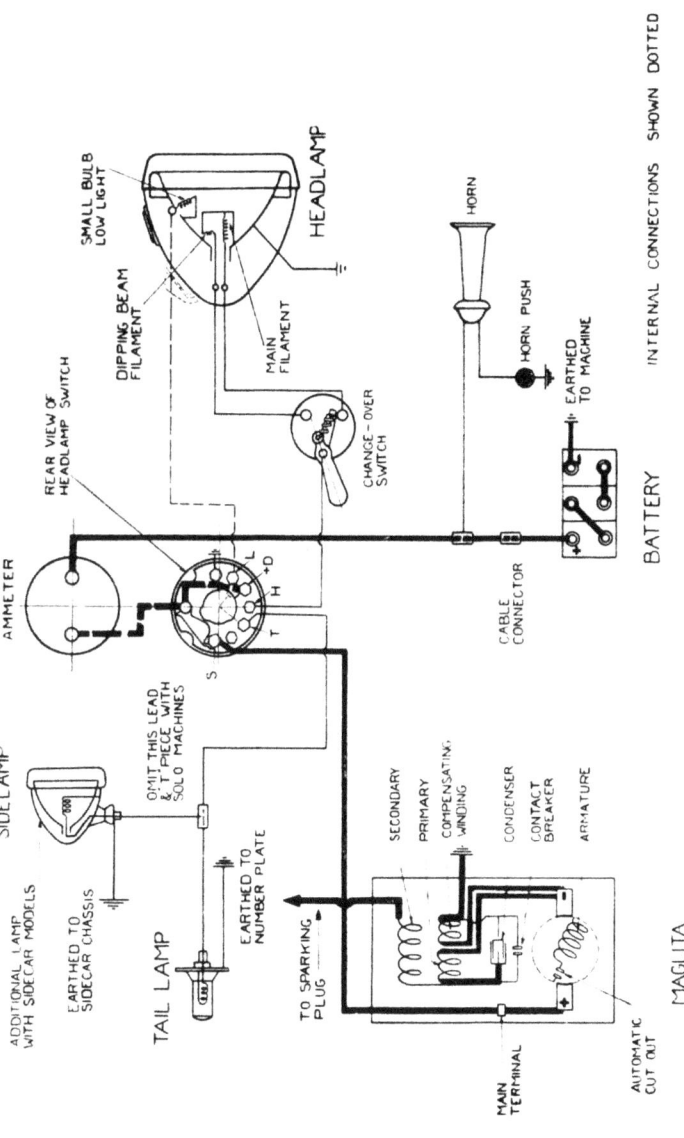

Fig. 64. Wiring Diagram for Lucas M.L. "Maglita" Type F.D. Lighting and Ignition Equipment with M 40 Headlamp

(*Joseph Lucas, ltd.*)

The switch is shown in the *L* position, providing full dynamo charge, low light, sidecar and tail lights. The other switch positions are given on page 97. Internal connections are shown dotted.

All cables are taken to the switch at the back of the headlamp, and this switch is easily removed by undoing two screws, when it can be withdrawn complete with cables.

The lamp front is readily removable as it has a bayonet type fixing. The parabolic reflector is also removable from its three supports. To ensure correct replacement, one of the slots in the reflector rim is marked "top." Focussing of the lamp is provided for by a special main bulb adjustment. Clockwise and counter-clockwise rotation of the bulb causes it to move towards and away from the reflector, respectively. A spring stop in the holder indicates every complete bulb rotation by a click action. The main

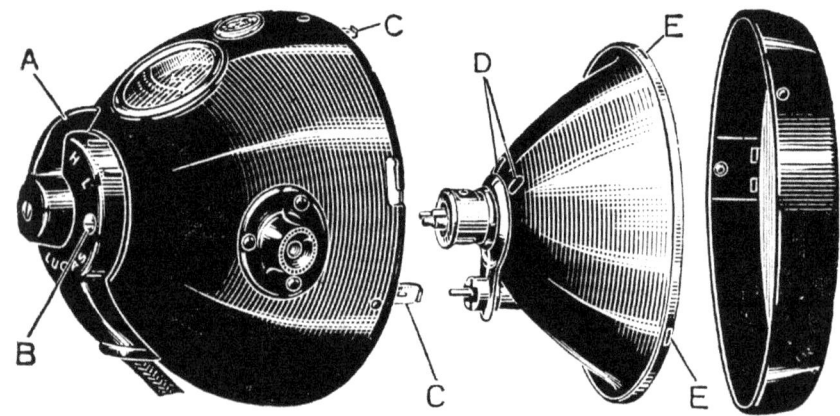

(*Joseph Lucas, Ltd.*)

FIG. 65. LUCAS HEADLAMP (TYPE H52) DISMANTLED

A—Switch   C—Reflector supports   E—Reflector rim slots
B—Fixing screw   D—Ammeter lighting holes

bulb is a 24-watt Lucas No. 624DVMC, while the pilot bulb is a 3-watt B.A.S. No. 8S.

The S.51 Headlamp. This headlamp, which is used in conjunction with the Matchless instrument panel is entirely free from switches or instruments. In other respects it is very similar to the H.52 lamp, and has exactly the same type of focussing adjustment for the main bulb. The parabolic silvered reflector and the lamp front also have the same type of bayonet fixing, enabling them to be quickly detached. Where the generator is an M.S. "Magdyno," the main double filament bulb is a No. 624DVMC; and where an F.D. "Maglita," a 12 watt No. 612DVMC. In both cases the pilot bulb is a B.A.S. No. 8S.

The M.40 Headlamp. This type of lamp, which is of M-L design and used in conjunction with the Lucas M-L. type F.D. "Maglita," houses the ammeter and rotary control switch, as in

the case of the H.52 headlamp. It has a double filament main bulb giving anti-dazzle control by a handlebar switch, and a pilot bulb. The control switch has the following four positions—
"Off"—Lamps off, and "Maglita" not charging.
C—Lamps off, and "Maglita" charging. ($1\frac{1}{2}$-2 amp.)
H—Headlamp (driving light), tail lamp, and sidecar lamp (when fitted) on; "Maglita" charging.
L—Headlamp (pilot light), tail lamp, and sidecar lamp (when fitted) on; "Maglita" charging. ($3\frac{1}{2}$ amp.)

Focussing is carried out by adjusting the position of the main bulb holder after the clamping lever is slackened. The lamp front is secured by a screw and can be removed together with the reflector. The main bulb is a Lucas No. 612DVMC, and the pilot bulb is a B.A.S. No. 8S.

Tail Lamps. Two types of tail lamps are used on Matchless machines, type PT31 on the lightweights, and type MT110 on all other models. The construction of both is very similar.

The front portion of the MT110 lamp is let into a circular hole in the rear number plate. The bulb holder is mounted on a rubber diaphragm which most effectively prevents vibration damaging the filament. The PT31 tail lamp also has a patent rubber cushioning device for bulb protection. Both lamps are constructed so that the bulb holder can be used as an inspection lamp. Armoured cable, and not rubber covered cable, is therefore used, the armouring forming the necessary "earth return." The PT31 lamp used with the "Maglita" takes 3-watt bulbs, while the MT100 lamp takes a No. 8S bulb of the same wattage.

Sidecar Lamp. The R370 reflector sidecar lamp, fitted to the near-side mudguard on all sidecar outfits, has a silvered reflector with a $3\frac{3}{4}$ in. diameter front. There is no internal wiring, contact being made by springs of special design. To enable the bulb to be correctly focussed, there are several alternative positions for the holder. A 3-watt bulb is used, type No. 8S.

Batteries. Batteries used on the lightweights are of the PUW5E type with a capacity of 8 amp.-hr. On other machines the PUW7E type with a 12-amp.-hr. capacity is used. The new "Milam" moulding material entirely eliminates leakage. Special separators ensure free diffusion of the electrolyte and a low internal resistance. The unique vent construction allows the free escape of the gas at reduced pressure, without carrying away the acid solution or allowing the ingress of dirt.

DYNAMO MAINTENANCE

Before removing the cover for any reason, it is advisable to disconnect the positive lead of the battery to avoid the danger of reversing the polarity of the dynamo or short-circuiting the battery. To correct polarity, run engine slowly with switch in "c" position and press cut-out contacts together.

If at any time a "Magdyno" equipped motor-cycle must be ridden with the batteries disconnected, or in any way out of service, it is essential to run with the switch in the "OFF" position.

With the "Maglita" the lamps, in case of emergency, can be run direct off the generator, by disconnecting the battery and turning the control switch to the full "on" position. Under these circumstances the engine speed should be kept down below about 2,500 r.p.m., as otherwise the lamps may burn out. Never run the generator direct with the switch in the "dim" position, as this is likely to burn out both the pilot and tail bulbs. If direct running is necessary, put the control switch to full "on" either before starting up or while the engine is turning over very slowly. Always turn the control switch to the "off" position after stopping the engine, as this prevents the possible discharging of the battery in the event of the cut-out sticking.

Brushes. It is very important to make sure that the brushes work freely in their holders. This can be easily ascertained by holding back the spring lever and gently pulling each flexible lead, when the brush should move without the slightest suggestion of sluggishness. It should also return to its original position directly the lead is let go. When testing the brush in this way, release it gently, otherwise it may get chipped. The brushes should be clean and "bed" over the whole surface; that is, the face in contact with the commutator segments should appear uniformly polished. Dirty brushes may be cleaned with a cloth moistened with petrol.

The brush springs should be inspected occasionally to see that they have sufficient tension to keep the brushes firmly pressed against the commutator when the machine is running. It is particularly necessary to keep this in mind when the brushes have been in use a long time and are very much worn down. Do not insert brushes of a grade other than that supplied with the machine, and do not change the tension springs. It is advisable to inspect the brushes about every 3,000 miles.

Commutator. The surface of the commutator should be kept clean and free from oil or brush dust, etc. Should any grease or oil work its way on to the commutator through over-lubrication, it will not only cause sparking, but, in addition, carbon and copper dust will be collected in the grooves between the commutator segments. The best way to clean the commutator is, without disconnecting any leads, to remove from its box one of the main brushes and, inserting a fine duster in the box, hold it, by means of a suitably-shaped piece of wood, against the commutator surface, causing the armature to be rotated at the same time.

LUCAS ELECTRIC LIGHTING EQUIPMENT

Electromagnetic Cut-out. The cut-out automatically closes by means of solenoids the charging circuit, as soon as the dynamo voltage rises above that of the battery. When the dynamo voltage falls below that of the battery, the reverse action takes place,

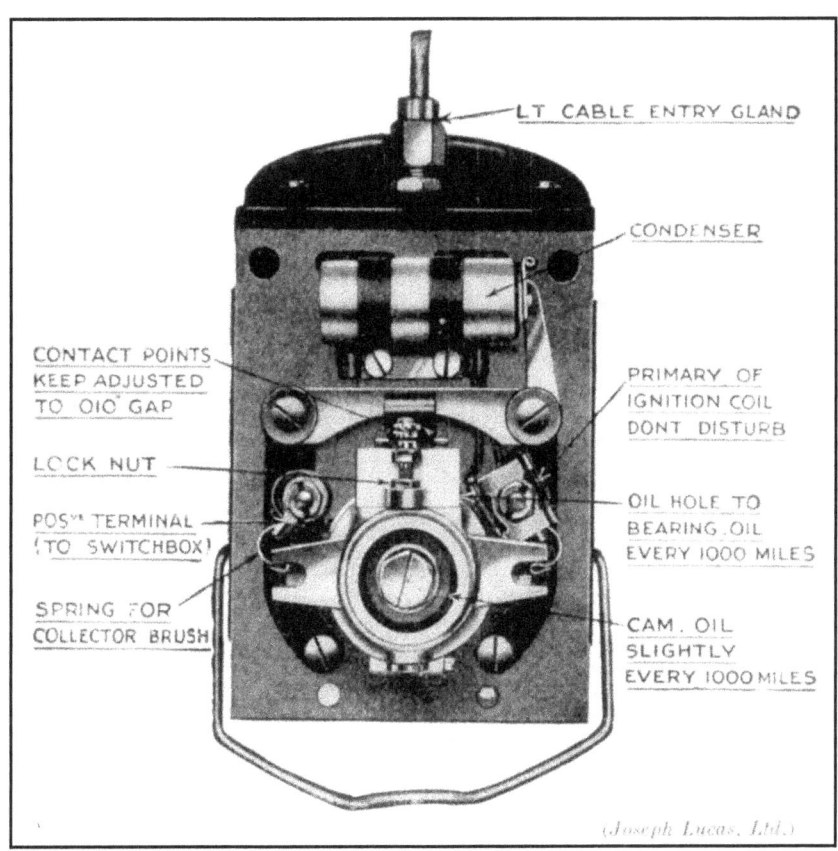

FIG. 66. CONTACT-BREAKER SIDE OF F.D. "MAGLITA," SHOWING SOME POINTS REQUIRING ATTENTION

that is, the cut-out opens and thereby prevents the battery from discharging itself through the dynamo.

The cut-out is accurately set before leaving the makers, and should not be tampered with or adjusted. Should the cut-out fail to close the circuit on accelerating the engine, the cause of the damage is likely to be found elsewhere. There is no relation between the operation of the cut-out and the state of charge of the battery.

Absence of Fuses. In order to simplify the system as far as possible, no fuse is provided. If all the connections are kept clean and tight, there is no possibility of any excess current causing damage to the apparatus.

Lubrication. The armature bearings are packed with grease by the manufacturers and require no attention until a big mileage has been covered, when it is desirable to return a "Magdyno" or "Maglita" to a Lucas Service Department for cleaning and re-lubricating. For contact-breaker lubrication, see page 121.

A Warning. On no account attempt to remove the dynamo armature unless this is done by a person having sound electrical knowledge, as de-magnetization of the magnets will probably be caused.

CARE OF LAMPS

Cleaning Reflectors. The reflectors are protected by a transparent and colourless covering, which enables any accidental finger marks to be removed with a soft cloth or chamois leather without affecting the surface of the reflectors. On no account should a metal polish be used on Lucas reflectors, as this is liable to ruin the surfaces. If the ebony black of the outer body becomes dull in service, the original lustre can be restored by the application of a little good furniture or car polish.

Focussing Headlamp. The best method of focussing is to take the motor-cycle to a straight, level road, find the correct bulb adjustment, and then move the lamp in its adjustable mounting until the best road position is obtained. The driving light should be switched on when focussing is carried out. Special care should be taken to see that the filament is in its correct position relative to the reflector.

Replacement of Bulbs. Always use Lucas bulbs with Lucas reflectors. When it is found necessary to replace the main headlamp bulb, screw it out two or three turns in an anti-clockwise direction. This will release the pressure on the bulb contacts and enable the bulb to be withdrawn easily. Care should be taken that the bulb is fitted the correct way round, i.e. with the dipped beam filament above the centre filament. The correct type of bulb for each lamp is given in this chapter with the brief lamp specifications. Spare bulbs are best carried in a Lucas bulb case.

CARE OF THE BATTERY

It is of the utmost importance that the battery should receive regular attention to keep it in good condition.

The following are the most important maintenance hints—
1. Keep the acid level $\frac{1}{4}$ in. above the top of the plates.
2. Add only distilled water, never tap water.

3. Test the condition of the battery by taking readings of the specific gravity of the acid with a hydrometer.

4. The battery must never be left in a discharged condition.

Topping-up. At least once a month the vent plugs in the top of the battery should be removed and the level of the acid solution examined. If necessary, distilled water, which can be obtained at all chemists and most garages, should be added to bring the level above the tops of the plates, but well short of the bottom of the vent plugs. If, however, acid solution has been spilled, it should be replaced by a diluted sulphuric acid solution of specific gravity, 1·285. It is important when examining the cells that naked lights should not be held near the vents, on account of the possible danger of igniting the gas coming from the plates.

Storage. If the equipment is laid by for several months, the battery must be given a small charge from a separate source of electrical energy about once a fortnight, in order to obviate any permanent sulphation of the plates. In no circumstances must the electrolyte be removed from the battery and the plates allowed to dry, as certain chemical changes take place which result in permanent loss of capacity.

Testing the Condition of the Battery. It is advisable to complete the inspection by measuring the specific gravity of the acid, as this gives a very good indication of the state of charge of the battery.

An instrument known as a "hydrometer" is employed for this purpose. These can be bought at any Lucas Service Depot. Voltmeter readings of each cell do not provide a reliable indication of the condition of the battery, unless special precautions are taken.

Battery-charging Period. It is difficult to lay down rigid instructions on this subject, as the conditions under which motorcycles are used vary considerably; and, obviously, the amount of charging a battery will require is directly dependent on the extent to which the lamps are used. The following suggestions will serve as a rough guide—

The switch should be left in the C position for about 1 hour daily. This time should only be increased if the period of night running is considerable, or when the battery is found to be in a low state of charge (if the specific gravity of the acid solution is 1·210 or below). The chief ill-effect of overcharging is loss of acid by gassing.

The battery must never be left in a fully-discharged condition, and unless some long runs are to be taken, it is advisable to have the battery removed from the machine and charged up from an independent electrical supply.

WIRING OF THE EQUIPMENT

Before making any alteration to the wiring, or removing the switch on the panel or from the back of the headlamp, disconnect the positive lead at the battery to prevent the possibility of short circuits.

The cables required for wiring up the equipment are assembled in the correct order before fitting to the machine, and are then braided together to form a complete cable assembly or harness. This method of wiring allows the cables to be easily clipped to the frame; and if it is necessary to take the electrical equipment right off the machine at any time the cables may be removed as a complete assembly. Another advantage is that the sheathing protects the cables against abrasion through vibration. This is important, as the equipment is wired on the "earth return" system, all cables being of the single conductor type, and any injury to the insulation is liable to cause a short circuit, which will quickly discharge and seriously damage the battery. The earthing leads from the headlamp and the negative battery terminal must be in good electrical contact with the frame of the machine. An earthing terminal is provided on the "Magdyno," to which these leads are conveniently connected. In the same way it is important to see that the base of the tail lamp and of the sidecar lamp (when fitted) are in good contact with a metal part of the machine. Special care must be taken when connecting up the battery of a "Maglita" set as connecting of the terminals wrongly can lead to demagnetization of the magnets.

All cables to the headlamp are taken directly into the switch, which can be easily withdrawn from the H.52 lamp body when the two fixing screws are removed. Care must be taken that the precaution of disconnecting the positive lead at the battery is taken before this is done.

The ends of all "Magdyno" cables are identified by means of coloured sleevings. The colour scheme is as follows: Battery, yellow and black; Dynamo, yellow; Dynamo-field, green; Tail-lamp, red and black; Earth, purple. A wiring diagram of the plain "Magdyno" set is given opposite. A small diagram is also fitted inside the lamp, and can be seen when the reflector is removed. When making a connection, proceed as follows: Bare about $\frac{3}{8}$ in. of the cable, twist the wire strands together, and turn back about $\frac{1}{8}$ in. so as to form a small ball. Remove the grub screw from the appropriate terminal and insert the wire so that the ball fits in the terminal post. Now replace and tighten the grub screw; this will compress the ball to make a good electrical connection. Other wiring diagrams will be found on pages 92, 95.

The cables to the battery are sweated directly to the battery terminals, thus obviating all chance of corrosion.

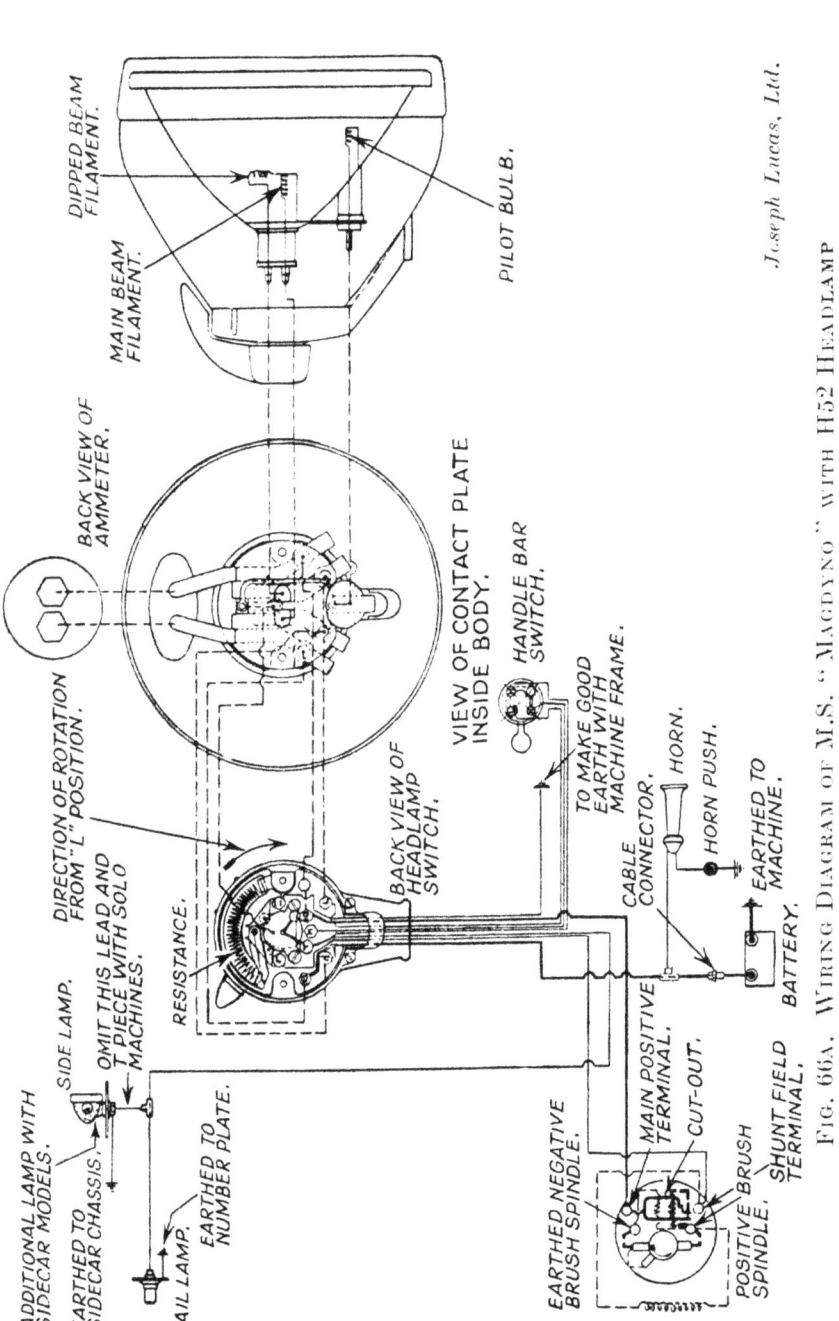

Fig. 66a. Wiring Diagram of M.S. "Magdyno" with H52 Headlamp

CHAPTER V

MAINTENANCE AND OVERHAULING

IN this chapter, which has conveniently been split into four sections for ease of reference, novices and experienced riders should find all essential information relating to Matchless maintenance and overhaul, which, together with the data and numerous illustrations in Chapter I, should enable a rider to find out everything he can reasonably want to know having regard to the care of his own particular model.

ROUTINE ADJUSTMENTS

There are a number of minor adjustments which it is desirable that the Matchless rider should attend to every few hundred miles, or when circumstances necessitate these adjustments being made. If the rider values his machine, however, he will not wait till adjustment *has* to be made, but will carefully inspect his machine as a matter of routine and make the necessary adjustments before they become absolutely essential.

Cleaning. It requires a considerable amount of time to keep a motor-cycle in anything approaching "showroom" condition, but it is the author's opinion that, unless a machine be kept reasonably clean, the fullest pleasure and maximum efficiency cannot be obtained from it. Apart from the question of pride of ownership, dirt covers a multitude of defects and greatly accelerates depreciation in respect of market value. This is, of course, obvious. If neglected, a motor-cycle rapidly becomes shabby and an eyesore. After a ride in dirty weather, cleaning may take at least an hour. On no account should a machine be left soaking wet overnight. A serious amount of rusting may ensue.

It should be noted that chromium plating does not require and should not be treated with metal polish, for it does not oxidize in the same manner as nickel plating. The chromium-plated parts should be treated similarly to the enamel, and the surfaces will then improve with cleaning.

Periodical Inspection of Nuts. One of the most important points in connection with the care of a motor-cycle is to look over the machine frequently and apply a spanner to any nuts which have worked at all loose.

Valve Clearances. In order that the valves shall seat properly and have the correct degree of lift at all running temperatures,

MAINTENANCE AND OVERHAULING

it is extremely important that the correct clearances should exist between the valve stems and the tappet heads, or rocker ends, as the case may be, according to whether the engine be of side-valve or overhead-valve type. The clearances (see "Specifications," Chapter I) should be checked now and again with the feeler gauge on the magneto spanner, although it is unlikely that adjustment will be needed, unless a big mileage has been completed, or the engine is new or the valves have been recently ground-in. The clearances for the exhaust valves on most engines, it will be noted, are larger than the inlet valve clearances, due to the fact that the exhaust valves are subjected to greater heat during the exhaust strokes, and therefore expand to a slightly greater extent. In the case of the side-valve "Silver Arrow" and overhead-camshaft "Silver Hawk," however, the special cylinder head and induction design maintains all valves at approximately the same temperature and, therefore, the same clearances are used for inlet and exhaust valves. On the overhead camshaft machine hardly any clearance is permissible, and this small clearance between the end of each valve stem and the corresponding rocker-arm adjustable grub screw must be made while the engine is *cold*, for as the engine warms up the camshaft axis becomes slightly higher, due to rocker-box expansion, and the valve clearances therefore increase. On all side-valve engines and the push-rod operated overhead-valve engines the tappets should be adjusted when the engine is *warm*, not hot.

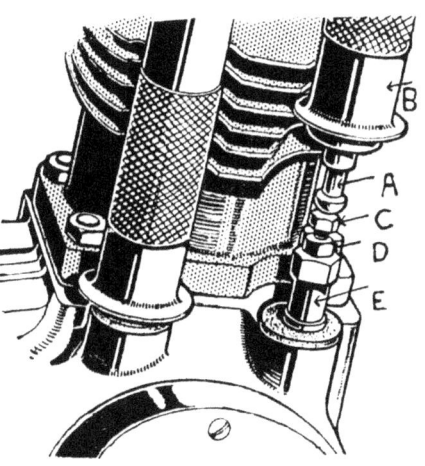

FIG. 67. TAPPET ADJUSTMENT ON THE O.H.V. MODELS

A—Push-rod
B—Push-rod cover
C—Adjustable tappet-head
D—Lock-nut
E—Tappet guide

To check and adjust the exhaust valve clearance, proceed as follows: Remove the valve cover in the case of the side-valve and overhead-camshaft engines, or telescope the push-rod cover in the case of an overhead-valve engine, until the spring catch retains it in position (Fig. 67). Now turn the engine over until compression is felt in the cylinder concerned just after the inlet valve has closed, and then raise the exhaust valve lifter gently or put the decompressor, where fitted, into the "on" position, and further rotate the engine until the piston ascends to the top dead-centre position when both valves are fully closed. Move the decompressor into the "off" position or drop the exhaust valve lifter, and proceed to check the clearance by inserting a feeler gauge of the correct thickness between the base of the valve stem or push-rod and the tappet head (side-valve and overhead-valve), or rocker grub screw end (overhead-camshaft). Finally, however, be certain that the exhaust valve lifter or decompressor is in no way determining the height of the tappet above its cam. There should be an appreciable amount of backlash (about $\frac{1}{16}$ in.) at the handlebar control of the exhaust valve lifter. The feeler gauge blade should just go in without binding. If it binds or goes in loosely, an adjustment is required. To adjust the tappets (side-valve and overhead-valve) hold the tappet head (C, Fig. 67) with one spanner, and with the other loosen the lock-nut securing the adjustable head. Then screw the adjustable head up or down, according to whether the feeler blade indicates that it is necessary to increase or decrease the valve clearance, and finally retighten the lock-nut and once again check the clearance, as the last operation is liable, if care be not taken, to upset the adjustment. On the overhead-camshaft, four-cylinder engine the valve rocker grub-screw lock-nut is loosened, the screw itself turned till the desired adjustment is found, and the lock-nut retightened.

Proceed similarly with the checking and adjustment of the inlet valve clearance. Multi-cylinder Matchless models require the above routine to be performed for each cylinder. Finally give the machine a run when a noticeable improvement in performance should be observed. Incorrect valve clearance affects the valve lift as well as the valve timing, and some engines are very sensitive on this point.

Exhaust Valve-lifter Adjustment. As already mentioned, it is important that there should not be an entire absence of backlash at the exhaust valve-lifter lever with the exhaust valve fully closed, which would inevitably prevent the exhaust valve from seating properly, and thus cause loss of compression and burning of the valve and its seating, accompanied probably by intermittent banging in the exhaust pipe and silencer. There should be about $\frac{1}{16}$ in. backlash at the handlebar control, and the desired adjustment may be made by loosening the lock-nut on the cable adjuster stop and screwing the adjuster in or out, as required, a few turns.

The Sparking Plug. Difficult starting or occasional misfiring can usually be traced to a dirty or defective sparking plug. The life of a plug is considerable, but the points of the electrodes gradually burn away and eventually the gap becomes enlarged

MAINTENANCE AND OVERHAULING

considerably, and it is necessary to reset the points with the aid of a feeler gauge. The correct gap is ·020 in., except for coil ignition, where it is ·027 in. Excessive gap at the plug points means that the voltage required from the magneto is higher; and this not only renders starting difficult, but — what is worse — causes brush discharge inside the magneto. This discharge eventually causes internal corrosion, and the efficiency of the magneto is impaired. From time to time the plug should be removed and thoroughly cleaned with petrol, both inside and outside. All deposits of soot or charred oil must be eliminated. The insulation should be examined for cracks or flaws, and in very humid weather should be wiped dry with a rag before starting-up. The accepted method of testing for current at the plug terminal is to place a wooden-handled screwdriver, with steel blade, across the terminal and just touching the cylinder fin, when a spark should be visible on rotating the engine. To test the plug itself, remove it with the high tension lead still affixed, clean it, lay it on the cylinder, and note whether it sparks satisfactorily when the engine is rotated. If it does not, scrap it. On a twin-cylinder engine a faulty plug may quickly be detected by shorting each plug in turn with a screwdriver. Always fit the correct type of plug. (See Chapter I.)

The Contact-breaker. The magneto should not be interfered with unnecessarily, for it is a very delicate instrument, and functions best when left well alone; but at regular intervals, say every 1.000 miles, the contact-breaker cover, or distributor cover on the "Silver Hawk," should be removed and the contacts (see Figs. 53 and 55) should be examined, and their gap checked with a 12 thou' feeler gauge, except in the case of the "Maglita" or M-L magneto contacts where a 10 thou' gauge is advised. If the clearance is excessive, the timing will be advanced and the primary circuit will not be closed for the correct period, and occasional misfiring is very likely. In the case of a multi-cylinder engine it is imperative that the "break" corresponding with each cylinder is of the same magnitude. Provided the contacts are kept clean and, above all, *free from oil*, they will probably need adjustment only at long intervals. It is not desirable to alter the setting unless the gap varies considerably from that of the magneto spanner gauge. If adjustment is necessary, rotate the engine round slowly until the points are seen to be fully opened and then, using the magneto spanner, slacken the lock-nut and rotate the fixed contact screw by its hexagonal head until the correct gap is obtained, as indicated by the feeler gauge (NOTE: 15 thou' is correct for the "Hawk"); then screw up the lock-nut firmly.

If, when the contact points are examined, it is found that they have become burned or blackened (owing probably to the presence at some time or other of dirt or oil), they may be cleaned with very fine emery cloth, and afterwards with a cloth damped with petrol. All dirt and metal dust must be wiped away entirely. Where the contacts are found to have become seriously pitted, it may be advisable to go over the surfaces with a dead smooth file, but only the very smallest amount of metal must be removed. Bad pitting is usually due to a faulty condenser. Removing the contact-breaker unit will assist filing the contacts quite true, which is imperative. Instructions for removing the Lucas contact-breaker and its rocker-arm will be found on page 136, and advice on timing the "break" on page 137. Should the ignition switch suddenly decline to work, a worn carbon brush fitted on the inside of the contact-breaker cover may be suspected, or, alternatively, a weak spring which fails to keep the brush in contact with the contact-breaker retaining screw.

Any sign of incipient rusting on the contact-breaker spring should be checked immediately, as rust and corrosion are frequent causes of broken contact-breaker springs.

In the case of the M-L magneto and "Maglita" contact-breaker, it is as well occasionally to examine the plunger and control spring, and to grease these thoroughly, as any rusting here may possibly cause binding of the control and sticking of the tappet in its guide. Similarly, it is advisable on Lucas and Lucas M-L magnetos, or "Magdynos" and "Maglitas," to lubricate occasionally the cam ring so as to reduce wear on the fibre rocker heel. In the case of the Lucas DFV4 coil ignition unit and the K.L.V. magnetos, the distributor also requires lubrication at regular intervals. Full in-instructions for the lubrication of Lucas ignition equipment will be found in the lubrication section of this chapter.

Cleaning the Slip Ring. The high tension pick-up or pick-ups, as the case may be, should be removed occasionally from the magneto or "Magdyno," and the slip-ring track and flanges cleaned by holding with a suitable instrument a soft cloth moistened with petrol against the ring while the engine is slowly rotated by hand. Before replacing each pick-up be sure that the spring holding the carbon brush in contact with the ring is free, and that the brush is not unduly worn.

The Distributor. On the four-cylinder Matchless fitted with the DFV4 coil-distributor unit, the distributor moulding should occasionally be removed and the electrodes cleaned with a dry duster, special care being taken to remove all deposits. The metal segments themselves may be cleaned with a rag moistened in petrol.

Clutch Adjustment. In the event of clutch slip being experienced, the adjustment of the clutch-operating cable should be suspected. When correctly adjusted it should be possible to move the clutch actuating lever (to which the lower end of cable is attached) to and fro slightly with the fingers, and if this free movement cannot be felt the cable stop should be adjusted accordingly. To slacken off the adjustment on all other gearboxes, the ball-ended screw attached to the actuating lever which operates on the clutch thrust rod end may be unscrewed a trifle.

Should this screw be disturbed, it must subsequently be securely locked in position by means of the lock-nut. With the clutch properly adjusted there should be $\frac{1}{32}$ in. clearance between the end of the short clutch rod and the ball-ended adjuster screw. An additional adjustment is, of course, provided by the cable stop. Should the clutch, on the other hand, develop harshness even with correctly adjusted chains, the clutch plates should be carefully removed and smeared with a mixture of powdered graphite and water worked up into a paste. Oil should not be used under any circumstances, as it will damage the friction inserts, which are cheap though somewhat difficult to refit. Clutch slip, which is invariably diagnosed by the whole clutch warming up, may, of course, be due to insufficient tightening of the spring or springs, in which case the remedy is obvious.

Gear Control Adjustment. On all models except the "Silver Hawk," which has a patent automatic spring tensioning device for the primary chain with a non-movable gearbox, an adjustment in the position of the gearbox made to compensate for primary chain stretch involves, as a rule, an adjustment of the gear control rod. It is exceedingly important that the gear control is maintained correctly adjusted, and it is sound practice to check the adjustment occasionally, although if it be erroneous to a large extent, difficult gear changing and a tendency for the gear lever to jump out of middle gear is usually present. Before actually proceeding to adjust the control, ensure that the small lever on the gearbox itself is firmly locked to its shaft.

Adjusting " Silver Arrow " Gear Control. Firstly remove the split-pin and washer from the upright connecting-rod yoke upper end pin (i.e. the pin passing through the end of the gear lever), and slack off the lock-nut securing this gear rod yoke end. Then place the gear lever into *third* gear position, and after removing the top yoke end pin, the split-pin of which has already been removed, lightly pull and push alternatively the gear rod by hand in order to feel the action of the gearbox indexing plunger (H, Fig. 58). As the sliding mainshaft and layshaft dog wheels move across either side of the correct third gear position *the resistance of the spring indexing plunger can be felt quite definitely*, and the exact position when the plunger end engages the third gear groove on the periphery of the cam plate must be accurately determined. Having established this position, and without allowing any further upward or downward movement of the connecting rod, screw up or unscrew the yoke end until its eye is in line with the hole in the end of the gear lever so that the pin can be freely inserted. Before locking the yoke end into position, it is advisable to again obtain by hand the exact position of third gear as already described, and check the length of the rod for correct setting, after which the yoke end may be secured by means of its lock-nut and the pin refitted. Do not overlook the replacement of the split-pin. It should be understood that the gear quadrant notches in themselves are in no way intended as accurate guides for gear control adjustment, which should be effected independently of the *exact* position of the gear lever relative to the quadrant. Further, it should be realized that once the correct adjustment for third gear position has been obtained, the remaining gears will automatically be correct as regards adjustment.

Adjusting Gear Control (Models C, C/S, X/3, X/R3). Although the four-speed gearbox itself is of the same pattern as that used on the spring frame Matchless models, a somewhat different system of coupling the gearbox actuating lever to the gear change lever results in a reversal of the gear change positions on the quadrant, and a somewhat different method of adjusting the gear control is necessitated. To check the gear control adjustment proceed as follows: Remove the split-pin securing the gear rod to the gear lever and then, while rocking the rear wheel gently to and fro so as to rotate the layshaft dog wheels, place the gear lever into *bottom* (1st) gear position. Having done this, remove the upper gear rod yoke end pin, from which the split-pin has already been removed, and while still rocking the rear wheel to and fro, exert a downward push on the gear rod to ensure that the bottom gear dogs are in full engagement. Now slack off the locking-nut securing the upper gear rod yoke end, and screw this yoke end up or down the rod as required, until while holding the gear lever back against the rearmost end of the bottom gear quadrant notch, the rod is about $\frac{1}{16}$ in. too long to permit of the pin being inserted. Now insert this pin, and while rocking the rear wheel to and fro, work the gear lever through the gate until the top (4th) gear position is reached. Once again remove the yoke end pin, and while still gently rocking the rear wheel to and fro, pull the gear rod upwards this time to ensure the top gear dog wheel being in full engagement with the mainshaft sliding dog wheel. Then, while holding the gear lever against the foremost end of the top gear quadrant notch, try fitting to it the gear rod end yoke, and take careful note as to whether the rod is as much too short to permit of the entry of the yoke end pin as it was too long at the bottom gear position. If this is not so the length of the rod requires adjusting.

It may be mentioned here that the designer has purposely

MAINTENANCE AND OVERHAULING

made the movement of the gear lever between the extreme ends of the gate greater than is necessary in order to provide for wear that may in time develop in the various gear joints, although with proper lubrication this wear is extremely slow. It is absolutely essential, therefore, that at all times this excess movement should be equally divided at each end of the gate, that is to say, *the gear rod length must be adjusted to be as much too long in the bottom gear position as it is too short in the top gear position*, in each case while the gear lever is held against the respective extreme ends of the gate.

Adjusting Gear Control (Models R/7, D, D/S). On the three-speed B.W. and F.W. Sturmey-Archer gearboxes adjustment of the gear control is extremely simple. All that it is necessary to do to check the adjustment is to place the gear lever in neutral and note whether, when the rear wheel is gently rocked to and fro, it is possible to grate the dogs of the bottom (1st) gear and middle gear (2nd) by moving the gear lever *an equal distance either side of the neutral position*. If the distances are not equal, the gear rod should be shortened or lengthened as required by unscrewing or screwing up the upper yoke in the usual manner.

Primary Chain Adjustment. There is no adjustment whatsoever for the primary chain on the new four-cylinder Matchless (see page 33), but on all other models chain stretch is taken up by drawing the gearbox rearwards the necessary amount by means of a drawbolt or thrust screw, after first loosening the gearbox fixing bolts which enter slotted holes in the rear engine cradle plates or frame lug. In order to verify the chain tension it is, of course, first necessary to detach the chain case which encloses the chain. With a correctly-adjusted primary chain there should be a total whip or movement at the middle of the lower chain run when lightly pressed up or down of about $\frac{3}{8}$ in. This deflection should be tested for a number of positions and, if there is a variation in chain tension, the adjustment should be secured at the tightest position.

When there is an undue amount of slack, there is a danger of the chain jumping the sprockets or breaking when accelerating or decelerating. Chains which are too tight waste power, wear unduly due to crushing stresses on the rollers, and cause excessive strain on the bearings and chain wheels. Remember that primary chain adjustment affects the secondary chain adjustment, and before adjusting the secondary the primary should be inspected and, if necessary, adjusted first. Also do not forget that sliding the gearbox, as a rule, interferes with the gear control adjustment.

Secondary Chain Adjustment. This is effected by drawing the rear wheel backwards in the rear fork ends. In the case of the secondary chain, although not running at as high a speed as the primary, incorrect tensioning produces exactly the same ill-effects, and it should not be overlooked that a loose secondary chain, if it jumps the sprockets at high speed, can have disastrous consequences. When adjusted correctly there should be about ¾ in. total whip at the centre of the lower chain run when the chain is lightly moved up or down in its tightest position. To adjust the secondary chain on all models except the "Silver Arrow" and "Silver Hawk," proceed as follows: Slack off the rear spindle nuts, and then, after first ascertaining that the primary chain does not require adjustment, adjust the chain tension correctly by screwing up the two adjuster bolts in the rear fork ends, taking great care to screw up the adjusters absolutely evenly in order that correct alignment of the rear wheel is maintained. Perfect rear wheel alignment is imperative both from the point of view of the tyres and also the secondary chain itself, which would otherwise suffer serious wear. After a series of secondary chain adjustments have been made, it may be found that the rear wheel spindle approaches perilously near the end of the fork slots. In this case a chain should be shortened, and the adjusting bolts of the rear wheel should be unscrewed right back. Usually, however, by the time a chain elongates seriously it becomes worn out and requires replacement. A rough-and-ready method of testing a chain for wear is to hold a length between the hands and observe to what extent the chain may be bent sideways.

On the spring frame models the deflection of the frame affects slightly the tension of the secondary chain, and, in consequence, it is essential when checking or making adjustments to the latter to set the frame in the normal position assumed when the rider is seated with the compression springs slightly compressed. To ensure this it is necessary to sit upon the machine with the wheels resting on the ground, and tighten the frame dampers until their friction is sufficient to keep the springs compressed when the rider's weight is removed. The prop stand should then be brought into use, and if the compression springs are still kept in the normal riding position it will be noticed that the rear tyre is well clear of the ground.

Adjusting Magneto Chain. The magneto chain only requires adjustment at rare intervals or when dismantling. Comparatively slow running under ideal conditions prevents rapid wear, unless the sprockets are badly aligned. In the case of the spring frame models, a shaft drive with a flexible coupling is used instead of a chain. With a correctly tensioned magneto chain there should be a total whip or movement in the centre position of the free chain run of approximately ¼ in.

To adjust the magneto chain on the Big Twins, firstly remove the chain case cover and slack off the four gearbox fixing stud nuts and screw the special double-headed adjuster nut clockwise to tighten the chain, or *vice versa* to slacken. This causes the magneto platform to slide along the engine cradle plates. After obtaining the correct adjustment be sure to tighten down securely the four gearbox stud nuts, and when replacing the cover see that the faces are quite clean.

On Model R/7, which has the magneto mounted on a platform at the front of the engine, adjustment is effected, after removing the chain case cover, by varying the position of the magneto on its platform, slotted bolt holes being provided to allow of this. Correct chain adjustment is made by slackening off the two nuts only on the underside of the platform and sliding the magneto backwards or forwards as required.

In the case of Models C, C/S, the driving chain is properly tensioned by tilting the magneto bodily by means of its hinged platform and screwed adjuster bolt. To tighten the chain, unscrew the upper adjustment nut about half a turn and tighten the underneath nut a corresponding amount. If necessary repeat the operation, but be sure to have the two nuts securely tightened. On Models D, D/S, although the magneto drive is taken off the engine shaft on the opposite side of the engine, a similar type of hinged magneto platform to that on Models C, C/S is used, and the foregoing instructions are applicable.

Coupling-up a Chain. Chain replacement, after removal for cleaning, is enormously simplified if the obvious precaution be taken to unite the two ends to be joined so that the whole of the chain tension is resisted by the teeth. Do not neglect to replace the spring link with the closed end facing the direction of chain travel.

Bowden Controls. Few things have a greater adverse effect on the performance of a machine than badly adjusted or slack control cables, especially where the carburettor is concerned. With the cables properly adjusted by the screw stops at the top of the mixing chamber, a very slight movement of the throttle lever or twist-grip from the fully-closed position should cause the throttle slide to commence to ascend. The same remark applies in regard to the air lever and ignition lever. Immediately slackness is noticed, the backlash should be taken up by adjusting the cable stops. In the case of the clutch and exhaust valve-lifter controls, an appreciable amount of backlash at the levers is desirable for obvious reasons.

Adjusting Fork Action Damper. The action of the damper fitted on the front forks can best be adjusted while the machine is in motion and travelling over a badly corrugated surface. The ebonite damper hand nut (Fig. 12) should be screwed sufficiently tight to make the fork action sluggish under these circumstances.

With this adjustment, little or no variation should be required for riding on average road surfaces.

Adjusting Front Fork Spindle Bearings. Provision is made for taking up side or endwise wear of the various fork spindle bearings. The need for such adjustment will be made apparent by a click or creaking noise when the steering head is abruptly turned. First by placing the fingers partly over the spindle link end, and partly upon the lug through which the spindle passes, while the steering head is turned, ascertain which spindle or spindles require adjustment. Then after slacking off both end nuts, turn the spindle bodily by means of its hexagonal end, left-hand or anti-clockwise to tighten. Do not turn, at the most, more than one-half a revolution before a re-trial with the end nuts tightened, as it is essential to guard against over-tightening, when the fork will become stiff in action or most likely refuse to function at all. It should be explained here that the fibre washers fitted between the spindle lug ends and the spindle side plates are not intended for frictional purposes, but to prevent actual seizure in the event of the spindles being excessively tightened. The necessary damping action is provided independently as described above.

Steering Head Adjustment. The steering head should occasionally be tested for adjustment by exerting pressure upwards and downwards from the extreme tips of the handlebars with the steering damper well slacked off. Should any perceptible shake be felt it must immediately be taken up, or the bearings may suffer damage. On the other hand, if the bearings are excessively tightened, steering will be stiff and the machine will handle generally unsatisfactorily. To guard against unconsciously over-tightening the head bearings, it is advisable to jack up the front of the machine with a suitable box. To adjust the bearings, first loosen the top nut on the steering column and then screw down the nut immediately below until all shake has entirely disappeared, when securely lock in position by means of the upper nut.

Adjustment of Spring Frame. Although wear of the inner friction discs (Fig. 12) is almost negligible, nevertheless once every season or, say, every 5.000 miles, the two clamping bolts in the top bridge lug should be slackened off, and the hand-adjusting ebonite nuts screwed up as tightly as possible, in order to draw the spindles out of the clamping lug, when the pinch bolts should again be securely retightened and the damper hand-nuts readjusted to give the desired degree of friction. The amount of friction required to give the maximum comfort varies according to the road conditions. For all normal conditions, it will be found quite satisfactory to adjust the dampers in a similar manner to that prescribed for the front fork damping adjustment. (See page 113.) The two rubber buffer stops (*B*, Fig. 12) limit the spring frame movement, but only an exceptional jolt will compress the springs sufficiently to bring these into action. The remedy is to apply more friction.

Wheel Bearings. All Matchless motor-cycles are provided with taper roller bearings (see Fig. 17) for both front and rear wheel hubs, and care should be taken to see that these bearings are correctly adjusted. Periodically, the rider should jack up each wheel in turn and test the amount of bearing play by attempting to rock each wheel sideways with one hand, while holding the frame or handlebars firmly with the other. *A roller hub bearing is properly adjusted when there is just the slightest amount of play perceptible.* On no account, even though the wheel may spin round apparently without friction, should this play be omitted, for with roller bearings it is possible to impose enormous crushing stresses upon the rollers by excessively tightening the adjuster cones.

To adjust either front or rear wheel hub bearings, first slacken off the spindle nut on the left-hand side, and then loosen the outer of the two lock-nuts on the inner side of the fork ends. Having done this, the inner nut which is integral with the bearing cone should be turned with a thin fixed spanner clockwise or anti-clockwise, according to whether it is desired to tighten or loosen the bearing adjustment respectively. Always keep the bearings well lubricated.

Brake Adjustment. Correct adjustment of the brakes is of considerable importance from the point of view of skidding, tyre wear, and the ability to obtain powerful retardation with a minimum of physical effort. It is important when adjusting interconnected brakes after a big mileage to *see that front and rear brakes are correctly synchronized.* Unless this is done one of the brakes will obviously be applied before the other, with the result that a considerable proportion of the potential braking power will be lost, and when the brake pedal is applied rather suddenly on a wet road a skid may ensue. Synchronization of front and rear brakes does not imply adjusting each brake by means of the knurled adjuster nuts, so that the anchor plate friction linings commence to expand against the brake drums simultaneously on application of the pedal. On the contrary, because the foot operation of the front brake is effected through a Bowden cable while the rear brake is applied by a rod, it is necessary to adjust the controls so that the front brake is applied slightly in advance of the rear one.

To adjust the interconnected brakes, jack the machine up so that both wheels are quite clear of the ground, and then rotate by hand the front and rear knurled adjusting nuts so that with the brake pedal released the front wheel is just free to revolve unimpeded, and when it becomes difficult to move against the application of the brake the rear braking effect is only just noticeable. When correctly adjusted, both wheels must, of course, be able to revolve freely when no pressure is applied to the foot pedal, and upon applying a moderate pressure it should be observed that application of the handlebar front brake lever does not cause any additional movement of the front brake expander lever on the off-side of the anchor plate, this indicating that the brake in question is in full engagement. Any tendency for the back wheel to squeak or skid denotes that the adjustment of the front brake foot-operated cable is insufficiently in advance of the rear, and in such a case the remedy is to tighten up the front adjustment slightly or, alternatively, to slacken the rear.

In the case of Model D, each brake is adjusted independently by means of the knurled adjuster nuts after first jacking up the wheels.

Tyres. Check the tyre inflation pressures (see Specifications) about once a week by means of a pressure gauge, and see that both front and rear tyes are inflated to the recommended pounds per square inch. Unless the correct tyre pressures are maintained for both solo riding and passenger work, the covers will not give their maximum service, and the rider will not obtain the best results either as regards the performance of the machine or personal riding comfort.

On the spring frame models serious over-inflation will not produce the riding discomfort that would be caused on other machines having no spring suspension, and for this reason it is important to pay particular attention to the tyre pressures. If a tyre, when travelling and bearing its full share of the load, comes into contact with an obstruction, the impact (which is the product of the load carried and the velocity) may reach an extremely high figure and produce an excessively localized strain on the cover material, and a resultant fracture or concussion burst. The tread rubber itself, owing to its nature, may show no perceptible signs of bruising or damage as the result of even the most severe blow.

From time to time inspect the covers with the machine jacked up, and remove all small flints carefully with a sharp penknife. Any but superficial rubber cuts are a menace to the whole cover structures and should be efficiently repaired. Covers retain their strength, only so long as the whole of their plies remain unbroken. If two or three strands are severed, the whole covers are weakened and bursts may ensue. The penetration of wet and road dirt also results in rapid deterioration of the casing material, as does the leaving of a machine unjacked for unreasonable periods, or allowing the tyres to stand in a welter of paraffin or oil.

Tuning the Amal Carburettor. Although, as a general rule, a Matchless model is dispatched from the factory with the carburettor correctly adjusted, the rider may in special circumstances

MAINTENANCE AND OVERHAULING

desire to check its setting and, if necessary, to tune it. *Neither the float chamber needle nor the jets should, however, be interfered with without good cause.* The action of the Amal carburettor has already been described on page 77, and Fig. 52 shows a sectional view of the instrument. The following notes are given on the assumption that the reader understands fully the principle and working of the Amal. With regard to tuning, there are four separate ways by which adjustment can be made: (*a*) main jet (three-quarters to full throttle); (*b*) pilot air adjustment (closed to one-eight throttle); (*c*) throttle valve cut-away on the air in-take side (one-eight to one-quarter throttle); (*d*) needle position (one-quarter to three-quarters throttle). The diagram (Fig. 68) clearly

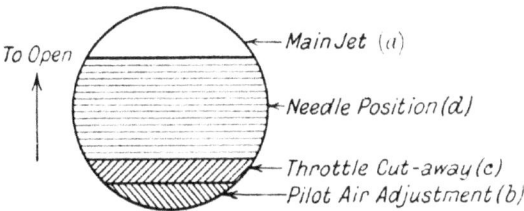

FIG. 68. RANGE AND SEQUENCE OF ADJUSTMENTS—AMAL CARBURETTOR

indicates the part of the throttle range over which each adjustment is effective.

1. To check or obtain the correct main jet setting, start up the engine and, after allowing a few seconds to warm up, fully retard the ignition lever and fully open the throttle. If black smoke issues from the exhaust, and it is now possible to open the air lever beyond the one-third or one-half open position to obtain even running, it would indicate too rich a mixture, and the needle attached to the throttle valve must be lowered or lengthened by releasing the flat strip retaining cotter and engaging it with a notch farther down. Several notches are provided. On the other hand, if the engine commences to spit back with the air lever fully closed and stops altogether as the air lever is opened to about one-third, it denotes that the mixture is too weak, and the needle attached to the throttle valve must be raised a trifle. When correct, the engine should commence to hesitate and spit back through the carburettor immediately the air lever is opened more than about one-third, but should run satisfactorily on the fully closed air position. *Under no circumstances should the engine be run for more than a few seconds* in this fully retarded ignition and fully opened throttle position, or the exhaust valve or valves will suffer.

Where the mixture is found to be too rich and lowering of the needle fails to effect a cure, a throttle valve with less cut-away should be used. Similarly in the case of an excessively weak mixture after making fruitless adjustment with the needle valve, one with a greater cut-away should be fitted. Each Amal valve is stamped with two numbers, the first indicating the type number of the carburettor, and the second figure the amount of cut-away in sixteenths of an inch, e.g. 6/4 is a type 6 valve with $\frac{4}{16}$ in. (i.e. $\frac{1}{4}$ in.) cut-away. In cases where alteration in needle height and throttle valve cut-away fail to give satisfaction, different main jet sizes should be experimented with.

2. To check or obtain the pilot jet setting, start up the engine and close the air lever fully and the throttle as far as possible without stopping the engine. Leave the ignition lever on almost full advance. Then, after allowing the engine to warm up thoroughly, screw up or unscrew the throttle stop (Fig. 53A) until the desired idling speed is obtained, afterwards taking up any slack in the throttle cable if necessary by the adjuster stop. Then proceed to obtain even firing by turning the pilot air adjusting screw in the necessary direction (screwing-in enriches the mixture, and, *vice versa*, unscrewing weakens the mixture). It must be understood that adjustment to this screw affects the mixture only on very small throttle openings. The adjustment is not very sensitive, and no difficulty should be found in finding the best setting, when the locking-nut should be tightened down to prevent further movement by vibration. It should not be imagined that because the engine sometimes stalls when starting up from cold that the pilot jet adjustment is necessarily at fault. It is usually due to fuel condensation. Once the pilot jet has been accurately set it should not require further attention except in extremes of temperature.

Where an air filter is attached to a carburettor formerly without one, the main jet opening can usually be advantageously reduced by 10 per cent, and for racing purposes an increase of 10 per cent is recommended.

LUBRICATION

Just as important as the maintaining of correct adjustments and clearances for all working parts on a Matchless motor-cycle, is the paying of regular attention to the lubrication of the various components. The designers of the Matchless have taken special care to see that all parts which need lubrication *can* be lubricated. Thereafter the responsibility rests on the rider's shoulders.

Engine Lubrication. With the dry sump system used for all Matchless models, practically no attention is required other than regular replenishment of the oil tank (see page 61), verification of

MAINTENANCE AND OVERHAULING

the oil return, and occasional removal and cleaning of the filter situated immediately below the filler cap. This filter should be removed once every 500 miles and cleaned in petrol. It is also necessary once every season, or not less frequently than once every 5,000 miles, to remove the entire tank and wash it out thoroughly with petrol, after which fresh clean oil should be added. To avoid unnecessary waste it is quite satisfactory to arrange this clean out when the oil is at a low level in the tank, although normally it is highly desirable to add fresh oil to the tank frequently in preference to allowing it to run almost empty.

There is no adjustment on the D.S. system, but see that the pump plunger guide screw (b, Fig. 51) is always kept tightly screwed up and that there are no leakages at any of the pipe unions. Also see that the glass on the sight-feed bowl is not cracked or broken, in which case the sight-feed would probably fill right up and overflow. A temporary measure would be to connect the two pipe ends with a piece of rubber tubing. On the overhead-valve engines grease-gun lubrication is provided for the rocker box, and there is an adjustment for the automatic inlet valve guide lubrication. If lubricating oil escapes at the crankcase joints, and the exterior of the engine becomes saturated with oil, suspect a faulty crankcase breather. If the disc breather is at fault, which would probably be indicated by the absence of front chain lubrication, remove it from the crankcase, clean it, and adjust it.

Rocker-box Lubrication. A charge of good heat-resisting grease such as Price's H.M.P. should be injected by the grease-gun provided in the tool kit through the nipple (G, Fig. 36) at the back of the rocker box once every 500 miles. On the overhead-camshaft engines the rockers are automatically lubricated from the engine.

Valve Guide Lubrication. In the case of the Matchless sidevalve and overhead-camshaft engines, completely enclosed valve chests, which are in communication with the crankcase and bevel box respectively, ensure that some of the oil mist finds its way on to the reciprocating valve stems and so prevents these working dry.

On the two overhead-valve engines a continual supply of fresh oil is positively fed to the inlet valve guide from the oil pump itself. As mentioned on page 75, an auxiliary oil feed is taken (via the sight-feed where fitted) from the pump housing to a "T" piece mounted on the top of the rocker box from whence some of the oil goes direct to the upper cupped push-rod ends to return to the timing case through the telescopic push-rod covers, while some is diverted to the inlet valve via a special channel cut in the cylinder head and rocker box. This oil supply may be increased or decreased by rotating the adjuster screw in the "T"

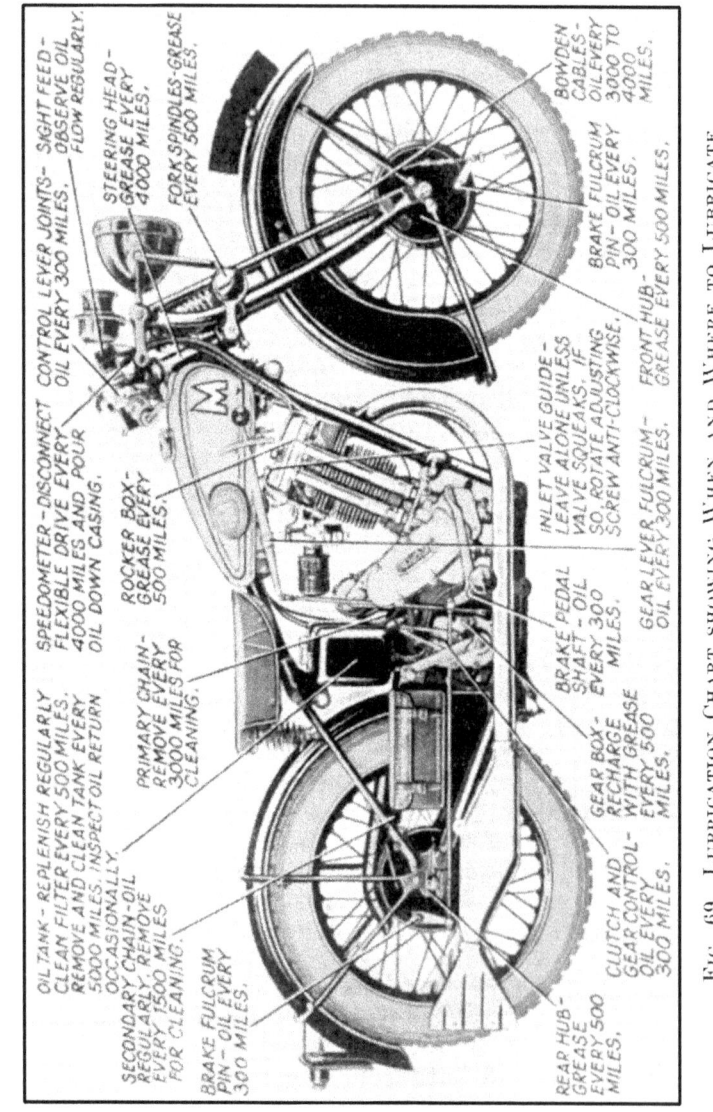

Fig. 69. Lubrication Chart showing When and Where to Lubricate the Matchless

The above chart, illustrating a De Luxe C/S O.H.V. model, is applicable in general to the whole present range, but is intended as a guide rather than to be scrupulously followed. In the case of the S.V. machines, there is, of course, no rocker box to lubricate and no adjustment for the supply to the inlet valve guide. On the O.H.C. model the rocker box is automatically lubricated but the primary chain is not.

MAINTENANCE AND OVERHAULING 121

piece anti-clockwise or clockwise respectively. The supply should not be interfered with unless the inlet valve commences to squeak, in which case a turn or two should be given to the screw in an anti-clockwise direction.

Magneto and Dynamo Lubrication. No lubrication of the dynamo or magneto armature bearings is necessary until at least 20,000 miles have been covered, as these are initially packed with heat-resisting grease. It is advisable, however, in the case of the Lucas magnetos and "Magdynos" to withdraw the cam ring and place a few drops of thin machine oil on the piece of felt contained in the contact-breaker housing pocket about once every 5,000 miles. The oil is automatically fed by means of a wick passing through a hole in the cam ring to the cam ring inner surface, and so provides just sufficient lubrication to prevent rapid wear of the fibre rocker-arm heel and a resultant increase in the gap between the contacts. The rocker-arm bearing itself requires no lubrication whatever, and scrupulous care must be taken to avoid letting any oil find its way on to the contact points. On all contact-breakers a few drops of oil should also be placed on the outer cam ring surface.

In the case of the Lucas M-L magneto and "Maglita" contact-breaker, an *occasional* spot of oil should be applied to the cam surface on which the reciprocating vertical tappet runs, as this will prevent rusting and wear. In the case of the "Maglita," a drop of oil should be placed in the oil hole under the contact-breaker, for the bearing, once every 1,000 miles.

Distributor Lubrication. The Lucas DFV4 distributor and contact-breaker unit driven off the "Silver Hawk" dynamo shaft has a grease-box for lubricating the distributor shaft bearing. This box should be packed with a good quality high melting-point grease such as Price's H.M.P., and the cap should be given one turn about every 500 miles. About every 3,000 miles add a few drops of thin oil to the hole provided in the housing for lubrication of the four-lobe contact-breaker cam, and also add a few drops for the timing control.

Bowden Controls. It will forestall the time when the Bowden cables snap if a certain amount of oil be applied about once every 300 miles to the handlebar lever joints, and those points where the cables are apt to bind or chafe at the handlebar controls. It will also pay to oil the entire lengths of the cables every 3,000-4,000 miles. By doing this, longevity and smooth action of the cables is ensured.

By means of a specially designed oil-gun (obtainable from the manufacturers), it is now possible to flood the inner wire with lubricant in a few seconds. Oil is injected through a small bared patch on the outer casing, and is forced through the special wire casing on to and along the inner wire. All Bowden cables on every Matchless model are fitted with small metal clips which may be observed fitted approximately to the centre of each. These clips cover the small bared patch referred to, and to apply the gun it is only necessary to slide the clip along the casing to enable the specially constructed gun to be clamped with the bared patch occupying a central position on the rubber pad on the gun nozzle. A few turns of the screwed plunger is then all that is required. Engine oil is suitable.

Lubricating Primary Chain. On the "Silver Hawk," about once every 500 miles, the oil plug on the top right-hand side of the chain case should be removed, and a quantity of clean engine oil poured in. The lower chain run should be entirely submerged.

On all other models the primary chain is entirely protected and automatically lubricated by a pipe leading from the crankcase breather, and an inspection should be made occasionally to see that this breather is functioning correctly. For all ordinary purposes, the oil mist which settles out in the chain cover and is led by a suitable duct into the path of the chain is sufficient, but if the maximum chain service is desired, it is advisable once every 3,000 miles to take off the chain cover, remove the chain, and thoroughly wash it in paraffin. After carefully draining the paraffin off by allowing the chain to hang vertically and wiping the chain, it should be immersed in a bath of molten tallow, or, as a poorer substitute, ordinary engine oil. If the latter method is used, the chain should be allowed to remain in the oil overnight in order to allow the lubricant to penetrate to all the link joints. When replacing the chain, see that it is correctly tensioned. If the chain is treated in this manner it should give at least 10,000 miles of satisfactory service.

Lubricating Secondary Chain. Before starting out on a run some engine oil should be applied, if the secondary chain appears at all dry, by applying an oilcan spout to the small hole on top of the chain guard while rotating the rear wheel. Once every 1,500-2,000 miles in summer, and once every 1,000 miles in winter, the chain should be removed, cleaned and lubricated in the manner described above for the primary chain. If treated thus it should give at least 15,000 miles of satisfactory service.

The Magneto Chain. On all Matchless models the chain is automatically lubricated.

Fork Spindles Lubrication. About every 500 miles the fork spindles bearings should be flooded with a good quality grease, such as Tecalemit or Wakefield "Castrolease." This process takes a few seconds only by means of the special grease-gun provided, which merely requires holding the nozzle end against the rounded nipples on the fork spindles and giving a few sharp strokes.

Steering Head Lubrication. The ball bearings in the steering head require to be lubricated about once every 4,000 miles by applying a grease-gun to the nipple provided on the front of the head. Do not neglect these bearings, as any stiffness will spoil the steering.

Wheel Bearings. About every 500 miles the lubricators in the centre of both front and rear hubs should have a small quantity of grease forced through them by the grease-gun. Wakefield " Castrolease " is suitable.

Brake and Gear Control Joints. Approximately every 300 miles an oilcan should be applied to the two brake anchor plate fulcrum pins and the pedal shaft itself. Thin cycle oil should be used. It is also advisable to lubricate all joints and pivots in the brake and gear control mechanism, paying special attention to the pins coupling the gate-change gear operating lever to the small lever mounted on the gearbox itself, and also the operating lever fulcrum. See that, in regard to the last-mentioned, the fixing screw is tightened sufficiently to ensure the gear lever moving firmly through the gate, the notches of which may also be oiled slightly with advantage.

Gearbox and Clutch. Second in importance to proper engine lubrication is the correct lubrication of the countershaft gearbox, whose function it is to transmit the whole of the engine thrust to the rear wheel.

Once every 500 miles, or more often when a large amount of riding is undertaken in very hilly districts necessitating the frequent use of the lower gears, the Sturmey-Archer three-speed lightweight gearboxes should be recharged with a grease-gun full of Wakefield "Castrolease Light" *via* the small grease nipple. It will facilitate entry of the grease if the kick-starter is gently depressed a few times. Occasionally the grease plug should be removed and the oil level (the same as for model A/2) checked.

On the "Silver Arrow" the correct oil level is *just above the bottom of the threaded hole into which the plug screws.* Therefore, when the plug is removed the grease should overflow slightly when the machine is standing level, and if a grease-gun full of Mobiloil "D" every 500 miles fails to maintain the correct level, the supply should be increased accordingly. At the same interval (i.e. about every 500 miles), a few strokes of the grease-gun should be applied to the small nipple fixed to the clutch worm. While this is being done, the engine should be allowed to tick-over in neutral, for the grease injected goes direct to the high-speed dog-wheel bearing, which is only called into use when running on the lower gears or in neutral.

On all other Matchless four-speed models the correct level of grease in the gearbox is *from one-third to half full.* In the case of less frequent lubrication than a grease-gun every 500 miles, the lightweight four-speed box should be charged with ½ pint of Mobiloil "D" and recharged with ¼ pint every 1,000-1,500 miles. With the heavyweight box, an original charge of ¾ pint and recharging with ¼ pint every 750-1,000 miles is recommended.

DECARBONIZING

The period for which an engine will run satisfactorily without being decarbonized depends to a large extent upon driving conditions and the way a mount is handled, but in most cases, after the rider has covered 1,500-2,000 miles, it will be found that the accumulation of carbon deposits on the piston crown and in various parts of the combustion chamber results in an engine losing its original "kick," and there is a marked decline in general all-round performance, accompanied by a tendency for knocking under the slightest provocation.

In connection with decarbonization there are three types of engine to be taken account of: (a) the side-valve engine; (b) the overhead-valve engine; (c) the overhead-camshaft engine. The general procedure of decarbonizing is much the same in each case, although structural variations render the operations somewhat different. All Matchless engines have detachable cylinder heads except Model D, and it is unnecessary to remove the cylinder or cylinders when decarbonizing, although about once every 5,000 miles this procedure is necessary in order to examine the piston rings and clean the grooves in which they operate.

The S.V. Engines. These include the two Big Twins, where each piston may be decarbonized separately after removing each cylinder head in turn; the "Silver Arrow" twin, where the monobloc head is required to be lifted off; Models R/7 and C, where ordinary detachable heads are used; and Model D, which has no detachable head necessitating the entire cylinder to be withdrawn off the crankcase.

The O.H.V. Engines. On the two push-rod operated overhead-valve engines, decarbonizing entails the removal of the detachable heads after first taking off the rocker-boxes and push-rods.

The O.H.C. Engine. On the "Silver Hawk," before decarbonizing can be undertaken, it is necessary to remove completely the one-piece cam and bevel-box, and then to withdraw the monobloc cylinder head casting, as in the case of the "Silver Arrow." The petrol tank is also best removed.

Initial Preparations. Jack the machine up and, if the engine exterior is very dirty, go over it with a rag damped in paraffin, taking special care to clean the parts about to be dismantled, and see that a clean box or other receptacle is at hand in which

MAINTENANCE AND OVERHAULING

to place temporarily the various parts. Put the engine on compression and begin stripping off those parts which obstruct easy removal of the cylinder, cylinder head, heads or block as the case may be.

Removing Cylinder Head (S.V. Models). To prepare for a top overhaul on all except Model D, all that is necessary is to remove the sparking plug or plugs, and then to unscrew all the cylinder-head retaining bolts when the detachable head, heads, or block

FIG. 70. MATCHLESS SINGLE-CYLINDER S.V. ENGINE WITH CYLINDER AND CYLINDER HEAD REMOVED FOR DECARBONIZING
The engine illustrated is a model N/7

may be lifted clear by prising off in some cases with a screwdriver, care being taken to prise upwards, not downwards, to avoid damaging the fins. This gives instant access to the piston crown or crowns, and also to the valves. It is quite unnecessary to interfere with the carburettor. In the case of the "Silver Arrow" both cylinder stays must be removed. Be very careful where a C. and A. gasket is not fitted not to damage the joint faces when removing the cylinder head.

Removing Cylinder Head (O.H.V. Models). Firstly, remove the exhaust pipes, and then unscrew the top cap of the Amal carburettor mixing chamber and withdraw the air and throttle slides. Next unscrew the nut securing the petrol pipe to the petrol tap, and, after removing the two nuts securing the carburettor to the cylinder head flange, withdraw the entire unit with pipe attached. Next remove the small tie bar attached to the overhead rocker housing support bolt and frame lug. Then raise the lower portion of each push-rod cover tube to permit the small spring plunger on the top portion to engage with the hole in the lower portion, which engagement will retain the tubes in this telescoped condition. (Fig. 67.) Having done this, unscrew the three special bolts by which the overhead aluminium rocker

FIG. 71. PREPARING FOR "SILVER HAWK" CYLINDER HEAD REMOVAL

housing is fixed, and after disconnecting the three oil pipe unions, withdraw the housing together with the push-rods and their protective covers. Next remove all cylinder head fixing bolts, when the head is free to be lifted clear of the cylinder. It may, perhaps, be necessary to give the head a sharp tap upwards to release the spigoted joint, which often becomes rather firmly fixed owing to carbon deposits.

Removing Cylinder Head (O.H.C. Model). On the "Silver Hawk" it is necessary, as in the case of the overhead-valve engines, to remove the rocker-box first. In this instance the rocker-box and bevel-box are cast as one. Therefore before the rocker-box can be detached the bevel drive from the vertical shaft to the camshaft must be disconnected by releasing the union between the vertical shaft cover and the bevel-box, which allows the small bevel to be withdrawn with the bevel-box when the latter is lifted clear, for this bevel shaft has an Oldham coupling. To remove the cylinder head, undo all the rocker-box and cylinder-head fixing bolts after disconnecting the petrol pipes and exhaust pipes, and gently raise upwards and backwards till clear.

Removing Cylinder. In the case of Model D, when decarbonizing, there is no alternative but to remove the entire cylinder since no detachable head is provided. Firstly, remove the carburettor from the cylinder flange by undoing the two nuts, after first removing the petrol pipe from the top of the float chamber with petrol turned off, and after taking out the throttle and air slides. Then proceed to remove the exhaust pipe, which has a push-in attachment at the exhaust port. Having done this, remove the valve caps, as they are most easily unscrewed with the cylinder in position. Avoid using very powerful leverage upon them if it is found that they are stiff, or the cylinder may suffer distortion. A number of light but rapid taps on the end of the valve cap spanner should be given with a hammer, and if this fails to shift them, introduce a little cold water into the hollow of each cap while the engine is hot and, simultaneously, apply the spanner. Only adopt this method as a last resort. Stiff valve caps can be entirely obviated if their threads be occasionally oiled. Both valves themselves may now be separately removed, if desired, by taking off the valve chest cover plate and applying a proprietary valve extractor such as the Terry, so that its hooked end rests on each valve head and the lever portion is placed under each valve spring cap, so that on depression of the lever the valve spring is compressed sufficiently to enable the cotter to be removed. On this and on all other side-valve Matchless engines the valves may, if preferred, be removed from the valve chest after first withdrawing the cylinder, cylinders, or cylinder bloc, as the case may be, without the aid of a special tool, the valve springs being compressed by inverting the cylinder and pressing the spring caps with a suitable implement. Now place the piston on almost bottom dead-centre with the connecting-rod big-end slightly to the rear of the centre position and proceed to remove the four cylinder holding-down bolts, after which the cylinder may be gently drawn off, care being taken to avoid putting any strain on the connecting rod or permitting the piston skirt to fall sharply against the connecting rod as the last ring emerges from the barrel mouth, which is heavily chamfered to enable the rings to be gently withdrawn or inserted. Having removed the cylinder, immediately wrap a piece of rag around the piston and connecting rod to prevent their sustaining damage, and also to prevent any foreign matter entering the crankcase.

In the case of the Big Twins, cylinder removal is accomplished in a similar manner to that described above, each cylinder being dealt with in turn after first removing the exhaust pipes, carburettor, and induction manifold. Care must be taken to avoid interchanging any of the parts of the two cylinders. Removal of the cylinder barrels on Models C, R/7, and the two overhead-valve models is quite straightforward once the detachable heads have been removed, but in the case of the last-mentioned machines be careful not to lose the hardened end caps for the valve stems, and avoid damaging the ground faces of the cylinder and head. If the cylinder head, when dismantled, shows signs of leakage at the joint (i.e. blackening) it must be ground-in similarly to the

FIG. 72. THE "SILVER ARROW" ENGINE WITH CYLINDER HEAD AND BLOC REMOVED FOR DECARBONIZING

valves. The valves on these engines may be removed unless a special extractor (Fig. 73) be used by laying the head face down, after packing the valve heads, and pressing on the valve spring caps until the split collets can be withdrawn. The overhead valves must on no account be interchanged, and this remark applies in regard to all Matchless valves which though theoretically perhaps interchangeable, in practice definitely are not so.

To remove the cylinder bloc on the "Silver Arrow," after detaching the head, proceed as follows: Firstly remove the valve chest cover and then take off the exhaust manifold and pipe, and also withdraw the throttle and air slides from the carburettor which itself may be left in position. Then, after disconnecting the petrol pipe and removing the five cylinder-bloc holding-down nuts, the cylinder bloc may be lifted clear.

Removing the Carbon. Thoroughness in decarbonizing well repays the labour expended. The more completely the carbon is

MAINTENANCE AND OVERHAULING

removed, the better will the engine performance be, and the longer will it be before further decarbonizing again becomes necessary. It is inadvisable, however, to decarbonize the piston ring grooves more than about once every 5,000 miles, when the cylinder as well as the cylinder head should be removed. When undertaking an ordinary top overhaul every 2,000 miles, the carbon deposits on the piston crown and on the inside of the cylinder head need alone be scraped off. To do this a moderately sharp penknife, or the end of a screwdriver, should be employed. Every trace of carbon should be carefully removed. Be careful, however, not to employ excessive force on the piston, or its comparatively soft aluminium surface will be deeply scratched. When decarbonizing the cylinder head, do not overlook the exhaust ports which are usually heavily sooted or carbonized, and, as before-mentioned, see that the face on the overhead-valve head is not scratched. A good method of holding the head when decarbonizing it is to fit a hexagon steel bar screwed at one end into the sparking plug hole. The cylinder head may then be held in a vice by means of the bar. If a bar is unavailable, an old sparking plug makes a good substitute. After the deposits have been removed, clean the surfaces with a calico rag damped in paraffin.

In the case of Model D where the entire cylinder has to be removed, the top of the piston may afterwards be rubbed with *very fine* emery cloth until a perfectly smooth surface has been obtained. This method of finishing off may also be used for the detachable heads on all models, but the pistons should not be thus treated except when the cylinder itself is removed, enabling all abrasive particles to be afterwards eradicated. Emery particles which get down on to the rings may cause bad scoring of the cylinder walls. On Model D, the deposits on the integral cylinder head may be reached by a long screwdriver inserted through the cylinder mouth. Care should be taken not to allow the screwdriver shank to scratch the part of the cylinder included in the piston stroke. See also that all carbon is removed from the valve caps, which may afterwards be cleaned with emery cloth.

In the case of the multi-cylinder models each piston must be dealt with in turn, and the cylinder heads or cylinder bloc combustion chambers, in the case of the "Silver Arrow" and "Silver Hawk," must be scrupulously cleaned. Detachable exhaust manifolds enable carbon deposits in the exhaust ports to be readily removed.

When occasion is had to remove the piston or pistons, do not attempt to remove carbon from the outside of the skirt. Only the crown, the inside, and the piston ring grooves should be scraped and cleaned. The latter may be cleaned of all deposits after the rings have been removed by running a small, sharp flat-ended tool round their circumferences. Only a tool of the right size should be used, or the shape of the grooves may be spoiled.

Piston Removal. The fully-floating gudgeon pins may usually be pushed out by hand after removing with a small pair of pliers the spring circlips on both sides, when the piston or pistons may be lifted off. On no account interchange the pistons, and mark them on the inside so that they are replaced correctly. On the "Silver Arrow" piston the slope at the crown is an indication of its correct position relative to the connecting rod.

Examining and Removing Piston Rings. The piston rings are the main-guard of the engine compression, and they must therefore be full of spring, free in their grooves, and set with their slots opposite each other (i.e. at 180 degrees). If both rings are bright all over they should be left alone. If, on the other hand, they are dull or stained at some places, they are not in proper contact with the cylinder walls. Possibly they are stuck in their grooves with burnt oil, and will function properly if the grooves are cleaned. If vertically loose in their grooves or very badly marked, the rings must be renewed. Piston rings are of cast iron and, being of very small section, must be handled with exceptional care, or they will be fractured. They cannot safely be opened out wider than will allow them to slip over the piston crown. Therefore, to put them on or to remove them requires the insertion of small metal strips. Be most careful to note the order in which the rings are removed to ensure correct replacement. When fitting new rings, thoroughly clean the grooves into which they fit, as any carbon deposit left at the back of new rings forces them out and makes them too tight a fit. Paraffin usually loosens stuck piston rings.

Removal of Valves. As mentioned on page 127, all side valves can be removed from the cylinder valve chests without the use of a special tool, all that is necessary being to invert the cylinder, after detaching the head, and press on the valve spring caps until the valve cotters can be taken out, thus releasing the springs.

With the overhead-valve engines the valves may be removed in a similar manner, but owing to the fact that very powerful duplex coil springs are used, it is far better policy to compress the springs with the aid of the special Matchless valve extractor, shown at Fig. 73. To remove a valve, the tool is placed over the detached cylinder head so that the recessed boss at one arm fits over the valve spring cap, while the pointed end of the adjustable screw is brought to bear upon the valve head centre by rotating clockwise the small tommy bar. A few turns will compress the duplex spring sufficiently to enable the split collet to be removed, assisted by a tap on the valve spring.

Grinding-in the Valves. Generally speaking, on the side-valve

MAINTENANCE AND OVERHAULING

engines the valves require to be ground-in once every alternate decarbonization (i.e. every 4,000 miles), while on the overhead-valve type they require to be ground-in at every decarbonization (i.e. once every 1,500-2,000 miles). On the side-valve engines removal of the cylinder is advised, but on the overhead-valve type this is, of course, unnecessary.

Valves of the side-by-side type have, of course, to be *pressed down* on their seatings when using a screwdriver, while those of

FIG. 73. SHOWING USE OF MATCHLESS O.H.V. EXTRACTOR

the overhead type have to be pulled up against their seatings. Be very careful not to interchange the valves.

Only grind-in valves when necessary, using *fine* valve-grinding compound mixed with oil or paraffin; only a small quantity is necessary, and do not revolve the valves round and round, but give a quarter turn backwards and forwards, frequently raising the valve from its seat and dropping down in a different position. A small hand vice will be found a convenient tool for holding the valve stem on an overhead-valve engine, and very great care must be taken after this operation to remove all traces of valve-grinding compound. The valve stems may be cleaned with *very fine* or worn emery cloth. Do not use coarse grinding compound for grinding-in valves.

Do not grind-in valves excessively, but see that all pitmarks are removed from the valve face. Finish off with a fine powder. Wash cylinder, valve caps, compression tap, and valves and springs, etc., in clean paraffin, *taking great care to remove all traces of emery or grinding powder.* Dry with a clean, smooth cloth. All is now ready for reassembling. Always check the tappet or valve clearances after grinding-in the valves and reassembling.

Grinding-in Cylinder Head and Barrel Faces. If either seatings have been damaged in removal of the head, it will be necessary to regrind these in, in the same manner as one would a valve. To grind in the cylinder head, the four studs should be removed. This may be done by screwing two nuts on the studs, using one as a lock-nut against the other. The holes from which the studs have been taken should then be filled with grease, so that the grinding compound is kept out of the threads. The head and barrels should then be rubbed together, similar to the grinding-in of valves. A good joint may be made between the head and the barrel by smearing a little seccotine on the faces.

Reassembly (S.V. Engines). When reassembling a side-valve engine, which is almost exactly the dismantling process reversed, push gudgeon pin into piston until it comes flush with inside of boss of piston; slip piston over connecting rod, then tap gudgeon pin *gently* in, making sure that the pin has entered the small end bush, which should be oiled. Refit the spring circlips. The piston rings should be spaced so that gap of top ring faces front and gap of bottom ring faces rear. Smear piston thoroughly with oil and see that there is plenty behind the rings. Wipe top of the piston clean. The cylinder or cylinder bloc should be smeared with oil and then refitted to crankcase. If paper washer is torn, fit a new one. It should be smeared with seccotine or gold size.

If any difficulty is experienced in getting piston rings to enter cylinder, obtain assistance to hold the cylinder while the rings and piston are eased in. In the case of the "Silver Arrow," the mouth of each cylinder is generously chamfered to allow of the easy entry of the piston rings, and when applying the cylinder, the pistons must be introduced in line with the bore, and not at right angles to the base as on all other models. Screw down cylinder nuts, giving each a half turn alternatively and diagonally. Fit the detachable head, taking care not to omit the copper-asbestos washer, and to retighten the cylinder fixing nuts evenly in the manner shown by Fig. 74, tightening all finger-tight first. Screw in sparking plug, refit exhaust lifter cable where fitted and the exhaust system. Attach oil pipe, valve cover, carburettor, and high tension wire to plug. The work is now complete. Start

MAINTENANCE AND OVERHAULING

engine and run gently until warm. Then check tappet clearances (see page 105) and check cylinder holding-down nuts for tightness.
Reassembly (O.H.V. Engines). When refitting the piston take great care to see that this is replaced in the same position from which it was removed. Refit the barrel in the manner as indicated in the case of refitting the cylinder on the side-by-side valve engine. The base of the barrel should be smeared with a little gold size or seccotine. Paper washers should be used to ensure a perfectly oil-proof joint. It is important to see that the six bolts holding the head to the barrel are tightened down evenly, and that the small stay is locked to the frame afterwards. Replace

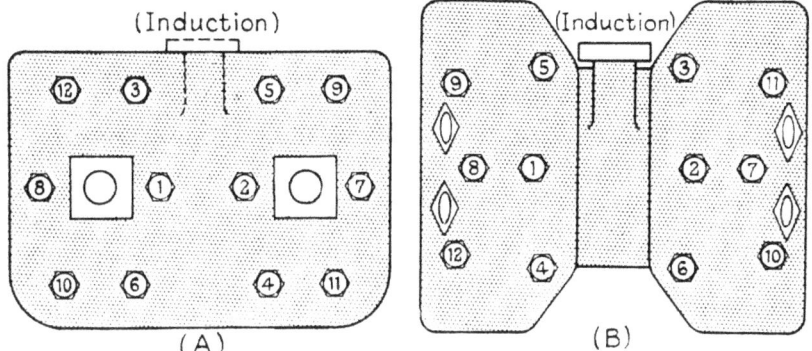

FIG. 74. THE CORRECT ORDER OF TIGHTENING THE MONOBLOC CYLINDER HEAD FIXING NUTS

At *A* and *B* are shown the order for the "Silver Arrow" and "Silver Hawk" heads, respectively

the sparking plug. The rocker-box and push-rods with their covers may then be refitted. Should the push-rods be difficult to fit, shorten the tappets as much as possible.

To refit the rocker-box and overhead gear, the details given for the removal of these should be reversed. It should be noted that the front bolt securing the overhead rocker housing is provided with a somewhat coarser pitch than the others, and must therefore be replaced correctly. When refitting the cylinder head to the barrel, *it is important to see that both the face of the cylinder barrel and the cylinder head are perfectly clean*, and free from dust particles. These should not be cleaned with even fine emery, but just wiped over with a perfectly clean piece of cloth. Finally, refit the two exhaust pipes, carburettor, and the pipe leading to the "T" piece on the rocker-box. Do not interfere with the inlet valve lubrication adjustment. Having completely reassembled the engine, check the valve clearances, warm up and go over the various nuts once again.

In the case of the overhead-camshaft engine, the cylinder head bolts must be tightened with great care in the order shown at Fig. 74 before replacing the bevel- and cam-box and readjusting the vertical shaft drive.

Maintaining Compression. If piston rings and valves are OK, the only other possible sources of leakages are the valve caps and the sparking plugs (presuming the head is firmly bolted down). The washers belonging to these parts should be replaced as soon as they become at all worn or distorted, and a jointing medium should be utilized when screwing up the plugs and valve caps. If suspected, test for compression leakage by putting thick oil on to the sides of the joints and noting the presence or absence of bubbles with the engine running.

MAINTENANCE AND OVERHAULING

Maintenance of the Amal Carburettor. Periodical cleaning is necessary to maintain efficient functioning of the carburettor, and should be carried out in the following sequence—

Disconnect petrol pipe. Unscrew holding bolt Q (Fig. 52) and remove float chamber complete. With box or set spanner, slacken the mixing chamber union nut E. Mixing chamber complete may now be removed from engine, either by unscrewing the pin (if clip fixing) or the nuts (if flange fitting). Unscrew mixing chamber lock ring, and pull out throttle valve needle and air valve. Remove main jet P and needle jet O. Mixing chamber union nut E may then be removed and jet block complete pushed out. If this is obstinate, tap gently, using a wooden stump inside the mixing chamber. Unscrew float chamber cover W and slacken lock-screw X. Withdraw the float by pinching the clip V inwards, and at the same time pull gently upwards.

Generally it is sufficient to wash all the parts in clean petrol, but if the carburettor has had extended service, check the following—

(*a*) FLOAT CHAMBER NEEDLE U. If a distinct shoulder is visible on the point of seating, renew this as soon as convenient.

(*b*) THROTTLE VALVE. Test in mixing chamber, and if excessive play is present it is advisable to renew this without delay.

(*c*) THROTTLE NEEDLE CLIP. This part must securely grip needle. *Free rotation must not take place*, otherwise the needle groove will become worn and necessitate a new part being fitted. *Be sure to refit the clip in the same groove.*

(*d*) JET BLOCK. If trouble has been experienced with erratic "idling," ascertain by means of a fine bristle that the pilot jet J is clear, and that the pilot outlet M in the mixing chamber is unobstructed.

MAINTENANCE AND OVERHAULING

To Reassemble. Refit jet block F with washer on underside, and screw on lightly mixing chamber union nut E. Screw in needle jet O and main jet P. Open air lever $\frac{7}{8}$ in., throttle lever half-way; grasp the air slide between the thumb and the finger; *make sure that the needle enters the central hole in the adaptor top.* Slightly twist the throttle valve until it enters the adaptor guide, when on pushing down the valves the air valve should enter its guide. If not, slightly move the mixing chamber top, when the air valve will slide into place. Screw on mixing chamber lock-nut. *No brute force is necessary.*

Attach carburettor to the cylinder, pushing right home, and examine washer if flange fitting. Insert holding bolt Q, and thoroughly tighten union nut E by means of a fixed spanner. Refit float and needle, holding the needle head against its seating by means of a pencil until the float and the clip V are slipped into position. Make sure that the clip enters the groove provided. Screw on the cover lightly, and lock in position by means of lock-screw X. Fit holding-bolt in float chamber with one washer above and one below the lug. Screw holding-bolt into mixing chamber and lock securely. Clean petrol pipe and filter if fitted, and replace. It will be necessary to re-check the pilot setting if this has been disturbed.

Care of the Lucas Magneto (or Magneto Portion of " Magdyno "). When undertaking an annual overhaul, the following points should be attended to—

(*a*) Polish the contacts—if of tungsten, with fine emery cloth; if platinum, with a dead smooth file. To render the points accessible for cleaning, it is necessary to withdraw the contact-breaker from its housing by unscrewing the hexagon headed retaining screw by means of the magneto spanner. The whole contact-breaker can then be pulled off the tapered shaft on which it fits. Now push aside the locating spring and prise the rocker-arm off its bearing, as shown in Fig. 75, when it will be possible to begin cleaning the points. Do not interfere with the spring-retaining screws. Before removing the rocker-arm, note whether the breaking of the contacts is at all sluggish by putting pressure on the fibre heel. If this is found to be the case, the bearing pin should be cleaned with very fine emery cloth and afterwards moistened with a little oil. When replacing the contact-breaker, care should be taken to ensure that the projecting key on the tapered portion of the contact-breaker base engages with the key-way cut in the armature spindle, or the whole timing of the magneto will be upset. The hexagon-headed screw should be tightened up with care; it must not be too slack (for it is part of the primary circuit), nor must undue force be used.

(*b*) If the machine has done a season's riding, remove the

driving end bearing plate and resoak the felt washer in good quality grease or replace with a new one.

(c) Remove the high tension pick-up by swinging aside the flat retaining spring, and polish the moulding with a clean cloth. See that the carbon brush is working freely in its holder and that it is not unduly worn. Clean the slip-ring track and flanges by holding a soft cloth damped with petrol by means of a piece of wood on the ring while the engine is being slowly and very carefully rotated. A magneto run with a carbon brush absent, or sticking, produces nitric acid internally (due to the sparking), which destroys all the lubricant, and attacks both the metal and insulation of which the armature is composed. If the brush is accident-

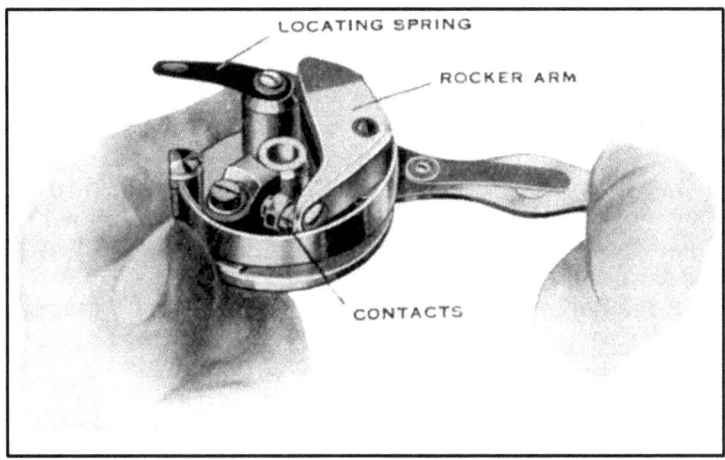

Fig. 75. Removal of Lucas Contact-breaker Rocker Arm

ally broken, care must be taken that no pieces are allowed to remain inside, or serious damage will result.

(d) Examine the high tension cable, and replace if the rubber shows signs of disintegrating.

(e) See that the contacts "break" to the correct extent (·012 in.). It is seldom necessary, nor is it desirable, to dismantle the magneto. The armature of a magneto cannot be removed without loss of magnetism from the magnet and, unless facilities for remagnetizing are available, it is best not to dismantle. If you must dismantle, first remove the pick-up and the safety spark screw, or a broken slip-ring may result.

Care of the M-L Magneto. The handling of the M-L magneto (see page 107) is very similar to that of the Lucas just described; but, of course, the contact-breaker mechanism is of different design. Special care should be taken to see that the action of the vertical tappet is quite free.

MAINTENANCE AND OVERHAULING

Lucas H.T. Pick-ups. With "Magdyno" and Lucas magneto pick-ups use only 7 mm. cable. Do not attempt to use a thicker cable pared down to fit.

Dismantling Lucas Spring Magneto Control. Should it become necessary at any time to dismantle the spring control and Bowden cable, proceed as follows: First remove the contact-breaker cover, held in position by a spring arm, and then withdraw the cam ring. Next, unscrew the fixing screw, which is sunk flush with the surface of the end plate. Finally pull the Bowden cable until it comes right out, together with the cable stop (which screws into the end plate), lock-nut, end plate, and plunger.

Removing Bowden Cable from M-L Magneto. To remove the cable from the instrument, do not attempt to remove the cam from its housing. It is only necessary to undo the hexagon nut, which forms the abutment for the outer casing of the Bowden cable. If the cable and plunger to which it is attached are drawn upwards to their fullest extent, it will be found that the nipple into which the end of the cable is soldered comes above the top of the boss on the cam cage housing. The nipple may then be slipped sideways out of the hole in the plunger in which it fits, thus detaching the cable entirely.

Magneto Timing. Accurate magneto timing is important. For all normal road uses, the spark settings given at the end of the engine specifications, Chapter I, should be closely adhered to. On page 142 are given in degrees the maximum advances corresponding to these stroke settings. Only for genuine racing purposes is it advisable to increase the spark advance. Always remember that should the timing be so far advanced that maximum explosion pressures are reached with the crank in true top dead-centre position, the big ends come in for a terrific hammering for which they are not designed. If the magneto, "Magdyno" or "Maglita," has been removed for any purpose or the drive disturbed, it will be necessary to re-time it, and to do this proceed as follows in the case of a single-cylinder engine.

Set the piston so that it is at the top of the compression stroke and as near the top dead-centre position as possible. Verify that it is on the compression and not the exhaust stroke by noting whether both valves are fully closed with the normal clearances at the tappets or rockers, as the case may be. Now remove the magneto chain case cover, and loosen the sprocket fixed on the tapered end of the magneto armature. Probably the sprocket is rather stiff, in which case a sharp tap should be given one of the teeth after undoing the nut a couple of turns. Preferably a piece of brass or other soft material should be interposed to prevent damage. Keep the magneto chain on, and, if it has perchance been removed, refit it. Then remove the sparking plug, and to ascertain that the piston is exactly on top dead-centre, insert a pencil or piece of wire through the hole. Make a mark on the pencil or wire and measure carefully, and place another mark $\frac{7}{16}$ in. (or whatever the exact magneto advance is) above the first one. Rotate engine sprocket backwards until the top mark occupies the place previously held by the bottom mark, the piston having obviously descended $\frac{7}{16}$ in.; then remove the contact-breaker cover and set the contact-breaker so that the points just commence to separate with the spark lever on *full advance*.

To find the exact point of break, place a thin piece of paper between the closed points and turn the armature forwards until the paper is just released, and no more, on pulling it gently. When first tightening the spindle nut, the magneto should be held from rotating by means of the contact-breaker until the taper in the sprocket bites on the spindle. To time accurately by the degree method, an engine timing disc is necessary.

Having timed the magneto, check the gap at the contacts; replace contact-breaker cover; and then, after tensioning the magneto chain, replace the chain case cover. The magneto chain should not be tensioned by means of the magneto-retaining screws on the hinged platform to an extent such that a bending moment is imposed on the armature spindle. It should be adjusted as described on page 112. The ignition timing may easily then be checked by again placing the piston on top dead-centre, or $\frac{7}{16}$ in. below top dead-centre on the twin-cylinder models, and moving the ignition lever backwards and forwards from the fully retarded position to about one-third full advance, when the contact points should be observed definitely to part. Finally replace the contact-breaker cover and the sparking plug and test the engine. It should give plenty of power at fairly low speeds without any tendency for pinking on top gear with the ignition lever in the three-quarter advanced position. If on starting up, a series of loud explosions occurs in the exhaust system, it is probable that the ignition has been timed on the exhaust, and not the compression stroke.

Retiming the ignition on the multi-cylinder Matchless models entails a very similar procedure to that described above for the single-cylinder models, but it is of vital importance to *see that the ignition is timed correctly for the firing cylinder*, or in other words, the contact-breaker points must commence to open when the armature is rotated until the fibre pad on the contact-breaker bell crank just engages the No. 1 cam on the cam ring. On the Big Twins, the No. 1 cam is *farthest* from the rear cylinder, while on the "Silver Arrow" it is the one on the right side, looking at the contact-breaker end of the magneto, or "Magdyno," and is adjacent to the high tension pick-up marked No. 1.

MAINTENANCE AND OVERHAULING

On the Big Twins the magneto timing is easily checked and adjusted, if necessary, after first loosening the magneto sprocket, which is a friction fit only, by unscrewing the armature locking-nut.

On the "Silver Arrow" or "Silver Hawk," it is necessary, in order to time the ignition, to loosen the front flexible coupling driving disc (G, Fig. 7), which is a friction fit on the camshaft or horizontal driving shaft, by unscrewing the nut (which has a left-hand thread) on the end of the shaft. To do this, it is necessary to separate the discs slightly by withdrawing the magneto backwards. The contact-breaker is then free to be rotated into the necessary position independently of the engine. Once the correct timing has been obtained, see that the disc locking-nut is securely retightened, and that the magneto or "Magdyno" is properly aligned (see below). Also, before finally fixing the magneto, once more set the pistons at top dead-centre, and observe that the contacts definitely part as the ignition lever is moved from the full retard to the full advance position.

A practical, but approximate, test for correct ignition timing is to start up the engine and fully retard the ignition. With the throttle fully open the engine should run at about 1,500 to 1,600 r.p.m. (i.e. at a speed corresponding to about 30 m.p.h. on top gear).

Magneto Alignment on the "Silver Arrow." Incorrect alignment of the magneto or "Magdyno" shaft with the protruding end of the camshaft to which it is coupled will cause rapid wear and ultimate failure of the rubber driving disc; and should it become necessary to completely dismantle the rear engine cradle plate and magneto platform assembly for any reason, it is essential that care is taken when refitting the magneto to ensure the necessary alignment. To ensure this, the erection must be completed with the exception of the actual fixing of the ignition unit. Now remove the coupling discs from both camshaft end and the magneto spindle, and clamp the magneto down on its platform with the two shaft ends almost touching one another, when any error in alignment can be seen at a glance. It should perhaps be explained that if the erection is properly carried out, there is little or no possibility of any variation in the vertical alignment, and no provision is therefore made in this direction. To correct errors in horizontal alignment, a strut bolt is provided to apply pressure to the near-side of the magneto. Owing to the angularity of the near-side clamp some movement of the magneto sideways occurs as the clamping screw is tightened, and therefore a balance between the pressure exerted by this clamp and the strut bolt has to be obtained in order to ensure that when the clamp is tight, the magneto spindle is exactly in alignment with the camshaft.

While making any adjustment to the length of the strut bolt it is advisable to slacken the clamping screw, but the actual checking of alignment must, of course, be made after retightening this clamp. Having correctly checked this alignment, the magneto may be removed and the coupling disc on same carefully tightened.

Removing " Silver Arrow " Camshaft. First remove magneto or "Magdyno" base fixing bolts, and slide the unit back upon its platform to disengage the coupling joint. It should be noted that in the actual process of withdrawing the camshaft, the magneto or "Magdyno" unit can be moved on its platform sufficiently to clear without disconnecting any of the various cables or controls. Next remove all bolts securing the sheet-metal timing-case cover, when the same is free to be removed, exposing timing gears. Next remove the nut securing the coupling disc (G, Fig. 7) to the projecting end of camshaft (this nut is screwed left-hand thread and must, therefore, be turned in a clockwise direction to release), and gently force the coupling disc off the tapered end of camshaft by means of a suitable lever. Now remove the nut securing the small helical worm pinion to flywheel axle (right-hand thread), and screw on to the threaded end of this pinion the special internally screwed extractor provided in the tool kit. Now turn the bolt which passes through the end of this extractor in a right-hand direction, when the pinion will be forced off the tapered end of the flywheel axle. Next remove the cylinder head and withdraw both valves and springs from the rear cylinder. Now remove the screws which locate the tappet guides for rear cylinder, and raise the guides sufficiently in their housing to allow the large gear wheel on camshaft to clear as it is being withdrawn. As explained on page 13, these tappet guides are a push-in fit only, and upon removing the locating screws (L, Fig. 8) it will be found possible to push them up as described. Lastly, remove the four nuts securing the aluminium cap (F, Fig. 7) which carries the rear end bearing for camshaft, and gently withdraw this cap. The camshaft is then free to be drawn out through the hole exposed. The re-assembly must be carried out in exactly the reverse order, and care must be exercised to avoid damage to the various joint washers. The camshaft gears are marked for re-setting purposes, and it is necessary to carefully slide the small worm pinion on to the flywheel axle with the marked tooth coinciding with the marked tooth space on the large pinion attached to camshaft, after which gently revolve the engine until the key on flywheel axle engages with the keyway in the small worm pinion, when the latter may be pushed on to the shaft tapered end and firmly secured with the fixing nut.

Dismantling O.H.V. Rocker-box. On the overhead-valve

MAINTENANCE AND OVERHAULING 141

engines, the rockers can be withdrawn complete with roller bearings (see Fig. 36) after undoing the four nuts and bolts securing the two rocker-box halves together. The roller bearings may then be slipped off each rocker-arm.

Valve Timing. On all Matchless engines the timing pinions or cam wheels are marked to ensure correct replacement. In order, however, to allay any suspicions the reader may have as to his own engine being incorrectly timed, a table is given overleaf showing the correct valve timings for all Matchless models. It should be noted that for the purpose of retiming the valves, normal tappet clearances should *not* be used.

Removing Rear Wheel. First, in the case of a spring frame or inclined engine model, put down the centre prop stand by holding same on the ground and gently pulling cycle backward. Next lean the cycle bodily to one side sufficiently to permit of the attachment of one side prop stand lengthening piece, after which lean the cycle to the opposite direction to apply the other side extension piece. On other models lower the rear stand. The rear wheel will now be well raised from the ground. Now disconnect the rear brake rod cross-head by withdrawing the split-pin by which it is attached to the brake-shoe expander lever, and also disconnect the rear chain connecting link, after which release the wheel axle nuts. The wheel is then ready to be removed by drawing same backward until the axle is free from the slotted fork ends, at the same time twisting the wheel in the fork to release the brake cover plate anchorage.

Removing Front Wheel. First put down prop stand with extensions as directed above, and then raise the front of cycle on to the front wheel stand, which it should be explained is not sufficient to provide a safe balance by itself. On other models jack up each wheel. Then remove the nut securing the expander lever, and gently force this lever off the splined end of the expander to which it is attached. Next withdraw the two cables from their slotted anchorage, and after slacking off both axle nuts, gently force out each washer from the recesses in the fork ends in turn with a stout lever, at the same time exerting pressure downwards upon the wheel, which will then fall out of position.

Dismantling Oil Pump. Should it be desired to remove the pump plunger proceed as follows: Unscrew the guide screw (Fig. 51) from the plunger housing and remove the two housing end caps, when the plunger may be eased out, large end first. When reassembling, the position of the groove on the plunger can easily be felt for while the screw is being introduced.

Wheel Alignment. If heavy tyre wear and freedom from skidding is to be avoided, it is essential to keep the wheels in proper alignment relative to each other and relative to the frame. The

MATCHLESS VALVE AND IGNITION TIMINGS

MODEL	Inlet Valve Opens Before T.D.C.		Inlet Valve Closes After B.D.C.		Exhaust Valve Opens Before B.D.C.		Exhaust Valve Closes After T.D.C.		Max. Ignition Advance		Valve Clearances for Timing
	Degrees	Inches	Degrees	Inches	Degrees	Inches	Degrees	Inches	Degrees	Inches	Inches
A/2	10	$\frac{1}{32}$	55	$\frac{19}{32}$	60	$\frac{23}{32}$	10	$\frac{1}{32}$	35	$\frac{3}{8}$	·008
B	20	$\frac{3}{32}$	65	$\frac{45}{64}$	65	$\frac{45}{64}$	25	$\frac{5}{32}$	48	$\frac{9}{16}$	·008
X/3	11	$\frac{3}{64}$	46	$\frac{39}{64}$	52	$\frac{49}{64}$	10	$\frac{1}{32}$	38½	$\frac{7}{16}$	·01
X/R3	11	$\frac{3}{64}$	46	$\frac{39}{64}$	52	$\frac{49}{64}$	10	$\frac{1}{32}$	38½	$\frac{7}{16}$	·01
R/7	14	$\frac{1}{16}$	57	$\frac{55}{64}$	53	$\frac{3}{4}$	15	$\frac{5}{64}$	40	$\frac{29}{64}$	·01
C	20	$\frac{1}{8}$	67	$\frac{55}{64}$	75	$1\frac{1}{16}$	28	$\frac{15}{64}$	40	$\frac{1}{2}$	·007
D	20	$\frac{1}{8}$	67	$\frac{13}{16}$	75	$1\frac{1}{16}$	28	$\frac{1}{4}$	37	$\frac{3}{8}$	·007
C/S	20	$\frac{1}{8}$	67	$\frac{55}{64}$	75	$1\frac{1}{16}$	28	$\frac{15}{64}$	40	$\frac{1}{2}$	·007
D/S	20	$\frac{1}{8}$	67	$\frac{13}{16}$	75	$1\frac{1}{16}$	28	$\frac{1}{4}$	37	$\frac{3}{8}$	·007

MAINTENANCE AND OVERHAULING

screw adjuster at the chain stays should be adjusted evenly on both sides.

When fitting or refitting a Matchless sidecar, place the sidecar in position, leaving all attachment nuts slack. The sidecar wheel should not run parallel with the machine wheels, or there would be a tendency for the machine to constantly pull to the left. The sidecar wheel should run in towards the machine ¾ in. (See Fig. 76.) To align correctly, two straight-edges 6 ft. long are necessary, which should be placed on the floor, one against the wheel rims of the machine, the other against the wheel rims of the sidecar. Now measure the distance between the edges immediately in front of the front wheel and at the rear of the rear wheel, the distance between the edges should be ¾ in. less at the front than at the rear. Finally retighten all nuts securely.

Adjusting Lucas H.F. "Altette" Horn. The horn is tuned by moving the adjusting screw in the centre of the front or grille. This screw is notched on its underside. Do not turn it through more than one or two notches at a time. The best adjustment can be found by trial. It should be noted that the centre screw is the only one provided for adjustment, and no other screw should be moved.

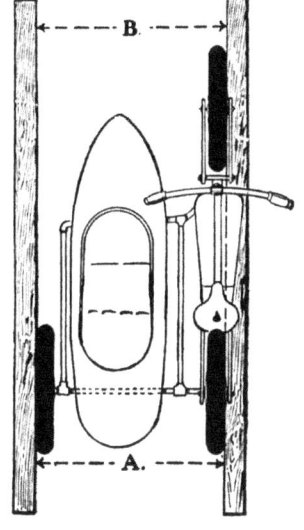

FIG. 76. SIDECAR ALIGNMENT

The distance B should be ¾ in. less than the distance A

The Annual Overhaul. Special points to be noted in the complete overhaul are as follows—

FRAME. Alignment, existence of flaws or cracks, play in spring forks, looseness of steering head, wear caused by friction of all attached parts, condition of enamel, spring frame damper adjustment.

WHEELS. Condition of rollers, cones, truth of wheels, alignment, loose spokes, condition of rims, wear of tyres.

CHAINS. Excessive wear, cracked or broken rollers, joints.

ENGINE. Oil leaks, compression leaks, main bearings, valves, valve guides and tappets, overhead-valve rockers, valve springs, valve seats and faces, cotters, condition of cylinder bore, piston, piston rings, play in big-end and small-end bearings, timing wheels, shafts and bearings, cams and camshaft.

GEARS. Condition of teeth on sprockets and pinions, damaged ball races and loose parts generally.

The examination should also include all control rods and cables, tank filters, clutch and brake linings, etc. To sum up, everything should be dismantled and readjusted and replacements made where necessary.

Fitting New Small-end Bush. The correct procedure is as follows: Get an old bush slightly smaller than the one which is to be extracted and a larger one for it to fit into. An iron bolt is then run through the connecting rod, and the two bushes placed one on each side of the latter. By slowly tightening a nut on the bolt with a long spanner, the bush in the connecting rod can be gently pressed out. A new bush may be fitted in like manner, and if a trifle large externally can be eased off with emery cloth. See that oil grooves are provided on the new bush.

Separating Crankcase Halves. Should the two crankcase halves of a Matchless engine be divided, it is essential that the oil pump plunger should first be withdrawn from its housing or damage to the pump plunger and drive will probably follow.

Dismantling Single-spring Clutches. The single-spring clutches consist of a main body which fits on to the splined mainshaft, and is secured by a nut. Should it be found necessary for any purpose to dismantle a clutch, the end cap, which takes the thrust of the push-rod button, should be removed by placing a tommy-bar in slots provided and tapping same sharply with a hammer. The clutch-rod button may now be withdrawn. The shaft nut should then be removed, together with the spring-cup washer. The clutch plates should be removed separately, also the sprocket and roller race. Fig. 14 illustrates a three-plate clutch dismantled.

When reassembling, care should be taken to replace the plates in the correct order. With the three-plate clutch the back plate, which is a plain metal plate, the tongues on which are shallower than any other plate, should be replaced first, followed by the roller race and clutch sprocket. When fitting the former, note that the roller-retaining ring should be nearest the rear chain sprocket; if this is not replaced correctly, it will not revolve freely or give a true bearing for the clutch sprocket. Then fit the dished metal plate, followed by friction plate (i.e. fitted with inserts), a plain steel plate, and a further friction plate; and finally, the outer plate, with the projection which registers in the hole in the spring cup. The spring cup should then be placed in position, together with mainshaft washers. The spring, spring collar, and retaining nut should then be fitted. The latter should be locked tight when the thrust button is in position; fix end cap, and the clutch is complete. With the multi-spring clutches, the procedure is similar to the above, but the six springs and their boxes must first be removed.

To Remove Four-speed Gearbox End Plate. First remove the kick-starter crank, after which the return spring and cover,

MAINTENANCE AND OVERHAULING

together with the tubular sleeve, may be withdrawn. In the case of all models with four-speed gearboxes (including the "Silver Arrow"), after slackening off the nut on the small clutch actuating lever (17, Fig. 56), the nipple can be slipped out of the arm. Next unscrew the cable adjuster from the slotted support stud attached to the gearbox end plate, or from the top of the V bracket on other models, after which all the end plate fixing nuts may be removed, leaving same free to be withdrawn. In the actual withdrawal process, pressure must be applied to the kick-starter axle end in order to prevent same, and also possibly the layshaft upon which it is mounted, being drawn out of position. The reassembly must be made in the reverse order, and particular care must be taken to securely tighten down the end plate fixing nuts. A tubular box key, if available, will be found most convenient for this purpose.

To Remove " Silver Arrow " Gearbox Entirely. First mark both high tension cables 1 and 2 to correspond with the figures stamped on " Magdyno " adjacent to the pick-ups; then detach both pick-ups which, as will be seen, are secured by the pressure of small flat springs. These springs are turned upon their supports to permit the removal of the bakelite pick-ups. Next remove the bakelite contact-breaker cap secured in a similar manner to the pick-ups, and withdraw the steel cam ring. Next remove the countersunk head screw which secures the advance and retard cable spring box to the "Magdyno," when this spring box may be gently withdrawn. Next unscrew the magdyno base bolts when, after sliding unit back on the platform to disengage the coupling and detaching the various dynamo cables including the negative battery cable, the entire unit may be removed. Next remove the battery clamp and disconnect the positive cable sleeve connector fitted about 6 in. from the battery terminal. This connection is covered by a rubber sleeve which can quite easily be moved to permit of disconnection. The battery may then be removed. Next remove the four small bolts which pass through the top of the magneto and battery platform, and also the two nuts by which the forward end of same is secured to the engine crankcase when the platform is free to be removed. Now remove the short front brake rod, and also detach the gear rod from the gear striker lever on the gearbox. Also detach the clutch cable nipple from the top of the clutch lever *via* the slotted hole in same, and unscrew the screwed cable stop from the slotted yoke at the top of the "vee" bracket, when the cable can be slipped through the slot provided. Now remove the left side footrest hanger, and, after removing the two nuts securing the outer half of front chain case, gently remove the latter, and detach the connecting links of both driving chains. Next remove the two bolts which pass through the slotted holes in rear engine plates, and slack off considerably all the nuts securing the off-side rear plate when, upon forcing the two plates apart to release the shallow tongue cut on the gearbox side, the entire box can be lifted clear. The replacement of all parts must be carried out in reverse order, and care must be taken to securely tighten all bolts securing the engine plates and the gearbox. The various dynamo cables are identified by means of coloured sleeves and must be fixed as shown on the wiring diagram. It will be found advisable to connect the advance and retard cable to "Magdyno" before this unit is actually fixed in position, and after fixing the cable spring box, care must be exercised to see that the cam ring is replaced with the narrow slot engaging with the projecting tongue on the advance and retard cable end, and by means of which the cam ring is revolved in its housing to provide the variable ignition setting controlled by the handlebar lever. Although a somewhat lengthy description is necessary for this gearbox removal process, it will in practice be found quite straightforward.

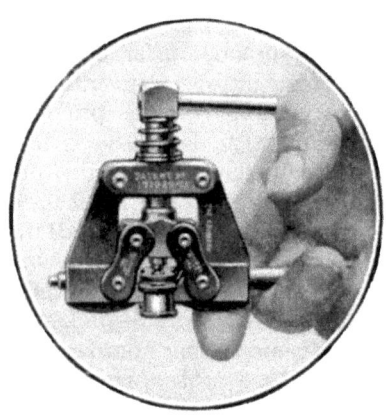

(*Coventry Chain Co,. Ltd.*)

FIG. 77. SHOWING HOW TO USE THE COVENTRY "UNIVERSAL" RIVET EXTRACTOR

To examine the interior of the gearbox it will, in any case, be necessary to disconnect the clutch wire from the operating lever.

Dismantling and Assembling Four-speed Gearbox. On those models where the gear operating lever is fitted through the gearbox cover, the gear control rod must also be disconnected by removing the gear connection pin which passes through the operating lever.

Then remove the gearbox cover nuts and the fork shaft lock nut, and draw off the gearbox cover. If this proves stiff give a few gentle taps on the inner side of the kick-starter crank with a mallet. Do not use a screwdriver to part the joint or oil may leak afterwards. The mechanism will now be exposed.

The kick-starter wheel can be lifted out, the low gear pinion must be drawn off the splined end of the axle, and the fork shaft should be unscrewed (it is formed with square head for this purpose). Then turn the striking forks to disengage them from the operating cam and lift them out with the next two pinions from each shaft. The layshaft and its splined on pinion can also be lifted out.

If it should be necessary to dismantle the cam gear, first unscrew the plunger stud, then the two set screws outside the box. This releases all the internal parts. Be careful to reassemble in the same relative positions.

The clutch must be dismantled and the clutch centre pulled off the splined end of the axle before the axle itself can be taken out. Then the sprocket locking plate screw may be removed with the locking plate, and the sprocket lock nut unscrewed (L.H. thread on H.W. gear and R.H. thread on L.W. gear). The rear drive sprocket fits over splines on the main gear wheel and can now be pulled off, so that the main gear wheel may be withdrawn from the inside of the box.

When reassembling, the operating cam must be in position first. Then fit the main gear wheel and axle sprocket and the axle with thrust washer. Next assemble the clutch. Now fit one of the forks to the axle sliding pinion and slip both over the axle and turn the fork to engage its peg in the cam.

Next fit the fork rod, and place the gearbox cover in position and test to make sure that the axle slider moves freely. Place the lever in high gear position, then remove the gearbox cover and note that the cam plunger is engaging the gear position correctly. The fork rod must now be removed and the cam turned to the second gear notch. Fit the layshaft dog gear on the layshaft and push on the layshaft pinion right up to its shoulder on the shaft. The recessed side of this pinion faces outwards to the bronze bush in the shell. Make sure that the dog gear revolves freely and fit the end of the layshaft in its bearing bush. Now fit the second fork to the layshaft slider and slip both into position and screw in the fork rod. Note that the cam must be in second gear to admit of the fork peg being turned into the cam slot. Next fit the axle dog gear and the low gear pinion. Push the latter down as far as the shoulder on the axle splines and again see that the dog gear revolves freely. Then fit the kick-starter wheel and gearbox cover and again test the gear operation. Place the outside lever in low gear this time, and then remove the cover and note that the low gear dogs are fully in mesh with the kickstarter wheel and that the cam plunger is correctly engaging the low gear notch. Finally, after complete assembly, test the gear control adjustment (page 109).

When referring to the gearbox cover in the preceding paragraph, the cover with all the kick-starter parts assembled should be inferred. The assembling of these parts in the cover does not call for any special notes. This cover can now be finally fitted up, the spring washers placed over the studs and the cover nuts screwed up. These nuts should be screwed up finger tight only at first, then proceed to tighten them up a few turns at a time going all round every one before finally tightening any one fully.

Chain Repairs. Always carry a complete chain repair outfit and some spare links. For removing chain rivets, the extractor shown at Fig. 77 is admirably suited, and is manufactured by the Coventry Chain Co. To use extractor, see that the point is level with the lower surface of the nut and open the jaws by pressing the tommy bar and handle towards each other, and insert the chain so that the jaws grip the roller, and the bottom of the inner plate rests upon the shoulders of the jaw. Turn the tommy bar until the rivet is forced through the outer plate. Repeat the operation on the next rivet; the outer plate can then be removed with the fingers and the chain connected up with the necessary spare part.

INDEX

ABSENCE of fuses, 99
Accessories, 57
Advance, magneto, 137
Alignment, magneto, 139
———, wheel, 141
"Altette" horn, 2, 143
Aluminium piston, 45
Amal air filter, 16, 118
——— carburetter, 76, 116, 134
Ammeter, 94
Anchor plate, brake, 22
Angularity, piston, 7
Annual overhaul, 143
Armature, 71, 91
Assembly, engine, 132
Auxiliary port, 74

BAFFLE, 11
Ballast resistance, 33
Batteries, 97, 100
Benzole-mixture, 61
Bevel box, 30, 126
Big end bearings, 8, 27, 34
Big twins, 4, 16
Bowden controls, 113
Brakes, 22, 65, 115
"Break," contact-breaker, 107
Breather, engine, 22, 31
Broken sight-feed glass, 15
Brushes, dynamo, 98
Buffer stops, 18
Bulbs, lamp, 100
Burned contacts, 107

CAMSHAFT, A/2, removing, 140
Carbon, removing, 128
Carburettor, 76, 116, 134
"Careless" driving, 66
Chains, 111, 122
Change of address, 59
Charging period, battery, 101
Circulation of oil, checking, 15, 61
Clutch, 20, 33, 108, 144
Coil ignition, 32, 72, 80
Condenser, 72, 82, 108
Contact-breaker, 79, 107
Controls, 62
Crankcase, splitting, 144
Crankshaft assembly, 9, 28
Cut-out dynamo, 32, 82, 99
Cylinder, removing, 127
——— head, removing, 125

DAMPER adjustment, fork, 113
Dangerous driving, 66
Decarbonizing, 124
Deferred payments, 2
De luxe equipment, 2
Dirty commutator, 98
Dismantling clutch, 144
Draining oil tank, 119
Driving licence, 58
Dry sump lubrication, 14, 73
Dynamo-coil-distributor, 32, 80, 121
Dynamo maintenance, 97

ELECTRIC horn, 2, 143
Electric lighting sets, 3, 90
Electro-magnetic cut-out, 82, 99
Electrolyte, 101
End caps, valve, 50
Engine compression, 134
——— lubrication, 118
——— number, 59
——— starting, 63
——— timing, 141
Exhaust stroke, 70
Exhaust valve-lifter, 106

FACE cam, 80
Fibre heel, 135
Filing contacts, 108
Firing angle, 7, 25
——— order, 31
Flexible magneto coupling, 12, 32
"Floating" rocker fulcrum, 30
Flywheel assembly, 9, 28
Focussing headlamp, 100
Fork damper adjustment, 113
——— spindles, 114, 122
Four-speed gear-box, 20, 33, 83

GEAR-BOX removal, 145
Gearboxes, Sturmey-Archer, 83, 109
Gear changing, 64
Grinding-in valves, 130
Groove, cam, 14, 73

HEADLAMPS, 94
Hire purchase, 2
Hub adjustment, 115
Hydrometer, 101

IDENTIFICATION marks, 59
Inflation, tyre, 116

Inlet valve guide lubrication, 119
Instrument panel, 3, 62
Interconnected brakes, 22, 65, 115

JETS, altering, 117
Jump-spark gaps, 83

KICK-STARTER attachment, 3
Knocking, 65

LICENCE, driving, 58
Lighting sets, 2
Lubrication chart, 120
Lucas "Magdyno," 90
—— "Maglita," 93
—— magnetos, 78

MAGNETO, care of, 135–136
——, principle of, 71
—— timing, 137
Monobloc engines, 6, 25

NEEDLE valve, carburettor, 117
Number plates, 59

OIL pump, 14, 73
—— replenishment, 61
Oldham couplings, 30, 127
Overhead camshaft, disconnecting, 126
—— valve engine, 50
—— valves, removing, 130

PANEL equipment, 3, 62
Parting crankcase, 144
Physical fitness, 58
Pillion riding, 66
Pilot jet, 63, 77, 117
Piston removal, 130
Plugs, care of, 106
Points, contact, 79, 107
Pre-ignition, 65
Primary chain, 111, 122
—— coil, 33, 72, 82
Priming engine, 63
Principle, four-stroke, 68
Pump, oil, 14, 73

RANGE at a glance, 1

Reflectors, cleaning, 100
Registration, 58
Removing cylinder, 127
Replenishment, 61
Resistance, ballast, 33
Reversed polarity, dynamo, 97
Rich mixture, 117
Rings, removing, 130
Rocker arm, C.B., removing, 136
Rocker box, 50, 126, 133
Routine adjustments, 104
Rubber coupling, magneto, 12
Running-in, 66.

SECONDARY chain, 111, 122
Sidecar alignment, 143
Sight-feed glass broken, 15
Slip ring, cleaning, 108, 136
Small-end bush, removing, 144
Sparking plug, care of, 106
Specific gravity, 101
Spitting-back, 117
Spring frame adjustment, 114
Starting-up, 63
Steering head adjustment, 114
Storage, battery, 101
Sturmey-Archer gearboxes, 83, 109

TAPPET adjustment, 105
Taxation, 58
"Tell-tale" lamp, 33
Three-plate clutch, dismantling, 144
Timing magneto, 137
Topping-up battery, 101
Tuning carburettor, 116
Two-port engine, 50
Tyres, care of, 116

VALVE clearances, 104
—— guide lubrication, 75, 119
—— timing, 141
Valves, removing, 130
Vertical shaft union, 126

WEAK mixture, 117
Wheel alignment, 112, 143
—— bearings, 24, 115
Wiring diagrams, 92, 95, 103
Worm, oil pump, 73

1933 & 1936 SUPPLEMENTS SECTION

PUBLISHER'S NOTE REGARDING THE 1931-1939 MODEL 'TIMELINE' CHART

The 1931 through 1939 model chart 'time line' shown on the following page was compiled from information that was available at the time of this 2018 publication.

While we have come to accept that the advent of the Internet has made information about anything instantly available, it's not always true. Case in point is the Matchless motorcycle models that were manufactured between 1931 and 1939. Consequently, we were left with researching the information from publications of that era. However, those publications were sometimes in disagreement with each other. In addition, some of the previous years' models were still in the dealers' showrooms when the new models were introduced, creating even more confusion as to when a particular model was introduced or discontinued. Adding to this confusion is the fact that some of the 'new' models were introduced ahead of their particular model year, these include the D5, D6 and D3 which are considered to be 1933 models but were actually released in 1932. From all this confusion and data we extracted as much of what we felt was reliable information and developed what we believe is a reasonable 'time line' by model type.

Unfortunately, information for the 1932 models is sadly lacking and even this publication makes no reference to them. While we cannot be sure, we suspect that the 1931 R7, DS and D models were continued for 1932 but, as we were unable to find absolute proof, they were omitted from the 1932 listing. However, our research indicates that these 3 models were discontinued for 1933. Consequently, we show them as no longer available (NLA) in the 1933 listing.

CC	OH/SV	CYL	1931	1932	1933	1934	1935	1936	1937	1938	1939	NOTES
250	SV	Single	R7									
250	SV	Single			NLA							
250	SV	Single			D7	D7	D7					
250	SV	Single					F7	F7				
250	OHV	Single	DS						G7	G7	G7	
250	OHV	Single			NLA							
250	OHV	Single			D2	D2	D2					
250	OHV	Single						G2	G2	G2	G2	
250	OHV	Single						G2M	G2M	G2M	G2M	COMP MODEL ALSO
250	OHV	Single				F4	F4					
350	SV	Single	D		NLA							
350	OHV	Single		D6	D6	D6	D6					
350	OHV	Single		D3	D3	D3	D3					
350	OHV	Single						G3	G3	G3	G3	COMP MODEL ALSO
350	OHV	Single								G4	G4	
400	SV	V Twin	A2	A2	A2	A2	A2					SILVER ARROW
500	SV	Single		D5	D5	D5	D5	D5				
500	SV	Single							G5	G5	G5	
500	OHV	Single	CS	CS	CS	CS	CS					
500	OHV	Single			D80	D80	D80					
500	OHV	Single						G80	G80	G80	G80	COMP MODEL ALSO
500	OHV	Single						G90	G90	G90	G90	COMP MODEL ALSO
600	SV	Single	C	C	C	C	C					
600	OHC	V Four	B	B	B	B	B					SILVER HAWK
990	SV	V Twin	X3	X3	X3	X3	X3					
990	SV	V Twin	XR3	XR3	XR3							
990	SV	V Twin						X4				
990	SV	V Twin							X	X	X	

1933 SUPPLEMENT

TO THE BOOK OF THE MATCHLESS

SINCE 1931, when this handbook was first published, considerable alterations have been made to the Matchless range which now numbers 12 machines, and it is the object of this Supplement to bring the book up to date for prospective buyers and owners of 1931-3 models. Of the nine machines manufactured in 1931 six (models A/2, B, X/3, X/R3, C, C/S) are retained this year with detail modifications only. The remaining three 1931 models have been dropped, but models D, D/S have served as the basis for

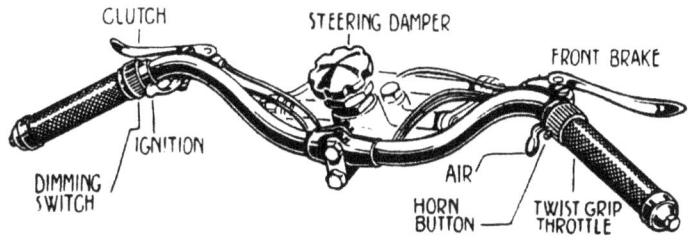

FIG. 78. SHOWING 1932-3 HANDLEBAR CONTROL LAY-OUT

two new 250 c.c. models. The other three new models (33/D5, 33/D6, 33/D3) were introduced last year and since weight is of no importance this year from a taxation point of view, Messrs. Colliers have made many detail improvements to them, especially in regard to appearance, equipment, and the strengthening of various parts. The sixth new machine is model 33/D80.

The 250 c.c. models are both eligible for the 30s. *per annum* tax. One is a side-valve (33/D7) and the other an overhead-valve model (33/D2).

Lucas electric lighting with electric horn is available on all models, a "Magdyno" set being fitted at £6 5s. extra, except in the case of model 33/D7, where a "Maglita" set is fitted at £5 15s. *De luxe* equipment (page 3) with illuminated instrument panel is also available for any model. This includes an air filter, except on models 33/A2, 33/XR3, 33/X3, and an ammeter, speedometer, ignition switch, and oil indicator on all models.

The Multi-cylinder Models. These have undergone the least alterations of all, though certain detail improvements have been made, some of which are common to the whole range. Model

33/A2 (the "Silver Arrow") has its monobloc Vee twin engine the same as originally introduced except that longer pistons are used and the exhaust port spacing is wider. Other alterations to this model are black tank panels with the "M" in chromium but not embossed, new, "clean" handlebars with integral controls (Fig. 78), a second gear ratio of 10·4 to 1. Model 33/B (the "Silver Hawk") has its four-cylinder overhead-camshaft engine unchanged but for slight modifications to the lubrication system. The fuel tank is altered similarly to model 33/A2; new handlebars are provided; second gear ratio is now 10·1 to 1.

Models 33/X3, 33/XR3 (The Big Twins), which incidentally are much used for police patrol work, are unchanged except for "clean" handlebars, entirely new fuel tanks, caged big-end roller bearings, "Invar-strut" pistons and closer gear ratios.

Models 33/C, 33/CS. No alterations have been made to the engines of these machines except for the use of special "Invar-strut" pistons and caged big-end roller bearings, together with a compression ratio of 5 to 1 for the 33/C engine. A new design of shock-absorber has been fitted on the engine shaft of both machines and second gear ratio has been raised from 10·6 to 8·7. Improvements to the C, C/S specification include new fuel tanks, oil tanks with fabric filters, improved silencers, oil-baths for the primary chains, quickly-detachable rear wheels, left-hand pedal control for the redesigned rear brakes (no longer interconnected with the front ones, but provided with water shields), and "clean" handlebars with integral controls.

NEW MATCHLESS FEATURES

Neater Controls. An excellent feature on all 1932-3 models is the fitting of a new type of "clean" handlebars of Matchless design with Bowden levers. The bars, which are adjustable for angle and of a slightly larger section than hitherto, are finished in highly polished black enamel with chromium-plated levers which are now integral fittings. As may be seen in Fig. 78, the throttle is operated by a long, thin twist-grip with a dummy to match. A new type rotary dimming switch and horn switch are also provided, and small trigger levers are now used for the ignition and air controls, which, with the throttle, open *inwards*.

New Fuel Tanks. A new design of bulbous saddle tank is fitted, and it has, except in the case of the "Silver Arrow" and "Silver Hawk," a different finish from that employed for 1932; an all-black highly polished stove-enamel finish with gold lining is used and the chromium initial "M" is embossed and held in place by two screws. A chromium-plated strip runs down the centre of the tank top. The new tanks are certainly of most striking appearance and have the same capacity as before (2½ gal.,

SUPPLEMENT

Fig. 79. The New Saddle Tank with Embossed Chromium "M"
This tank is specified on all 1933 machines except the "Silver Arrow" and "Silver Hawk"

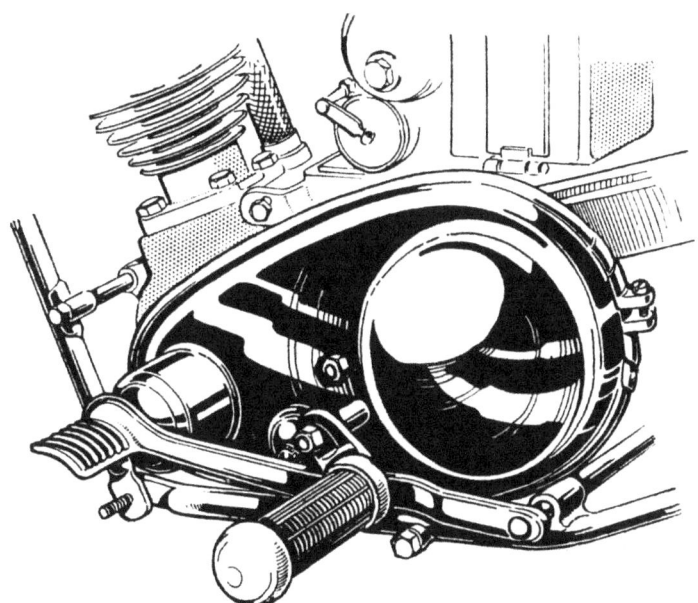

Fig. 80. Oil-bath Chain Case Fitted to 1933 Singles
Clamp details are shown in Fig. 80A. Model 33/D7 has a chain guard only and has not the 12 in. rear brake pedal fitted, as shown above, to the other D/5 class models

except on the "D" class models). Insulation from road shocks and vibration is provided by rubber buffers (Fig. 79), and larger knee-grips are fitted.

Chromium-edged Mudguards. All the 1933 "D" class models except the "250" side-valve have chromium-plated edges on the mudguards, which, besides giving an air of refinement to the machines, tends to prevent deterioration of the enamel. These edges are formed of brass mouldings rolled over the edges of the mudguards and riveted in place.

Oil-bath Primary Chain Cases. Black enamelled oil-bath primary chain cases of very neat design (see Fig. 80) are fitted to all 1933 single-cylinder models except model 33/D7. The lower chain run is entirely submerged in oil and the chain therefore operates under ideal conditions with a consequently great increase in its life and silent running. An inspection cap on the side of the chain case serves as an oil level indicator and enables the chain tension to be ascertained. The chain case is designed so that it can be readily taken apart. The two halves, which are steel pressings, are held together by a moulded rubber band with a metal clamp extending round the chain-case and tightened up by a nut and bolt conveniently placed at the rear (Fig. 80A).

Burman Gearboxes and Clutches. Pivot-mounted three-speed Burman gearboxes were introduced in 1932 for models D/5, D/6, D/3. This type of gearbox is retained this year for model 33/D5, but Burman four-speed gearboxes are now fitted to model 33/D2, and models 33/D6, 33/D3, 33/D80.

The three-speed Burman gearbox (type "WP") has a two-plate clutch and the four-speed model (type "HP") a three-plate clutch. Both gearboxes are of very similar design and have constant-mesh gears of oil-toughened nickel-chrome steel (not case-hardened), the necessary gear changes being obtained by means of dog clutches and locked by a patent rack and pawl mechanism (see Fig. 90) actuated by a bell-crank lever. The kick-starter is not mounted on the layshaft, but on a separate shaft, thus allowing a good second gear ratio to be obtained for starting purposes. The drive is taken through the mainshaft. The clutches are of the multiple-spring type with alternate cork-inserted and plain steel plates, the outer clutch spring plate having a recessed adjusting screw against which the floating plunger in the hollow mainshaft bears. Unlike the Sturmey-Archer clutches, the springs are adjustable for tension and a shock-absorber is fitted in such a way that the drive is transmitted from the clutch sprocket to the clutch through rubber buffers which give a radial movement of approximately 3/16 in. As may be seen in Fig. 90, to allow for expansion of the buffers dished recesses are provided.

Referring to Fig. 90, the action of the four-speed gearbox will be seen to be very simple. The mainshaft is splined for its whole length and the layshaft for only two short distances. Pinions 6, 7, 10, 11, are moved simultaneously by the striker 19 and pinions 9, 12 are keyed to their shafts. To obtain neutral the four sliding pinions are moved into the position shown, where both layshaft pinions are free of the layshaft splines. To obtain first gear the sliding pinions are moved to the extreme right so that the dogwheels 7, 8 are coupled and the drive is transmitted from the mainshaft to the gearbox sprocket 4 through pinions 8,

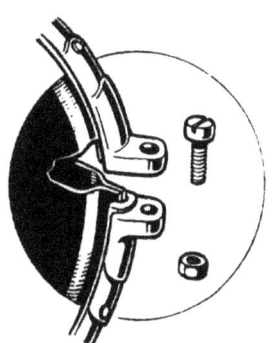

FIG. 80A. PRIMARY CHAIN CASE CLAMP

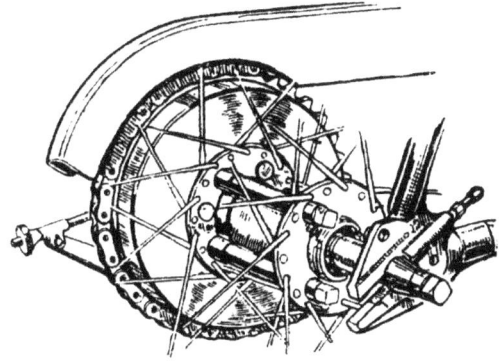

(*From " The Motor Cycle"*)

FIG. 81. QUICKLY-DETACHABLE REAR WHEEL

12, 9, 5. To obtain second gear the sliding pinions are moved ¼ in. to the left of the neutral position, when pinion 11 engages the layshaft splines and the drive is transmitted through pinions 7, 11, 9, 5. To obtain third gear the sliding pinions are moved ¾ in. to the left of neutral when pinion 10 engages the layshaft splines and the drive is taken through pinions 6, 10, 9, 5. Fourth gear is obtained by moving the sliding pinions to the extreme left until the dogwheels 5, 6 are coupled, thereby locking the gearbox sprocket sleeve 5A to the mainshaft and giving direct drive.

Optional Foot Gear Control. Positive-stop foot control may be had as an alternative to the hand control on all 1933 models with Burman gearboxes. 1932 Burman gearbox models may also be converted to foot control for a small extra charge. The 1933 Burman foot control ("T.T." type) comprises a short toe-operated lever with its fulcrum on an extension of the gearbox inner selector lever spindle. Also pivoted on the spindle is the casing of the foot control containing a double edged pawl engaging teeth cut on a sector keyed to the spindle, together with two springs which return the gear lever to the same position after every gear change. On the back of the casing are two bosses which bear against stops on the spindle bush and limit the lever movement. Foot control, rather similar to the Burman, may be specified also on model 33/CS.

Oversize Tyres. 26 in. × 3·25 in. "Firestone" cord tyres are fitted to all models except model 33/D7. Oversize tyres measuring 27 in. × 4 in. are available for all except the "D" class models.

Quickly-detachable Rear Wheels. Models 33/C, 33/CS have bolt-fitting quickly-detachable rear wheels. The method of securing the hub is shown in Fig. 81. To remove the rear wheel it is only necessary to undo the three tubular bolts and take out the centre spindle, when the wheel can be lifted clear of the three dummy studs and withdrawn.

Redesigned Brakes. All the "D" class models except 33/D7 have been fitted with entirely new brakes. Fig. 82 shows a partly sectioned front brake, but the rear is similar. A large flange is formed integral with the hub, and to this flange is secured by eight screws the $6\frac{1}{2}$ in. diameter brake drum proper which has some unusual features. It is made of centrifugally cast chromidium-iron alloy, an ideal braking surface because of its high co-efficient of friction, and has four deep ribs which serve the dual purpose of stiffening the brake drum and providing efficient cooling when descending long and steep hills. The brake anchor plate which houses the shoes has had its diameter increased so as to form a cover plate which entirely excludes mud and water. The rim of the cover plate is chromium-plated and this greatly enhances the appearance of the "D" class models. A brake pedal 12 in. long (see Fig. 80) operates the rear brake which is not inter-connected with the front one.

Transmission Shock-absorber. 1932-3 single-cylinder models have a face-cam shock-absorber fitted on the engine shaft to eliminate transmission snatch. As may be seen in Fig. 83, the magneto drive and engine sprockets are mounted on a splined sleeve which fits over the end of the mainshaft, and on this sleeve, able to slide axially, is a similarly splined face-cam member with its cams held by a powerful compression spring close to face-cams situated in a ring attached to the engine sprocket. The magneto sprocket (which, incidentally, is fitted as shown only in the case of model 33/D7) is, of course, integral with the splined sleeve, but the engine sprocket is free to rotate on it in so far as the compression spring will allow of relative movement between the face-cams. Thus, on opening the throttle suddenly some "slip" occurs, so smoothing out the transmission.

Fabric Oil Filters. The efficiency and reliability of the Matchless dry-sump lubrication system has been still further improved by the fitting to all 1932-3 oil tanks of a special detachable fabric filter (Fig. 84) through which all oil must pass before being returned to the tank. The filter, which is a felt cartridge about 7 in. long and 1 in. in diameter, has a capacity about ten

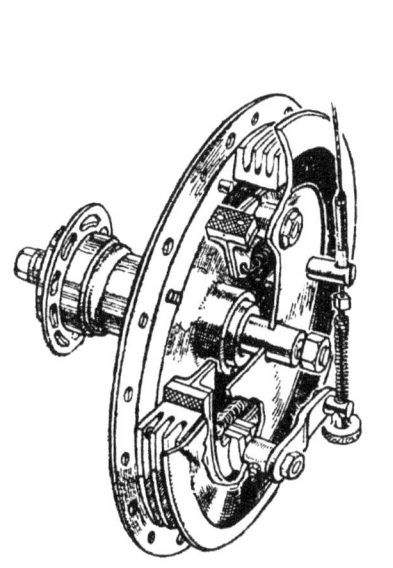

(From "The Motor Cycle")
Fig. 82. The New Matchless Brake with Ribbed Drum

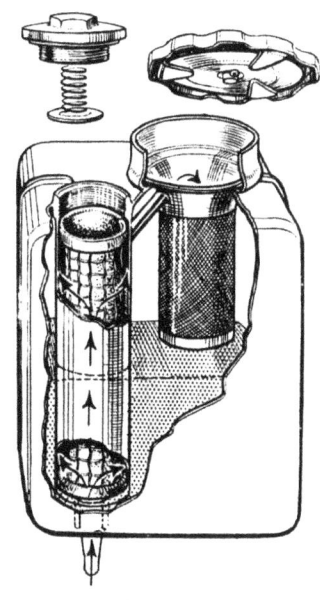

(From "The Motor Cycle")
Fig. 84. Showing Fabric Filter Fitted to the Oil Tanks

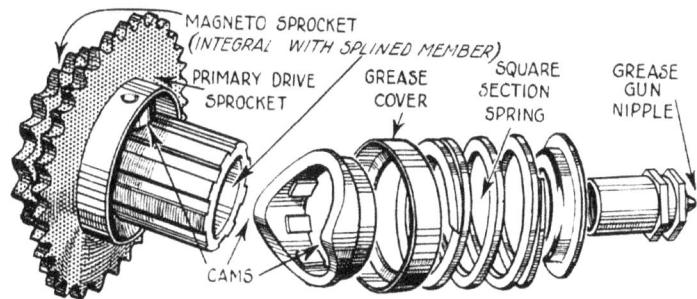

(From "The Motor Cycle")
Fig. 83. Component Parts of the Face-cam Type Transmission Shock-absorber Fitted to the Engine Shaft

times as great as the amount of oil actually filtered and is guaranteed to remove all impurities from the oil.

Matchless Engine Modifications. Models introduced 1931-2 and since retained and redesigned for 1933 have had in most instances the cylinder-head and cylinder finning made more massive, and all the small capacity "D" class engines except model 33/D7 have the ignition unit driven off the inlet camshaft and have a cast-aluminium chain-case for the drive. All overhead-valve engines which last year had valve-rocker return springs now have valve return springs enclosed in the push-rod covers. In place of the two-ring aluminium alloy piston with split skirt (Fig. 30A) used prior to 1932, a special type of three-ring piston known as the "Invar-strut" piston is fitted to all early 1933 engines except 33/D80, 33/D7, 33/D2, 33/D3, 33/D6, the "Silver Arrow" and "Silver Hawk." The piston, illustrated in Fig. 86, is self-compensating for varying temperatures and engines fitted with it can be driven hard for prolonged periods without risk of "drying-up." Small working clearances are used with the "Invar-strut" piston, and this entirely eliminates piston "slap." Later versions of the above engines have a self-compensating three-ring piston of Italian design having "Invar-struts." Big-end bearings, except on models 33/D7, 33/D2, 33/A2, 33/B, have been modified by the substitution of caged roller bearings for the shouldered crankpin bearing.

New Silencers. All 1932-3 models except the multi-cylinder models have an improved shape of silencer with integral fishtail. Internally the silencer is the same as that shown in Fig. 6. A high-level competition exhaust pipe with tubular silencer (Fig. 88) may be specified as an alternative to the standard exhaust system on all O.H.V. models, and also on model 33/D5 as an extra.

MODEL 33/D7

This remarkably low priced (£34) side-valve "250," introduced this year to take advantage of the 30s. *per annum* tax, for machines of under 250 c.c. capacity, has exactly the same specification as the 1931 model D described and illustrated on page 48, except for the following—

The 2·46 h.p. Side-valve Engine. As on the 1932-3 347 c.c. engine, the cylinder and cylinder-head are cast integral, with finned aluminium valve caps provided on the latter, but to obtain a decrease in capacity of 101 c.c. the bore and stroke have been altered to 62·5 mm. × 80 mm. The compression ratio has been raised to 4·9 to 1, giving a maximum speed of just over 50 m.p.h. The only other important engine alteration is the incorporation on the engine shaft of a face-cam shock-absorber. A decompressor for easy starting is retained.

Carburettor. This is a two-lever semi-automatic type 74/014 Amal with flange fixing direct to the cylinder and twist-grip throttle control. A size 70 main jet is used, together with a 4/4 throttle valve and needle position 3. Fuel consumption with this setting should work out at 100–120 m.p.g.

SUPPLEMENT

Lubrication. The dry-sump lubrication system remains unaltered but for the inclusion of a fabric filter in the oil tank.

Miscellaneous Items. Included in the specification are a 2 gal. saddle tank of new design, "clean" handlebars of graceful semi-sports pattern with integral fittings, a new silencer and "Firestone" cord tyres.

MODEL 33/D5

Something like a sensation was caused in the motor-cycle world, and history was made in the autumn of 1931 when Messrs.

FIG. 85. MODEL 33/D5 ("LIGHT 500")

Colliers placed on the market an amazingly cheap 500 c.c. motor-cycle (model D/5) complete with electric lighting and full equipment, weighing under 224 lb. This "Light 500" is retained for 1933 and its power/weight ratio, in spite of numerous improvements, has still been maintained at a level sufficient to give wonderful acceleration and a full throttle speed of about 65 m.p.h. Model 33/D5, which costs £38 10s., has the following specification—

The 4·98 h.p. Side-valve Engine. The power-unit, which has a bore and stroke of 82·5 mm. × 93 mm., is of straightforward Matchless design and very similar to the 5·86 h.p. engine described on page 43, though like model 33/D7 it has no detachable head and there are several other important differences. For instance, a caged double-row roller bearing is used for the big-end of the connecting-rod which now has fitted to the $\frac{7}{8}$ in. diameter gudgeon-pin a self-compensating "Invar-strut" piston (Fig. 86) with three narrow rings at the crown. The piston reciprocates in a heavily finned cylinder having the latest design of semi-turbulent combustion chamber with a compression ratio of 4·4 to 1. As may be seen in Fig. 85, the position of the sparking plug is somewhat unusual; it is situated in a cool position over the inlet port behind the valve cap, which, like the exhaust valve cap, has an aluminium "fircone" to assist cooling. The exhaust gases make their exit *via* a large diameter and heavily plated pipe and standard silencer with integral fishtail.

The valves operate in cast-iron guides and are protected and lubricated by the valve chest, which, as on all Matchless engines, is cast integral with the cylinder and has a detachable cover. There are no variations from standard Matchless practice in regard to either the two-cam timing gear or the dry-sump lubrication system. A decompressor is fitted, and the engine has a disc-type crankcase breather.

Carburettor. A two-lever, semi-automatic, pilot jet Amal type 76/004 is used (almost identical to the instrument illustrated on page 77). Twist-grip throttle control is standard and the recommended setting is: main jet size 180; throttle valve 6/5; needle position 3. With this setting 80-90 m.p.g. should be obtained solo, and 60-65 m.p.g. with sidecar.

Ignition. A Lucas magneto (unless "Magdyno" lighting is specified) is placed behind the engine and driven off the inlet camshaft at half engine speed by a chain enclosed in an aluminium chain case cast integral with the timing case cover. The plug fitted is a Lodge T.S.3 (1933 O.H.V. models have a Lodge H.1).

Frame and Forks. The frame, which is built of Aero quality butted steel tube, is a duplex cradle type of almost identical design to that used on the "C" class models (Fig. 32). It has, however, a $3\frac{1}{2}$ in. shorter wheel-base. The spring forks with finger adjustment to the shock-absorbers are of the same type fitted since 1930 and have fork stops.

Gearbox and Clutch. A three-speed, type "WP," Burman gearbox having constant-mesh gears is pivot-mounted similarly to the Sturmey-Archer gearbox in a rear extension of the engine plates, and is operated by a tank-mounted gear lever (with first gear position forward) or positive-stop foot control (12s. 6d. extra). The gearbox has an internal speedometer drive and the following standard solo gear ratios are provided—

First, 13·2 to 1; second, 8·1 to 1; third, 5·1 to 1. Sidecar gear ratios are: first, 15·0 to 1; second, 9·2 to 1; third, 5·8 to 1.

The clutch is a three-plate multiple spring type Burman with cork inserts and shock-absorber.

Transmission. Coventry "Ultimate" chains are used throughout, and the dimensions front and rear are $\frac{7}{16}$ in. × ·265 in. and $\frac{1}{2}$ in. × ·305 in., respectively. The front chain runs in an oil-bath chain case (Fig. 80). Besides the clutch shock-absorber, a face-cam shock-absorber is fitted on the engine shaft. The rear chain has an efficient guard.

Brakes. Both brakes are of an entirely new design (Fig. 82) with detachable cast chromidium-iron alloy brake drums of 6½ in. diameter provided with cooling fins and chromium-rimmed cover plates to exclude mud and water. No inter-connecting gear is used. The rear brake is operated by a 12 in. brake pedal on the off side, and the front one by a handlebar lever on the same side. Finger adjustment is provided for each brake.

Wheels and Tyres. The wheels which are built up of heavy gauge butted spokes have Timken roller bearing hubs and are fitted with 26 in. × 3·25 in. "Firestone" cord tyres.

Tanks. The fuel tank, which is a redesigned bulbous saddle type, with embossed chromium "M" (Fig. 79), has a capacity of 2 gal., sufficient for about 170 miles. The rectangular oil tank mounted over the gearbox and provided with a fabric filter (Fig. 84) holds 3 pints. Oil consumption works out at 1,300-1,500 m.p.g.

Miscellaneous Equipment. "Clean" semi-sports handlebars, adjustable for position, a Lycett "Aero" spring seat, large knee-grips and adjustable footrests ensure a comfortable riding position. Large domed mudguards with chromium-plated edges protect the rider from all dirt. The rear mudguard is detachable for tyre repairs. Included in the equipment are a steering damper, a spring-up central stand, tubular front stand, pump inflator, two large pannier tool-bags between the chain stays, and a very complete set of tools.

MODEL 33/D2

This rakish looking overhead-valve "250" is like the side-valve "250" eligible for the 30s. *per annum* tax and costs only £40 10s. It is, of course, much faster and on full throttle will attain a speed of 65 m.p.h. without difficulty. Model D/2, although a new model introduced this year, is really an improved version of the 1931-2 model D/S with its general specification developed on the lines of the "Light 500" already described. Its specification is, in fact, identical to that of model 33/D5 except in regard to the engine and gearbox. The rear brake pedal is also situated on the opposite side.

The 2·46 h.p. O.H.V. Two-port Engine. The bore and stroke are the same as on the 246 c.c. side-valve, namely 62·5 mm. × 80 mm., and the general design of the engine differs only a very little from the 1931-2 D/S engine (see page 53). The same type of crankcase, flywheel assembly and lubrication system are used, but the timing case cover is extended as on all present engines except 33/D7 to form a chain case for the magneto or "Magdyno" drive which is taken from the inlet camshaft. An "Invar-strut" piston is not used, however, in the case of this small capacity power unit. The cylinder finning has been considerably improved and the compression ratio raised to 6·5 to 1. The exhaust system may be of the type shown in Fig. 88 or 89.

Carburettor. This is a type 75/014 Amal semi-automatic, pilot jet instrument and has twist-grip throttle control. Recommended setting is: main jet, size 110; throttle valve, 5/4; needle position, 2. Fuel consumption is 100–120 m.p.g.

Gearbox and Clutch. The gearbox is a pivot-mounted, four-speed, type "HP" Burman, having constant-mesh gears and

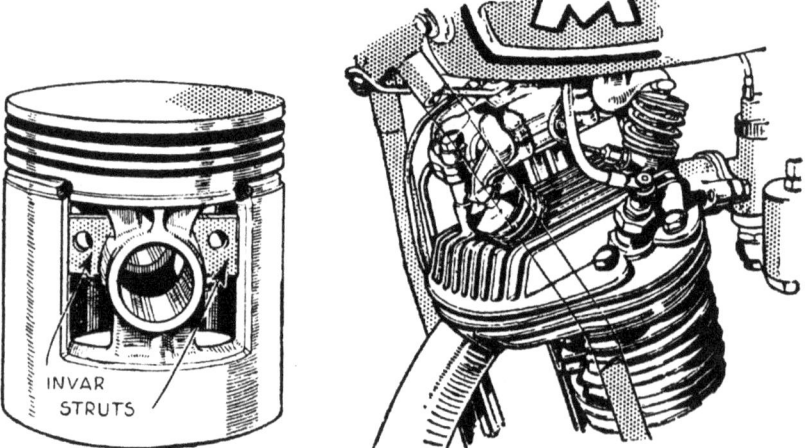

FIGS. 86 AND 87. SHOWING (LEFT) THE "INVAR-STRUT" PISTON AND (RIGHT) 1933 CYLINDER-HEAD AND OVERHEAD VALVE GEAR

The O.H.V. engine shown is a model 33/D6. Note pipe to inlet valve guide

hand or foot control at option. The standard gear ratios are: first, 16·6 to 1; second, 10·0 to 1; third, 7·8 to 1; fourth, 6·1 to 1. The clutch is a multi-spring, three-plate type similar to the two-plate type with cork inserts and shock-absorber.

MODELS 33/D3, 33/D6

These two 70 m.p.h. models, which should appeal strongly to riders who prefer the 350 c.c. class of overhead-valve machines, were originally introduced in 1932 and since then have had their specifications much improved, and it is now exactly the same as that of model 33/D2 except that a higher power engine is installed and a different set of four-speed gear ratios is employed. Models 33/D3, 33/D6 are identical except that the latter has a single-port engine. Their prices are £41 10s. and £40 10s., respectively.

The 3·47 h.p. O.H.V. Engine. This is a larger edition of the 2·46 h.p. engine with a bore and stroke of 69 mm. × 93 mm., respectively, the only important difference other than engine capacity being in regard to the big-end bearing which is of the caged roller type, and the compression ratio, which is 5·6 to 1.

FIG. 88. MODEL 33/D2 (WITH COMPETITION EXHAUST)

Model 33/D3 has a two-port detachable cylinder-head with hemispherical combustion chamber and two exhaust pipes, while model 33/D6 has a single port head. Like model 33/D2, the

FIG. 89. MODEL 33/D3 (TWO-PORT)

engine now has dry-sump lubrication with automatically lubricated inlet valve guide, enclosed and lubricated roller bearing overhead rockers, enclosed push-rods, a two-cam timing gear running in oil-bath, aluminium piston, inlet camshaft-driven "Magdyno," and a decompressor.

Carburettor. The carburettor is the same type as fitted to the

2·46 h.p. O.H.V. engine and has the same setting except that needle position 3 is advised.

Gear Ratios. The pivot-mounted, four-speed type "HP" Burman gearbox has the following ratios: first, 16·6 to 1; second, 8·9 to 1; third, 7·7 to 1; fourth, 6·0 to 1.

MAINTENANCE NOTES (1932-3)

Use of Foot Gear Control. With the very considerable leverage obtained on this type of control, care must be exercised when changing gear to avoid damaging the gear selectors or control mechanism. When changing gear, disengage the clutch and move the gear pedal simultaneously with a steady toe or heel and toe movement (1932 models) until the desired gear change down or up is obtained. Do *not remove the foot from the pedal* after the end of the travel has been reached *until the clutch has been re-engaged.*

Tyre Pressures. The correct inflation pressures for the front and rear tyres of all 1933 solo models except the Big Twins are 15-16 lb. per sq. in. and 20-22 lb. per sq. in. respectively. For the Big Twins, 16-18 and 22-24 lb. per sq. in. are recommended, front and rear. Where a sidecar is attached, 22-24 and 24-26 lb. per sq. in. are recommended for the rear tyre in the case of the single and multi-cylinder models, respectively. Sidecar tyres should be pumped to 15-16 lb. per sq. in., except on the multis where 16-18 lb. per sq. in. is desirable.

Tappet Clearances. All 1932-33 side-valve engines except the "Silver Arrow" should have their tappets kept adjusted so that with the engine *warm* there is a clearance of ·004 in. for the inlet valve and ·006 in. for the exhaust valve. On the new 2·46 h.p. and 3·47 h.p. O.H.V. engines the tappets should be adjusted so that with a *cold* engine there is just no clearance between the valve rocker ends and the hardened caps on the ends of the valve stems. It should be possible, however, to revolve these caps with the fingers. See that the decompressor is in the "off" position when making an adjustment.

Ignition Timings. The correct ignition timing for the 1933 2·46 h.p. S.V. Model D/7 engine is for the contact-breaker points to commence to open with the piston $\frac{1}{16}$ in. before *top-dead-centre* and the ignition lever fully retarded. The setting for the 1932 4·98 h.p. S.V. and the 3·47 h.p. O.H.V. engines is $\frac{1}{16}$ in. before T.D.C. on full retard, and for the same 1933 engines $\frac{1}{16}$ in. *after* T.D.C.

Cleaning Fabric Filter. About once every 500 miles not only should the filter below the filler cap of the oil tank be removed and thoroughly cleaned in petrol, but the hexagon-headed cap on top of the tank should be unscrewed and the fabric filter taken out and similarly cleaned.

Lubricating Transmission Shock-absorber (33/D7). To obtain smoothness of transmission the face-cam shock-absorber on the engine shaft of model 33/D7 must be kept lubricated. Every 300 miles, or more frequently if harshness of transmission develops, inject through the grease-gun nipple provided a charge of Wakefield's "Castrolease." On other models lubrication is automatic.

Lubrication of Primary Chains. On all 1933 singles except model 33/D7 the primary chain is enclosed in an oil-bath and therefore requires no attention other than occasional adjustment and replenishment of the case with engine oil.

Lubricating Burman Gearbox. All Burman gearboxes are sent out by the manufacturers charged with sufficient grease for at least 1,000 miles' running without attention. It is advisable every 1,000 miles to inject through the aperture uncovered by the removal of the grease cap on top of the gearbox 2-3 ounces of Wakefield's "Castrolease Medium," but the gearbox should not be completely filled, two-thirds full being the correct level. About every 5,000-7,000 miles remove and re-pack with grease the clutch sprocket roller bearing and also the mainshaft plunger.

Burman Clutch Adjustment. If clutch slip occurs, first suspect the clutch cable adjustment and if necessary adjust until there is the requisite $\frac{1}{32}$ in. clearance between the clutch rod (16, Fig. 90) and the ball in the actuating lever (17). If the cable adjuster is already screwed right home, the necessary clearance can be obtained by unscrewing the adjuster screw (15A) a trifle. Should clutch slip persist, it is probable that the spring adjuster nuts (15B) require tightening up and each of these should be given half a turn, when a retrial should be made. If necessary, repeat, but be careful to tighten all the nuts uniformly. The correct adjustment is normally seven complete turns from right home.

Should the clutch become difficult to free in spite of the cable not having stretched, wear may have occurred on the clutch rod, in which case the adjusting screw (15A, Fig. 90) should be slightly tightened up. The trouble may, however, be due to the clutch springs being over-tightened. A tendency for the clutch spring adjusting nuts to become unscrewed means that the springs have become fastened by means of mud or rust to the nuts, and the remedy is to clean the springs and nuts and also to polish the ends of the springs and grease them. If relative movement develops between the clutch sprocket and case, it indicates that the rubber buffers (3A) are worn and require renewal. A tendency for both the clutch sprocket and case to "rock" from side to side indicates that the roller race inside the clutch sprocket needs a new set of rollers. Only $\frac{1}{64}$ in. end play is permissible. Excess play

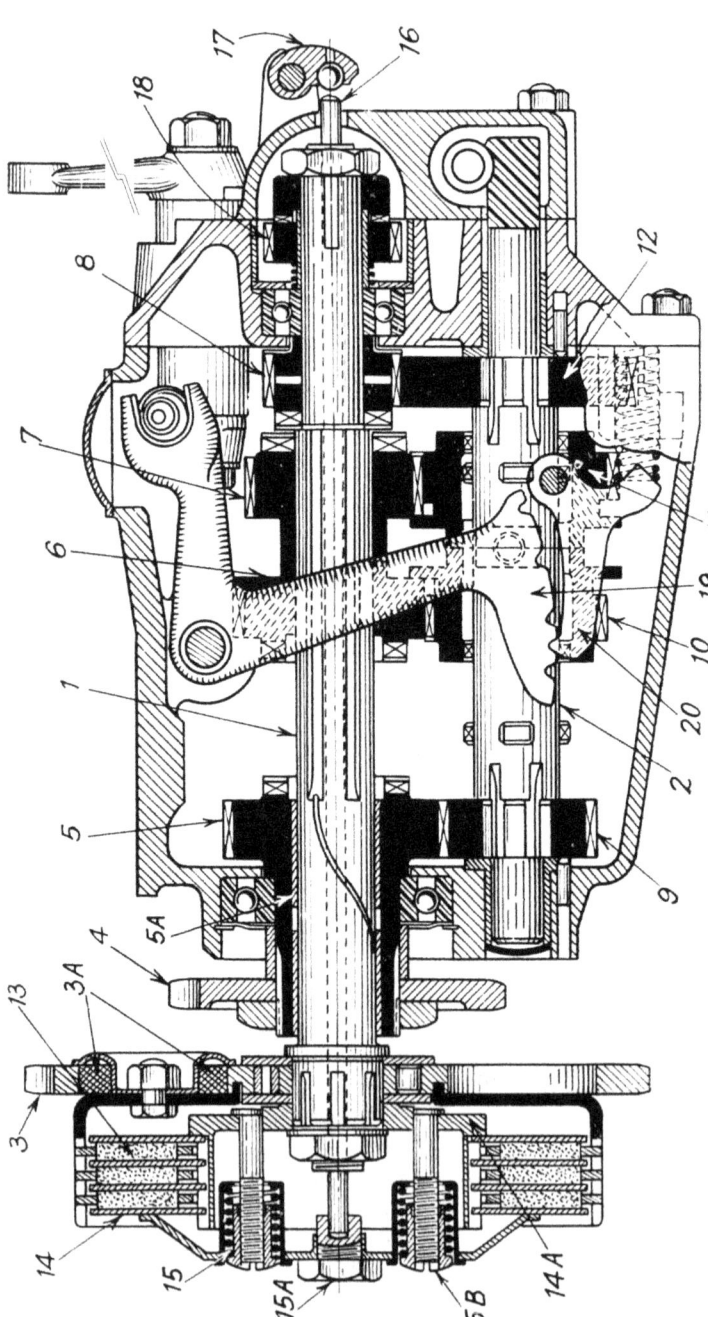

The key to numbered parts not given below will be found on page 84.

3A. Clutch shock-absorber.
6. Mainshaft sliding dogwheel (3rd gear).
7. Mainshaft sliding dogwheel (2nd gear).
8. Mainshaft dogwheel (1st gear).
10. Layshaft sliding pinion (3rd gear).
11. Layshaft sliding pinion (2nd gear).
12. Layshaft-driven pinion (keyed).
15A. Adjuster screw and lock-nut.
15B. Spring adjusting nut.
18. Mainshaft-driven k.s. pinion.
19. Striking fork with rack.
20. Spring-operated pawl.

may cause the tongues on the clutch plates to wear grooves in the clutch case.

Removing Quickly-detachable Rear Wheel. Prior to rear wheel removal on all models the mudguard should be detached. To remove the wheel on a model 33/C or 33/CS it is only necessary to unscrew the three tubular fixing bolts and remove the centre spindle when the wheel can be lifted clear of the studs. To avoid damage to these studs, however, it is advisable not to undo the spindle before removing the nuts and also to support the wheel while removing the spindle.

Adjusting Primary Chain. On all 1933 single-cylinder models, except model 33/D7, to test for $\frac{3}{8}$ in. up-and-down movement it is only necessary to remove the inspection cap. The pivot-mounted gearbox may then be swung bodily upon its lower fixing bolt the necessary amount after slackening the off side nut of the upper fixing bolt (unless the machine has foot control, when the near side nut should be slackened). Afterwards check the adjustment of the gear control.

Burman Gear Control Adjustment. After tilting the gearbox rearwards to take up primary chain stretch it is usually found, except on 1933 models with foot control, that some readjustment of the gear control is necessary. Incorrect adjustment causes rattle of the gear lever in its quadrant in second gear position and perhaps a tendency for the gear lever to jump out of gear and cause serious damage. To remedy matters, the length of the vertical rod should be adjusted until the gear lever is centrally positioned in the wide central gear quadrant notch. Should one complete turn of the coarse threaded connection give excessive lengthening, make the final adjustment by means of the finely threaded connection.

In the case of 1932 models with the Burman gearbox, the length of the short rod attached to the small lever on the foot change should be similarly adjusted so that the lever occupies a central position giving an equal amount of free movement backwards and forwards independently of the pedal.

Decarbonizing Hints. The decarbonizing instructions given on pages 124-134 are applicable to the 1932-33 models, but some additional hints are here given in regard to the new models.

To remove the cylinder in order to decarbonize model 33/D7, D5, 33/D5, which have no detachable heads, proceed as described on page 127 for model D. Remove the exhaust pipe and silencer, but leave the carburettor in position if desired after withdrawing the slides and disconnecting the petrol pipe.

Take off the plug, valve chest cover, and aluminium valve caps, when the cylinder may be slid off after the three retaining nuts have been unscrewed and the piston has been placed near bottom-dead-centre.

To remove the detachable cylinder-head prior to decarbonizing models D/3, D/6, 33/D3, 33/D6, 33/D2, owing to the closeness of the fuel tank to the rocker-box the fuel tank should be raised at its forward end immediately before removing the latter. This can be effected by undoing the two front tank fixing bolts. Proceed as described on pages 125-126, but here again the carburettor need not be removed if the slides are withdrawn. No tie bar now connects the rocker-box with the front down tube. On reassembling the 1932-3 engines do not forget to space the

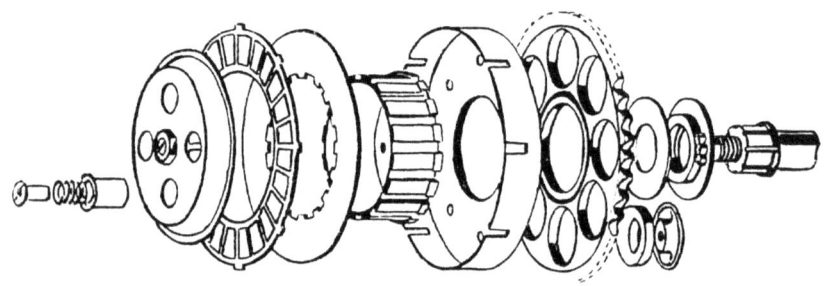

FIG. 91. SHOWING BURMAN CLUTCH ASSEMBLY

Only one friction and one driven plate are shown in the above sketch illustrating the relative positions of the various parts.

ring slots on the "three-ring" piston at 120 degrees to each other.

Retiming Ignition. It should be noted that on models D/5, D/6, D/3, 33/D7, the magneto or "Maglita" sprocket is provided with five keyways which in conjunction with the twelve sprocket teeth enables the ignition timing to be set with great accuracy. When dealing with the sprocket on a "Maglita" armature, on no account omit to grip the sprocket firmly by means of the two flats provided while tightening or loosening the fixing nut which has a locking washer held in place by a spring ring encircling the nut. To remove the ring, use a sharp instrument such as the blade of a penknife.

To Adjust Magneto Chain. The magneto chain on the Big Twins should be adjusted as described on page 112. All other 1932-33 models, except the spring-frame models, which have a shaft drive, have the magneto, "Magdyno," or "Maglita" fixed to a hinged platform which can be tilted as described in the case of models C, C/S on page 113 (third paragraph). The crankcase bolt upon which the platform pivots, and also the crankcase bolt upon which the adjuster screw is mounted, must first be slackened.

Dismantling Burman Clutch. To remove the clutch plates,

unscrew the spring adjusting nuts (15B, Fig. 90) and remove the springs, spring cups, and take off the spring plate, when the other plates may be withdrawn. If desired, the complete clutch assembly may be removed after taking off the spring plate by unscrewing the nut holding the clutch body on the castellated mainshaft.

Valve Timing. The correct valve timing for all the new single-cylinder models referred to in this Supplement is the same as for

Fig. 92. Power Unit of Model 33/D80

models D, D/S (see table on page 142) and should be checked with ·014 valve clearances.

MODEL 33/D80

On passing this Supplement for Press, the author finds that a new Sports "500," known as model 33/D80, has just been included in the 1933 Matchless range. The price of this very interesting machine is £43 15s. Owing to its exceptionally high power/weight ratio, model 33/D80 (which weighs only 300 lb.) possesses unusually good acceleration and general liveliness, and on full throttle will attain a speed of no less than 80 m.p.h.

The specification of model 33/D80 is similar to that of the other new O.H.V. "D" class models, but the engine (Fig. 92), which has a bore and stroke of 82·5 mm. × 93 mm. (498 c.c.) and a compression ratio of 6·2 to 1, has a somewhat different type of high efficiency two-port cylinder-head and other special features. Flange fixed direct to the inlet port is a down-draught Amal sports carburettor with horizontal mixing chamber. The rocker-box is of semi-circular form with duralumin rockers and an end plate with embossed "M," giving access to the rockers. In order to make the overhead valve gear readily accessible, the 2 gal. fuel tank is cut away on the off side to conform to the contour of the rocker-box. A Birmal Lo-ex three-ring, split skirt aluminium alloy, anti-slap piston is fitted, and the $\frac{7}{8}$ in. diameter gudgeon-pin works in a duralumin bush. A caged double-row roller bearing of extra large dimensions is used for the big-end, and the crankcase is ribbed on the driving side. The four-speed, pivot-mounted Burman gearbox, which has a multi-spring, shock absorber clutch, is fitted with foot control and has the following standard ratios: 12·9, 7·3, 6·23, 4·86 to 1.

1936 SUPPLEMENT

TO THE BOOK OF THE MATCHLESS

A TENDENCY towards greater standardization is noticeable in the 1936 range, which comprises a dozen models suitable for all temperaments and purses. Of last year's models the Big Twins and two side-valve singles (Models F7, D5) are retained with little alteration and constitute the 1936 "Tourist" range. All other 1935 models have been dropped and are replaced by a "Clubman" range of eight speedy and smart-looking O.H.V. singles with vertical engines. Only a brief description of the 1936 models is possible, as the primary object of this Supplement is to bring THE BOOK OF THE MATCHLESS up to date for Matchless owners.

THE " TOURIST " RANGE (S.V.)

The four "Tourist" models are Models 36/F7, 36/D5, 36/X4 and 36/X4 *de luxe* priced at (with electric lighting) £35 14s., £51, £69 15s., £73 10s. respectively.

The 250 C.C. Model 36/F7. This machine, which is the cheapest in the Matchless range, is, except for the smaller engine capacity, new silencer and coil ignition, very similar to Model 33/D7 (described on page 48). The bore and stroke are 62·5 mm. × 80 mm. and the well-proved D.S. lubrication system is retained. A detachable cylinder head is not provided. The specification includes a four-speed Burman gearbox, oil bath chain case, duplex cradle frame, spring-up centre prop stand, 25 in. × 3 in. tyres, 2 gal. fuel tank, etc.

The 500 C.C. Model 36/D5. Model 36/D5 closely resembles Model 36/F7, but the engine, which has a bore and stroke of 82·5 mm. × 93 mm., has a car type detachable head with semi-turbulent combustion chamber, a "Lo-ex" piston and Lucas "Magdyno" ignition. The oil tank is of improved shape, and the petrol tank holds 3 gal. A heavyweight four-speed Burman gearbox is provided and 26 in. × 3·25 in. tyres are fitted.

The 990 C.C. Model 36/X4. This "go-anywhere" family machine or fast solo remains substantially as hitherto (see page 34), but has been cleaned up and generally improved in detail. The engine, which has a bore and stroke of 85·5 mm. × 85·5 mm., now has forked type connecting rods instead of the side-by-side arrangement, and the big-end bearing has three rows of rollers. A Burman four-speed gearbox and tubular silencers are now fitted.

The 990 C.C. Model 36/X4 De Luxe. The specification of the *de luxe* Big Twin is identical to that of the standard Model 36/X4, with the exception that an instrument panel is mounted above the handlebars and chromium edged mudguards and an air filter are included.

THE " CLUBMAN " RANGE (O.H.V.)

The eight "Clubman" models are Models 36/G2, 36/G2M, 36/G3, 36/G3C, 36/G80, 36/G80C, 36/G90, 36/G90C, and their listed prices (lighting included) are £39 10s., £42 10s., £52 10s., £57 10s., £55, £60, £60, £65 respectively.

The 250 C.C. Model 36/G2. The general layout of this "two-fifty" and all other "Clubman" models is in accordance with orthodox Matchless design, but the O.H.V. two-port engine is of a new type. The bore and stroke are 62·5 mm. × 80 mm. and a "Lo-ex" piston is fitted. Features of a most compact and efficient engine include a heavily finned single-port cylinder, a down-draught carburettor, twin-camshaft timing gear, flat base tappets, an oval rocker-box with valve clearance adjustment at the tops of the push-rods, a new design of exhaust valve lifter. The D.S. lubrication system (see Fig. 94) is the same as on earlier engines, and Miller coil ignition is used. The specification includes a four-speed Burman gearbox, an oil-bath chain case, duplex cradle frame, spring-up centre prop stand, 3 gal. petrol tank, and 26 in. × 3·25 in. tyres.

The 250 C.C. Model 36/G2M. The only essential difference between this and the model just described is that magneto instead of coil ignition is specified. The magneto is driven by a chain enclosed in a chain case cast integral with the timing cover.

The 250 C.C. Model 36/G3. This machine, illustrated in Fig. 93, has a somewhat sturdier engine with a bore and stroke of 69 mm. × 93 mm., hairpin valve springs, magneto ignition. A heavyweight four-speed Burman gearbox is provided and the fuel tankage is 3 gal. Finned chromidium brake drums are incorporated.

The 350 C.C. Model 36/G3C. Except for the provision of a specially tuned engine with polished ports and combustion chamber, and the specifying of features adapted to competition and trials riding, this "Clubman Special" is similar to Model 36/G3.

The 500 C.C. Model 36/G80. This standard "five-hundred" has a similar general specification to the "three-fifties," but is powered with an improved version of the "Sports 500" engine. The bore and stroke are 82·5 mm. × 93 mm., the piston is a "Lo-ex," and the engine main shaft is carried on two journal ball bearings on the driving side and a flood-lubricated bronze bearing on the timing side. A two-port cylinder head is used

SUPPLEMENT

and the valve springs are of the hairpin type. The gearbox is a four-speed Burman.

The 500 C.C. Model 36/G80C. Similar to Model 36/G80 except that trials equipment is specified and the engine is specially tuned and has a polished combustion chamber and ports.

The 500 C.C. Model 36/G90. The "Super Clubman" is similar to the standard Model 36/G80, with the exception that a higher

Fig. 93. Typical of the New "Clubman Range"
(Model 36/G3)
A fast "three-fifty" with high-efficiency single-port sports engine

compression ratio, a tuned and polished engine are included, together with a 14 mm. plug.

The 500 C.C. Model 36/G90C. Equivalent to Model 36/G90 with trials equipment.

CORRECT LUBRICATION

The Matchless dry sump lubrication system as hitherto incorporates a double-acting oil pump (see page 73) which draws oil from the tank and forces it through the timing side main shaft to the main bearings and big-end, auxiliary oil feeds also being taken to the cylinder walls and timing gear.

Use These Engine Oils. For all 1936 Matchless engines the makers advise the use during the summer of Patent Castrol "XXL," Mobiloil "D," or "Aeroshell." For winter running the last two are quite suitable, but if Patent Castrol is preferred, Grade "XL" should be used. For racing, Patent Castrol "R" is best, but this should never be mixed with other oils. With regard to gearbox lubrication, use the winter grade of engine oil for Sturmey-Archer gearboxes and one of the following greases for Burman gearboxes.

Suitable Greases. For Burman gearboxes, secondary chains and general grease-gun lubrication, Castrolease Medium, Mobilgrease No. 2, and Shell Motor Grease Soft are eminently satisfactory.

Correct Engine Lubrication. This is assured provided you (1) use the right oil; (2) maintain the level above the half-full mark (do not fill above 1 in. below the return pipe with the engine cold); (3) check oil circulation at the return pipe orifice (at the indicator where an instrument panel is fitted); (4) keep the filters clean.

Clean Filters Every 1000 Miles. Every 1000 miles remove the filter below the filler cap and the fabric filter also, and thoroughly clean both with petrol. About once every 5000 miles (or once every season) drain and clean the tank and replenish with fresh oil. The draining can be arranged when the oil is at the lowest recommended level.

Grease Overhead Rockers Every 500 Miles. It is desirable to apply the grease-gun to the nipples for the O.H. rockers about once every 500 miles. Use a good heat resisting grease (see page 119).

" Magdyno " Lubrication. After a big mileage (say 20,000 miles) return the instrument to the makers and have the bearings repacked with grease. Apply a spot of oil (no more) to the heel of the contact-breaker rocker arm occasionally so as to minimize wear.

Dynamo Lubrication (Coil Ignition Models). Every 500 miles insert a drop of oil through the lubricator on the driving end of the Miller dynamo, and every 1000 miles press a little grease into the hole on the end of the commutator.

Dynamo Lubrication (Magneto Models). Deal with as for the Lucas "Magdyno."

Burman Gearbox Lubrication. About every 1000 miles inject one to two ounces of grease (see previous page) through the nipple on the gearbox top adjacent to the inspection cap, which is slotted at one end to permit of its being rotated on slackening the two fixing nuts. Do not fill completely; it is intended to run *two-thirds* full. Grease can alternatively be injected direct through the inspection orifice with a canister, and in the case of Model 36/D5 it is advisable to remove the extended sleeve nut on the right-hand end of the top gearbox fixing bolt, to permit of the application of the spout of the collapsible grease container. Also inject a little grease through the nipples on the gearbox end so as to lubricate the speedometer drive (where fitted), gear change mechanism and kick-starter spindle.

Sturmey-Archer Gearbox Lubrication. Keep the gearbox about *one-third to one-half full* by regular replenishment with engine oil (see page 175). All 1935-6 models have Burman gearboxes.

SUPPLEMENT

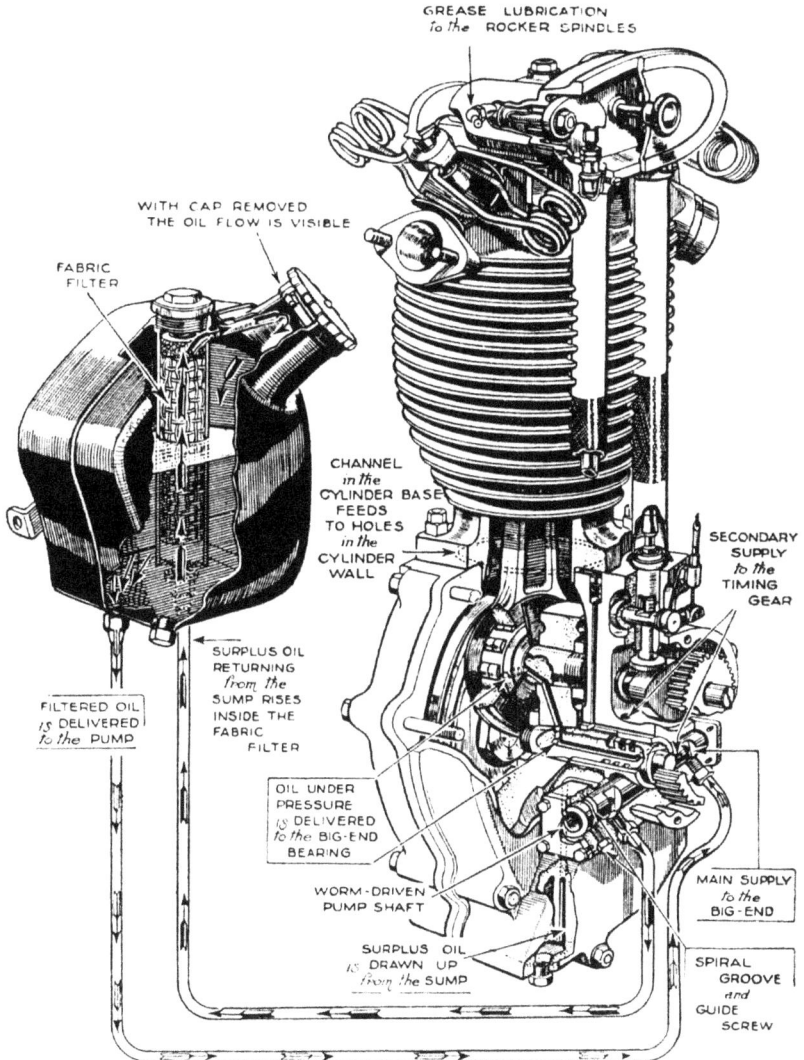

Fig. 94. How the "Clubman" Engine is Lubricated

Details of the "Clubman" engine are shown very clearly in the above illustration. Note the improved oil tank with fabric filter and the new design of exhaust valve lifter. But for these the 34-5/F engine is similar. On 1936 500 c.c. "Clubman" engines the rocker-box is of somewhat different shape, and on the 250 c.c. models hairpin valve springs are not provided. Always keep the pump guide screw done up tightly.

Inspect Level of Oil in Chain Case Weekly. The inspection cap orifice prevents over filling. Top up with engine oil as required. Deal with the secondary chain as described on page 122.

Dynamo and Magneto Chains. On coil ignition models the dynamo chain is enclosed in the oil-bath chain case and thus it follows that if the primary chain is correctly lubricated the dynamo chain is also. On magneto ignition models the chain case is packed with grease during assembly and no attention is required for about 5000 miles, after which fresh grease should be added.

Bowden Controls, Forks, Steering Head, Hubs, etc. Deal with these as described on pages 121-123, using one of the previously mentioned greases.

HOW TO DECARBONIZE

The general instructions for decarbonizing and grinding-in the valves given on pages 124-134 are applicable to 1936 models, but changes in design render certain dismantling procedure somewhat different. The following hints bring the original matter completely up to date.

Dismantling Side-valve Engines. As detachable heads are provided on all 1936 engines except Model 36/F7, undertaking a "top overhaul" is a matter of extreme simplicity. Only the sparking plug and cylinder head fixing bolts have to be removed to enable the head to be lifted off and the piston exposed. In the case of Model 36/F7, which has no detachable head, first remove the exhaust pipe and silencer. Then the carburettor mixing chamber should be unscrewed and the throttle and air slides withdrawn. Next remove the petrol pipe, plug, valve chest cover and aluminium fircone valve caps. Finally remove the three cylinder fixing nuts, put the piston near B.D.C. and draw off the entire cylinder as described on page 127.

Dismantling Overhead-valve Engines. When decarbonizing a "Clubman" engine, the first preliminary step is to disconnect the exhaust system and remove the plug, petrol pipe and carburettor slides. As the petrol tank obstructs matters, it should next be dealt with. Remove the three tank fixing bolts and, in the case of the 500 C.C. "Clubman" engines, drain the tank and remove the "U" pipe connecting the two halves. The tank may then be readily slid backwards until its stern rests on the saddle nose. A wooden block should be inserted beneath the front of the tank so as to keep it elevated sufficiently to enable spanners to be applied to the rocker-box fixing bolts and cylinder head stay fixing. On 250 c.c. models the tank need not be touched.

Slacken the cylinder head stay fixing bolt at the frame, remove the nut at the rocker-box end and push the stay clear. Now telescope the push-rod covers until they "stay put," as described on page 126. Remove the rocker-box fixing bolts and gently slide the rocker-box complete with push-rods and covers over towards the timing side. To remove the cylinder head, it is now only necessary to extract the four elongated retaining bolts. Be careful not to damage the hardened valve stem end caps or the soft copper gasket. Cylinder removal is perfectly simple.

To Decarbonize. Follow the instructions given on pages 128-130. The reference to Model D on page 129 applies, of course, to Model 36/F7.

Reassembly (S.V.). The instructions given on page 132 are applicable to 1936 "Tourist" engines.

Reassembly (O.H.V.). Reassemble the cylinder and piston as described on page 132 for the side-valve engines. Then refit the cylinder head, being careful to observe absolute cleanliness of the contacting joint surfaces. Tighten the head bolts firmly and evenly. When replacing the "Clubman" rocker-box assembly, it is wise to remove the inspection cover so as to verify that the upper ends of the push-rods are correctly located, and also to revolve the engine until the tappets are fully down. When refitting the petrol tank it is best to secure the rear part first. Finally check up the valve clearances as described in a later paragraph.

RUNNING ADJUSTMENTS

Are Tyre Pressures Correct? Test frequently with the gauge (not with a kick) and if the pressures do not correspond closely with those given below, rectify so as to ensure comfortable and economical riding (see page 116). For Model 36/F7 the best solo pressures for the 25 in. × 3 in. tyres are 14-15 lb. and 20-22 lb. per sq. in. for front and rear tyres respectively. In the case of Model 36/D5 with 26 in. × 3·25 in. tyres inflate to 14-15 lb. and 16-18 lb. per sq. in. front and rear respectively. Add an extra 2 lb. per sq. in. to the rear pressure only for pillion riding. With Models 36/X4, 36/X4 *de luxe*, having 26 in. × 3·25 in. tyres and fitted with a single passenger sidecar, the front pressure should be 15-16 lb., the rear pressure 20-22 lb., and the sidecar tyre pressure 16-17 lb. per sq. in.

In the case of the 250 c.c. "Clubman" models (36/G2, 36/G2M) front and rear solo pressures should be 14-15 lb. and 18-20 lb. per sq. in. respectively. On the 350 c.c. and 500 c.c. "Clubman" models use the same front pressure, but add 2 lb. to the rear one.

1934-5 Model 4F. Owners. On this machine, which has for practical purposes an inclined "Clubman" engine (and for which the instructions in this Supplement apply), take care not to leave the machine standing with the petrol tap turned on. If you do this you incur a decided risk of neat petrol dripping into the cylinder through the downswept inlet port and diluting the oil, perhaps causing an engine seizure or even a fire!

Suitable Plugs to Fit. For the "Tourist" models a Lodge TS3 or a K.L.G. 777 gives good results. For the "Clubman" models fit a Lodge H1 or K.L.G. KS5.

To Adjust Valve Clearances (S.V.). Remove the valve chest cover and with the spanner in the tool roll, hold each tappet and with another slacken the lock-nut which secures the adjustable tappet head. Then screw the head up or down until the correct valve clearance is obtained with each valve fully closed and the engine *warm* (not hot). For the Big Twins, clearances of ·004 in. and ·006 in. are recommended for the inlet and exhaust valves respectively. In the case of Model 36/D5 give a clearance of ·006 in. for both the inlet and exhaust valves, and on Model 36/F7 give clearances of ·012 in. for both valves.

To Adjust Valve Clearances (O.H.V.). As may be observed in Fig. 94, the "Clubman" engines have valve clearance adjustment at the tops of the push-rods and, in order to get at the adjustment, the rocker-box cover must be removed. Then rotate the engine until the valve needing adjustment is open and, after unscrewing the lock-nut, screw up or unscrew the adjustable push-rod end until the correct clearance is obtained, afterwards retightening the lock-nut. Check again afterwards in case this retightening has upset the adjustment. On the "Clubman" engines the correct clearance between the rocker ends and valves, when the valves are fully closed and the engine *cold*, is the nearest approach to *nil* possible. It should be possible with the fingers to revolve the hardened valve stem end caps without there being any perceptible up-and-down movement present.

Exhaust Valve Lifter Adjustment. Note the remarks on page 106. Details of the exhaust valve lifter mechanism on the "Clubman" engine are clearly shown in Fig. 94.

Inspect Contact Breaker Occasionally. Keep the contacts clean and free from oil and the "break" of the correct magnitude. On "Magdyno" and magneto ignition models the gap between the contacts when wide open should be ·012 in. Instructions on cleaning and adjusting will be found on pages 107, 135. On machines fitted with coil ignition the contact-breaker is housed in the timing case cover and is driven by the exhaust camshaft. It is of quite different design from the usual contact-breaker. About every 1000 miles the bakelite cover should be removed, the contacts examined and, if necessary, cleaned and adjusted. But do not interfere unless the gap varies considerably from the correct one, as indicated by a feeler gauge. The proper gap is ·018 in. to ·02 in. If the contacts are blackened, clean up with a piece of *very fine* emery cloth; if pitted, true up with a fine carborundum stone. To adjust the contacts, slacken the lock-nut and rotate the fixed contact screw as required and then retighten the lock-nut.

To Retime Ignition. On Lucas "Magdyno" and magneto models proceed as described on pages 137-138, noting that in the case of the Big Twins No. 1 cam is that *farthest* from the rear cylinder, and that in the case of the magneto ignition models the sprocket on the exhaust camshaft (a taper fit) is loosened, the contact-breaker being rotated with the fingers until the "break" occurs with the piston in the correct position before T.D.C. In this position retighten the camshaft sprocket. The ignition timing for the Big Twins is $\frac{3}{16}$ in. before T.D.C. on full advance. In the case of Model 36/D5 the correct timing is $\frac{1}{8}$ in. before T.D.C. on full advance. The timing for Model 36/G2M is $\frac{1}{4}$ in. before T.D.C. on full advance, and for Models 36/G3, 36/G3C, $\frac{7}{16}$ in. before T.D.C. on full advance. On the 500 c.c. O.H.V. Models 36/G80, 36/G80C, 36/G90, 36/G90C give an advance of $\frac{9}{32}$ in. to $\frac{5}{16}$ in. before T.D.C. on full advance.

To retime on 1934-6 coil ignition models, remove the bakelite contact-breaker cap and slacken the cam fixing screw. Then insert a small punch in one of the slots and gently tap with a *light* hammer until the cam is free on its taper. Set the piston at the correct position before T.D.C. and then turn by hand the cam *anti-clockwise* until the contacts begin to "break." In this position retighten the lock-nut and you are "all set." The correct ignition settings for Models 36/F7 and 36/G2 are T.D.C. on full retard and $\frac{1}{4}$ in. before T.D.C. on full advance respectively.

"Magdyno" Chain Adjustment. Maintain about $\frac{1}{4}$ in. whip at the upper chain run. To adjust on the Big Twins, after removing the chain case cover slacken off both the long headed bolts, passing through the rear engine plate below the "Magdyno." Then tilt the forward end of the "Magdyno" platform until the correct tension is obtained, finally retightening the securing nuts bolts.

To adjust the "Magdyno" chain on Model 36/D5, remove the chain cover, slacken the crankcase bolt on which the platform pivots and also the lower crankcase bolt upon which the adjuster screw is mounted and turn the latter until the "Magdyno" is tilted to give the correct chain tension.

Magneto Chain Adjustment. As with the "Magdyno" chain, maintain about $\frac{1}{4}$ in. whip. To adjust after removing the chain cover, slack off slightly the two crankcase bolts which secure the magneto platform and insert a lever or screwdriver under the front edge and tilt the magneto backwards until correct chain tension is obtained, finally tightening the two fixing bolts.

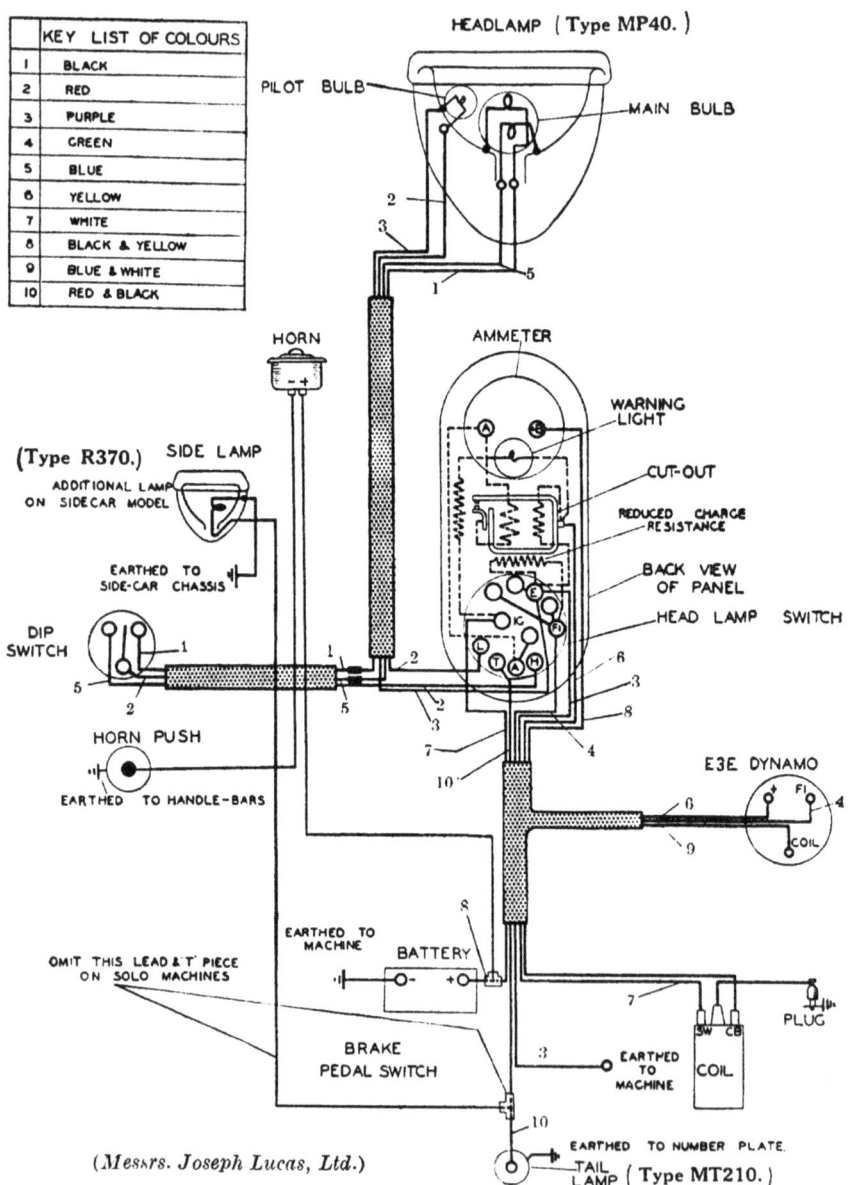

Fig. 95. Wiring Diagram for Models with Lucas Dynamo Lighting and Coil Ignition Equipment

Model 36/G2 has Miller equipment. The above W.D. also applies to magneto models with separate dynamo; in this case the ignition circuit is omitted.

SUPPLEMENT

Dynamo Chain Adjustment. To retension the dynamo chain it is necessary to rotate the dynamo in its cradle mounting until there is a whip in the centre of the top run of $\frac{1}{4}$ in. to $\frac{3}{8}$ in. To adjust the chain tension, first slacken the dynamo clamp bolt and then twist the unit bodily in its mounting *clockwise* to tighten. Note that it is possible to check the tension of both the dynamo and primary chains by passing the fingers through the oil-bath inspection cap orifice which can be released by unscrewing the knurled edge screw.

To Adjust the Primary Chain. It is possible to swing the gearbox bodily on its lower fixing pivot bolt, and to retension the chain proceed as follows—

First slack off the off-side nut on the top gearbox fixing bolt. Then slack off the nut on the adjuster bolt nearest the engine and turn the nut farthest from the engine *clockwise* until there is about $\frac{3}{8}$ in. to $\frac{1}{2}$ in. whip in the chain run as checked through the inspection cap orifice on the chain case cover. After retensioning the chain, tighten the nut on the adjuster nearest the engine, and also the top gearbox fixing bolt nut. Always adjust the primary before the secondary chain, and after making an adjustment on models with hand gear control, check and, if necessary, adjust the control as described below.

To Adjust Secondary Chain. If the chain has more whip than $\frac{1}{2}$ in. to $\frac{3}{4}$ in., retension it by drawing the rear wheel backwards in the slotted fork ends as described on page 111, being careful not to spoil the wheel alignment (see page 141). To check wheel alignment a taut piece of string or a wooden batten may be employed.

To Adjust Gear Control. After adjusting the primary chain by tilting the gearbox, an adjustment of the gear control is usually called for, except in the case of models with foot control, where the gear change lever is mounted direct on the gearbox. To adjust the hand gear control, proceed as described on page 169 of the 1933 Supplement, positioning the gear lever centrally in the *third gear* quadrant notch. Internal indexing on the Burman four-speed gearbox makes it simple to *feel* when the third gears are fully engaged.

Clutch Adjustment. If the clutch on a 1933-4 model with Sturmey-Archer gearbox refuses work, see that there is some free movement in the actuating lever to which the lower end of the cable is attached, and if necessary slacken the cable by means of the adjuster on the gearbox end plate. With the Burman clutch used on all 1935 and 1936 models, make any necessary adjustment as described on page 167 of the 1933 Supplement.

To Dismantle Clutch. In the case of the Burman clutch proceed as described on page 170 of the 1933 Supplement after detaching the outer half of the oil-bath chain case (see below). To dismantle an S.A. clutch (1933-4 models), unscrew the six screws holding the clutch springs and remove these, together with their boxes. Then lift off the spring box plate and withdraw the other plates. After reassembly, tighten up the screws fully, or some "drag" may occur.

Removing Oil-bath Chain Case Cover. To do this it is only necessary to remove the footrest arm and distance pieces, brake rod, yoke end pin and brake pedal, and then the securing pin in the aluminium band around the chain cover, when the outer half of the chain case can be detached. Replacement is simple, but be careful not to damage the rubber seal.

Steering Head Adjustment. Follow the instructions on page 114; be careful not to over tighten the bearings, or the steering will be stiff.

Front Fork Spindle Adjustment. This should be made exactly as described on page 114.

To Adjust Wheel Bearings. Deal with the roller bearings used for all hubs except those of Models 36/G2, 36/G2M as described on page 115. In the case of the two models mentioned, it is unnecessary to adjust with a slight "shake," as with roller bearings. To adjust, first slack off the near side axle nut and also the thin lock-nut on the inner side of the fork end, and then with the special spanner provided in the tool kit turn the cone *clockwise* until all "shake" disappears, after which slacken off slightly and retighten the lock-nut and axle nut firmly.

Rebushing Engine. This work is best entrusted to the makers, but should you by any chance decide to separate the crankcase halves be absolutely sure that you *first* withdraw the oil pump plunger. Failure to do this may cause serious damage.

Engine Timing. Do not experiment with valve timing, as this is a waste of time. The camwheels and engine pinion are clearly marked to ensure correct replacement.

To Remove the Camwheel. (Big Twins.) Before detaching the timing case cover place a receptacle below the crankcase to catch the oil as it runs out (on this engine the gears run submerged in oil). After removing the timing case cover revolve the engine until the marks on the camwheel and engine pinion coincide. Then raise the front inlet valve with a screwdriver or lever, when the camwheel may readily be withdrawn. When refitting the camwheel, if help is not available, keep the front inlet valve raised by packing or with a valve spring compressor. By holding all four camwheel levers up with the fingers it is now possible to insert the camwheel. See that the timing marks coincide.

VELOCEPRESS MANUALS - MOTORCYCLE

1930'S BRITISH MOTORCYCLE CARBS & ELEC COMPONENTS (BOOK OF)
1930'S BRITISH MOTORCYCLE ENGINES (OVERHAUL & MAINTENANCE)
1930'S BRITISH MOTORCYCLE GEARBOXES & CLUTCHES (BOOK OF)
AJS 1932-1948 SINGLES & TWINS 250cc THRU 1000cc (BOOK OF)
AJS 1945-1960 SINGLES 350cc & 500cc MODELS 16 & 18 (BOOK OF)
AJS 1955-1965 SINGLES 350cc & 500cc (BOOK OF)
ARIEL 1932-1939 PREWAR MODELS (BOOK OF)
ARIEL 1933-1951 (WORKSHOP MANUAL)
ARIEL 1939-1960 4 STROKE SINGLES (BOOK OF)
ARIEL 1958-1964 LEADER & ARROW (BOOK OF)
BMW R26 R27 (1956-1967) FACTORY WORKSHOP MANUAL
BMW R50 R50S R60 R69S (1955-1969) FACTORY WORKSHOP MANUAL
BSA BANTAM ALL MODELS FROM 1948 ONWARDS (BOOK OF)
BSA SINGLES & V-TWINS UP TO 1927 (BOOK OF)
BSA SINGLES & V-TWINS UP TO 1935 (BOOK OF)
BSA SINGLES & V-TWINS 1936-1939 (BOOK OF)
BSA SINGLES & V-TWINS 1936-1952 (BOOK OF)
BSA OHV & SV SINGLES 250-600cc 1945-1954 (BOOK OF)
BSA OHV & SV SINGLES 250cc 1954-1970 (BOOK OF)
BSA OHV SINGLES 350 & 500cc 1955-1967 (BOOK OF)
BSA TWINS 1948-1962 (BOOK OF)
BSA TWINS 1962-1969 (SECOND BOOK OF)
DOUGLAS 1929-1939 PREWAR ALL MODELS (BOOK OF)
DOUGLAS 1948-1957 POSTWAR ALL MODELS FACTORY SHOP MANUAL
DUCATI 160cc, 250cc & 350cc OHC MODELS FACTORY SHOP MANUAL
HONDA 50 ALL MODELS UP TO 1970 INC MONKEY & TRAIL (BOOK OF)
HONDA 90 ALL MODELS UP TO 1966 (BOOK OF)
HONDA 125-150cc TWINS C/CS/CB/CA FACTORY WORKSHOP MANUAL
HONDA 250-305 TWINS C/CS/CB FACTORY WORKSHOP MANUAL
HONDA C100 SUPER CUB FACTORY WORKSHOP MANUAL
HONDA C110 SPORT CUB 1962-1969 FACTORY WORKSHOP MANUAL
HONDA TWINS & SINGLES 50cc THRU 305cc 1960-1966 (BOOK OF)
HONDA TWINS ALL MODELS 125cc THRU 450cc UP TO 1968 (BOOK OF)
J.A.P. ENGINES 1927-1952 & MOTORCYCLES 1934-1952 (BOOK OF)
LAMBRETTA 1947-1957 ALL 125 & 150cc MODELS (BOOK OF)
LAMBRETTA 1957-1970 LI & TV MODELS (SECOND BOOK OF)
MATCHLESS 1931-1939 ALL MODELS 250cc THRU 990cc (BOOK OF)
MATCHLESS 1945-1956 350 & 500cc SINGLES (BOOK OF)
MATCHLESS 1955-1966 350 & 500cc SINGLES (BOOK OF)
NEW IMPERIAL ALL SV & OHV FROM 1935 ONWARDS (BOOK OF)
NORTON 1932-1939 PREWAR MODELS (BOOK OF)
NORTON 1932-1947 (BOOK OF)
NORTON 1938-1956 (BOOK OF)
NORTON 1955-1963 MODELS 19, 50 & ES2 (BOOK OF)
NORTON 1955-1965 DOMINATOR TWINS (BOOK OF)
NORTON 1957-1970 TWINS FACTORY WORKSHOP MANUAL
NSU PRIMA 1956-1964 ALL MODELS (BOOK OF)
NSU QUICKLY 1953-1963 ALL MODELS (BOOK OF)
PANTHER 1932-1958 LIGHTWEIGHT MODELS 250 & 350cc (BOOK OF)
PANTHER 1938-1966 HEAVYWEIGHT MODELS 600 & 650cc (BOOK OF)
RALEIGH MOPEDS 1960-1969 (BOOK OF)
RALEIGH MOTORCYCLES 1919-1933 (BOOK OF)
ROYAL ENFIELD 1934-1946 SINGLES & V TWINS (BOOK OF)
ROYAL ENFIELD 1937-1953 SINGLES & V TWINS (BOOK OF)
ROYAL ENFIELD 1946-1962 SINGLES (BOOK OF)
ROYAL ENFIELD 1958-1966 250cc & 350cc SINGLES (SECOND BOOK OF)
ROYAL ENFIELD 736cc INTERCEPTOR FACTORY WORKSHOP MANUAL
RUDGE 1933-1939 (BOOK OF)
SUNBEAM 1928-1939 (BOOK OF)
SUNBEAM 1946-1957 S7 & S8 (BOOK OF)
SUZUKI 50cc & 80cc UP TO 1966 (BOOK OF)
SUZUKI T10 1963-1967 FACTORY WORKSHOP MANUAL
SUZUKI T20 & T200 1965-1969 FACTORY WORKSHOP MANUAL
TRIUMPH 1935-1939 PREWAR MODELS (BOOK OF)
TRIUMPH 1935-1949 (BOOK OF)
TRIUMPH 1937-1951 (WORKSHOP MANUAL)
TRIUMPH 1945-1955 FACTORY WORKSHOP MANUAL
TRIUMPH 1945-1955 TWINS (BOOK OF)
TRIUMPH 1956-1969 TWINS (BOOK OF)
VELOCETTE 1925-1970 ALL SINGLES & TWINS (BOOK OF)
VESPA 1951-1961 (BOOK OF)
VESPA 1955-1963 125 & 150cc & GS MODELS (SECOND BOOK OF)
VESPA 1955-1968 GS & SS (BOOK OF)
VESPA 1963-1972 90, 125 & 150cc (THIRD BOOK OF)
VILLIERS ENGINE UP TO 1959 INC. 3 WHEELERS (BOOK OF)
VILLIERS ENGINE UP TO 1969 (BOOK OF)
VINCENT 1935-1955 (WORKSHOP MANUAL)

VELOCEPRESS TECHNICAL BOOKS – MOTORCYCLE

CATALOG OF BRITISH MOTORCYCLES (1951 MODELS)
INDIAN PONYBIKE, BOY RACER & PAPOOSE ILL PARTS LIST & SALES LIT
MOTORCYCLE ENGINEERING (P.E. Irving)
SPEED AND HOW TO OBTAIN IT (Motor Cycle Magazine UK)
TUNING FOR SPEED (P.E. Irving)

VELOCEPRESS MANUALS - THREE WHEELER'S

BSA THREE WHEELER (BOOK OF)

VELOCEPRESS MANUALS - AUTOMOBILE

AUSTIN-HEALEY 6-CYLINDER WORKSHOP MANUAL
AUSTIN-HEALEY SPRITE & MG MIDGET 1958-1971 WSM
BMW 600 LIMOUSINE FACTORY WORKSHOP MANUAL
BMW 600 LIMOUSINE OWNERS HAND BOOK & SERVICE MANUAL
BMW 2000 & 2002 1966-1976 WORKSHOP MANUAL
BMW ISETTA FACTORY WORKSHOP MANUAL
CORVAIR 1960-1969 WORKSHOP MANUAL
CORVETTE V8 1955-1962 WORKSHOP MANUAL
JAGUAR E-TYPE 3.8 & 4.2 WORKSHOP MANUAL
METROPOLITAN FACTORY WORKSHOP MANUAL
MGA & MGB OWNERS HANDBOOK & WORKSHOP MANUAL
MG MIDGET TC, TD, TF & TF1500 WORKSHOP MANUAL
PORSCHE 356 1948-1965 WORKSHOP MANUAL
PORSCHE 912 WORKSHOP MANUAL
TRIUMPH TR2, TR3, TR4 1953-1965 WORKSHOP MANUAL
VOLKSWAGEN TRANSPORTER, TRUCKS & WAGONS 1950-1979 WSM
VOLVO 1944-1968 ALL MODELS WORKSHOP MANUAL

VELOCEPRESS TECHNICAL BOOKS - AUTOMOBILE

FERRARI 250/GT SERVICE AND MAINTENANCE
FERRARI GUIDE TO PERFORMANCE
FERRARI OWNER'S HANDBOOK
FERRARI TUNING TIPS & MAINTENANCE TECHNIQUES
HOW TO BUILD A FIBERGLASS CAR
HOW TO BUILD A RACING CAR
HOW TO RESTORE THE MODEL 'A' FORD
MASERATI OWNER'S HANDBOOK
OBERT'S FIAT GUIDE
PERFORMANCE TUNING THE SUNBEAM TIGER
SOUPING THE VOLKSWAGEN
SOLEX CARBURETORS (EMPHASIS ON UK & EU AUTOMOBILES)
SU CARBURETORS (EMPHASIS ON UK AUTOMOBILES)
WEBER CARBURETORS (EMPHASIS ON ALFA & FIAT)

VELOCEPRESS BOOKS & GUIDES - AUTOMOBILE

ABARTH BUYERS GUIDE
COMPLETE CATALOG OF JAPANESE MOTOR VEHICLES
FERRARI 308 SERIES BUYER'S AND OWNER'S GUIDE
FERRARI BERLINETTA LUSSO
FERRARI BROCHURES AND SALES LITERATURE 1946-1967
FERRARI BROCHURES AND SALES LITERATURE 1968-1989
FERRARI OPP, MAINTENANCE & SERVICE H/BOOKS 1948-1963
FERRARI SERIAL NUMBERS PART I - ODD NUMBERS TO 21399
FERRARI SERIAL NUMBERS PART II - EVEN NUMBERS TO 1050
FERRARI SPYDER CALIFORNIA
HENRY'S FABULOUS MODEL "A" FORD
MASERATI BROCHURES AND SALES LITERATURE

VELOCEPRESS BOOKS – RACING

CARRERA PANAMERICANA - MEXICAN ROAD RACE (BOOK OF)
DIALED IN - THE JAN OPPERMAN STORY
IF HEMINGWAY HAD WRITTEN A RACING NOVEL
LE MANS 24 (THE BOOK THAT THE FILM WAS BASED ON)
VEDA ORR'S NEW REVISED HOT ROD PICTORIAL

AUTOBOOKS WORKSHOP MANUALS & BROOKLANDS ROAD TEST PORTFOLIOS

FOR A COMPLETE LISTING OF THE AUTOBOOKS & BROOKLANDS TITLES THAT WE CURRENTLY HAVE AVAILABLE, PLEASE VISIT OUR WEBSITE.

Our website www.VelocePress.com includes secure online ordering via PayPal and also provides detailed descriptions of the titles listed above.

Please check our website:

www.VelocePress.com

for a complete up-to-date list of available titles

www.ingramcontent.com/pod-product-compliance
Lightning Source LLC
Chambersburg PA
CBHW060347190426
43201CB00043B/1758